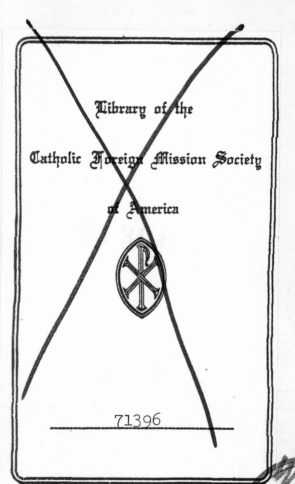

MACUMBA

Also by A. J. Langguth

JESUS CHRISTS

WEDLOCK

MARKSMAN

HARPER & ROW, PUBLISHERS
NEW YORK,
EVANSTON,
SAN FRANCISCO,
LONDON

MACUMBA

WHITE AND BLACK MAGIC IN BRAZIL

A.J. LANGGUTH

Frontispiece photograph by MANCHETE from PICTORIAL.

FIRST EDITION

Designed by Gloria Adelson

Library of Congress Cataloging in Publication Data

Langguth, A   J   1933–
   Macumba.
   1. Umbanda (Cultus) 2. Magic—Brazil. I. Title.
BL2592.U5L34 1975   299'.6   74–1830
ISBN 0–06–012503–9

75 76 77 78 79 10 9 8 7 6 5 4 3 2 1

MACUMBA

THE FIRST TIME I saw a spirit descend to earth and take control of a human body, I thought I was watching an epileptic seizure and turned my head away. It was a significant moment in my life, and I took it for a minor social embarrassment.

The victim, a girl, had been dancing for two hours when with no warning she staggered as though she had been felled by a hammer. She recovered balance but stumbled over the floor with her eyes rolling up somewhere under her brows, and behind their long fluttering lashes, the whites of those eyes looked like semaphores of pain.

I gave my attention to the palm leaves that had been strewn across the concrete floor, hoping that when I looked again she would have been removed from the hall.

The occasion was a spiritist ceremony in a suburb of Rio de Janeiro called rather patly Encantado—The Enchanted. I had arrived in Brazil at the start of the year, 1970, not at all interested in spirits, looking only for a few quiet months to rewrite a novel about marriage in the sixties.

Before I left Los Angeles, the editor had called from New York to impress on me that there must be more self-revelation from the narrator in my book. "He must open up," I was told. "Now he doesn't even have a name."

Despite the centuries of denials by writers, any editor as shrewd as David Segal assumed that a first-person narrative must be at least partly confessional, and I understood what he was urging on me. A few years before I had visited Rio and succumbed unconditionally, and now I expected its humid sunshine to open my pores and help me sweat myself across the pages of the revision.

Within a week of my arrival, I was joined by a young married couple I knew from London whom we can call, in the one use of made-up names here, Jane and Philip Gregory. The Gregorys arrived in Rio as guests of the Brazilian government since they were commissioned by a London gallery to buy quantities of Brazilian art. The purchases were quickly made but they stayed on, marking time until the carnival in February. It was Jane Gregory who induced me to come along with them to the ceremony in Encantado.

At first, pleading work, I said no; but, tall and imperious, Jane did not deign to argue. "You're coming, Langguth," she said. "Voodoo, you know. Curses. Magic. Blood. You will have to see one sometime in your life and it may as well be tonight."

Long before they left England, the Gregorys had reached the lees of their marriage, so that every dinner we shared ended in a row and either Philip or Jane jumped up angrily before dessert and strode off down Copacabana Beach. "It's like computer dating," I said after the first week. "I never know whom I'll be ending the evening with." They smiled nastily and launched their fight with added verve.

Once, it being Philip's turn to stomp away, Jane confided to me that she was expecting mail from a lover she had left behind in England. Would I collect the letters at her bank and slip them to her when Philip was chatting up a waitress or a chambermaid?

I framed several high-minded refusals before I gave in and did as I was told. Now Jane claimed to be inviting me to the ceremony in return for my favor, though more likely she didn't want to squander four or five hours of squabbling if there was to be no audience.

For my part, I understood voodoo to be a form of black mass, and my spiritual concerns at the time were so minimal that I wasn't faintly stirred by the prospect of religion either mocked or reviled.

All the same, Jane's last argument won me over. Why not go out that night and see the black men dance and chant and—if they must—kill a hen? It made for one less thing I would have to do in the days I got to Africa. So I left for the ritual, but with only the expectation that I'd be uncomfortable and bored.

The Gregorys were not people to reach in their pockets if another purse was open, and we were driven to Encantado in a black government limousine as the guests of a Brazilian diplomat on home leave from London. After extending his invitation to the Gregorys he seemed to be regretting it, for they were particularly snappish that night and to pass the time I was goading them more sharply than usual. During the fifty-minute ride, one of us in the back seat was either sulking or laughing too loudly.

Throughout, the diplomat's elegant wife remained serene, and while her husband fretted and reminded us that the evening was very solemn to the worshipers and that we could not leave early no matter how restless we might become, she said simply, "Never mind, you will like the dancing."

It was a stifling night, January being July south of the Equator, and in the back the three of us quickly wilted. Jane was wearing a beige pants suit that was darkening under the arms. Philip fared better since he rarely fastened the top four buttons of his silk shirts. My own blue cotton shirt was plastered against my back, and my trousers—"Too short!" Jane had scolded. "Why do American men choose to expose their ankles?" —were bunched up my thighs in accordion pleats.

In front the Brazilians, including their uniformed chauffeur, made no concession to the hundred-degree heat; for them no watery hairlines or beaded mustaches of sweat.

Since on the previous night it had been Jane who fled our table, Philip was taunting her about the treat that her foul temper had caused her to miss.

"It was nearly eleven o'clock," he said, looking around his wife's formidable shoulders to enjoy my discomfort. "The waiter had just brought our coffee when all at once Langguth looked at his watch and muttered, 'God!' He jumped up and ran out of the place, nearly knocking over a table and bowling down the waiters in his path, all the time shouting 'Taxi!' in the direction of the restaurant door. He couldn't have moved faster if his pants were on fire."

Jane raised an eyebrow. "Perhaps they were." All men were future grist; none escaped her stockpile. "Well, Langguth, and just what sent you rushing out at that speed at eleven P.M.?"

3

"I want to finish reading Proust before carnival."

They sniggered. I looked out the window and asked myself whether David Segal was insisting on more candor in life or merely on the printed page.

The car pulled up in front of a plain, sturdy house, where the chief of this spiritist center lived with his family. At the rear he had built a hall the size of a tennis court as a meeting place for the cult. He was introduced as a ranking official in the Brazilian mint, and he welcomed us with the sort of easy warmth that every visitor to Rio remarks upon.

"This is the night of worship of our goddess of grain," he explained as we walked through the kitchen, past bowls of corn, corn bread, popcorn.

"Ceres?" Jane asked.

"We call her by another name," our host said. "But it is true that the stories of many of our gods resemble those from Greek mythology."

It was the first intriguing thing I had heard about this voodoo, but we were being shepherded to our seats near the front of the hall and there was no time to follow up the matter. Much later I pieced together the stories of the gods that appear at the end of this book.

To my surprise, the diplomat's wife was led to a throne on a raised platform, where she sat, with no sign of embarrassment or hauteur, receiving low bows from the congregation and kisses on her outstretched hand. "My wife is a ——," the diplomat told us, using a Brazilian term I didn't catch. I suspect now that he called her a mãe do santo, a mother of the saint.

On the benches behind us skin colors were lighter than I had expected. Many honey-toned men and women had come to worship, along with many whites with a Mediterranean cast to their handsome features. I didn't know at the time that there were more than ten thousand of these spiritist centers in Rio alone, or that the magic, which had come to Brazil originally on African slave ships, by now touched the lives of every hue and caste.

To the right of the platform three men were playing the drums with their hands to a beat like a racing pulse. When we guests were seated, a door opened at the back of the hall and a line of women dressed in

4

white rocked down the aisle in a stylized samba.

Each wore half a dozen starched white skirts and a bandana to bind up her hair. Their ages spanned half a century, with the youngest a slender girl no more than seventeen. But while she was also the prettiest dancer she was not the most graceful. Two weathered black women swung their hips, spun on their toes, flared their petticoats wide, dipped and curtsied, all with a delicacy that made them beautiful.

The rhythm changed often, and sometimes the drummers beat so fast that all of the dozen women spun round and round until their skirts flew out and touched the next hem and the whirling circle became a vortex of white lace. I was leaking sweat and the incense kept me clearing my throat. But I wasn't bored. I didn't look at the Gregorys for fear of seeing small patronizing smiles.

Very likely I did them an injustice and they were as engrossed as I was, but just then I wasn't willing to take the risk. The drumbeat was dislodging something low in my chest, making a tentative and very slight fissure, and I didn't want to caulk that faint line yet.

At about this point, while I was assuming that the steady drumroll and the dizzying dance comprised the whole of the ritual, the young girl went off into her convulsion.

It took a few seconds for curiosity to overcome instinct, and when I looked again, the girl was being fitted with a gold crown made of papier-mâché. Other women also hung a pasteboard sword at her side. Then they led her down the aisle and out of the hall. She seemed unconscious as she passed us, her eyes still rolling with the frantic and purposeless movement one sometimes sees in the blind.

When the dancing resumed it took on greater fascination now that I knew what to expect. Within a few minutes a woman in her forties broke loose and charged across the platform. Again, the other women fenced her in and steadied her, less with their hands than with a protective field of energy that seemed to calm her and keep her on her feet. The violence of her attack had shaken her hair free. Now the others pulled the shawl from her shoulders and tied it like a sarong around her torso.

Before she could be taken away, another girl succumbed and the dancers left the woman alone, rocking slowly in place, while they attended to the new victim. Then the two of them, hair down over their shoulders and blinking their sightless eyes, were escorted together from the hall.

By this time there were nine dancers left in the circle, and I began to study each one for a telltale acceleration, that impression of being at the edge of her self-control, which would reveal her as the next one to lurch and spin. But with the phenomenon still new to me, unsettling and even frightening, I'd see the clues and look away again, hoping that I was wrong and missing those instants at which the spirit descended.

Another hour passed. Now I was entirely caught in the spectacle on the stage but not responding any more myself to the drums. My emotions, which I had always thought of vaguely as comprising a block that sat somewhere beneath the heart and above the groin, had solidified once more, and I was left with only my mind to try to make sense of this ecstasy I had witnessed.

For that is what it was. Not contortions of pain so much as a prolonged and violent orgasm. When it subsided, the women were left to recover from a state of being that looked to be, from the outside, exalted. I wondered whether men ever experienced that strange frenzy.

My interest wasn't in the least personal. With Prufrock, I knew that it could never devolve on me.

NEITHER THAT NIGHT nor for months afterward did I feel deprived that this spiritual experience was closed to me. Past the age of twenty, I hadn't worried much about my immortal soul, and my adult pleasures had proved to be less than transcendental. In fact, it had occurred to me in Malibu or on Copacabana Beach that since my happiest days were spent lying on the sand with an ocean echoing in my ear, the evolutionary process had very possibly taken me further than I might have chosen to go.

Back in Los Angeles, I would have said that I had forgotten my night with the Gregorys. But when I came to the end of a new novel and found myself endorsing the principle of ecstasy at the expense of morality, ordinary decency, even human freedom, I held the crazed women of Encantado responsible, and when I returned to Brazil eighteen months later, I set to work finding out more about this religion that could dislodge a human personality to make room for the spirit of an ancient god.

A novel set in Brazil had begun to suggest itself. One man dependent on drugs; a second man, a political prisoner, tortured by electric shocks; a girl in a state of religious possession—three strangers who would join and act out their story in some common ground of their unconscious minds, or their genes, or their bloodstreams. Some days it seemed possible, most nights pretentious, but before I could decide whether to go ahead, I would have to know much more about the faith.

The moment my Brazilian friends learned that I was interested in spiritism, they swamped me with stories about the magic, most of them so preposterous they snapped me back to disbelief. One man had seen a black pai do santo, a father of the saint, send a man hurtling across the room by using no more than his concentrated spiritual force. A mulatto, thirty or so, had spent a month shut up in a shack in central Brazil with eleven other believers. They lived entirely off the bull they had ritually slaughtered, speaking to no one, waiting one by one for their bodies to be taken over by the African spirits.

On the thirtieth day one of the most venerable gods, Obaluaé, appeared, covered with straw. He alone did not materialize by taking command of a human body in the shack. Instead, he came in his own form, cloudy and insubstantial, to bless the worshipers and send them home.

The faith had come west with the slaves, but generations of intermingling with Europeans and native Indian tribes such as the Tupi had not only produced a startlingly attractive people but had fused the Catholicism of Portugal with this magic from Africa.

The Yoruba tribe, from what is now Nigeria, was only one of the more than thirty African nations the Portuguese plundered for slaves, but it was the gods of the Yorubas who formed the core of a worship that has survived three hundred years on alien ground. The Yorubas called their gods the òrìsàs, the first *s* being pronounced as *sh*—oh-ree-shas. In Brazil the name was spoken the same way but spelled orixás. In Rio believers granted that the original center of the faith and still its most authentic repository was in the forests around the city of Bahia, now called Salvador, which was the capital of colonial Brazil.

The supreme divinity of the Yorubas was named Òrìsà-nlá (The Great Orisa) or Olódùmarè (The Almighty), a spirit that was unapproachable but essentially good. Since this Almighty was so remote from human affairs, the Yorubas made no dedications to him, but for lesser gods a blood sacrifice was considered effective and proper. Twice a month, for example, their blacksmiths killed dogs to propitiate Ogum, the god of iron.

Some of this history was told to me by men and women who had heard the stories from their parents or an old woman in their town. Whatever sounded confused or unreliable, I checked against books like John S. Mbiti's *African Religions and Philosophy* and Noel King's *Religions of Africa*. The texts not only filled in the gaps but confirmed observations of my own about the Brazilian character:

I read that the Yorubas were noted for their cleanliness, that their morning ablutions were part of a ritual to promote inner purity, and when the ceremonies were moved to Brazil, white-robed girls continued to rise before dawn to carry earthenware jugs of fresh water from the river to cleanse the hall and wash the body of every celebrant before the night's ceremony.

Historians had observed that the Tupi Indians were equally fastidious, and I knew what the coming together of these two well-scrubbed peoples had wrought in modern Brazil. In a country of fetishes, none outranked soap and water. Girls down to their last cruzeiro would spend it on a packet of lemon shampoo, and should any Brazilian, male or female, gain access to a shower, he was lost for an hour. Brazilians were the only people I had ever seen brush their tongues with toothpaste.

The cleanly Yorubas, along with most other West African nations, accepted the idea that friendly spirits returned to earth through mediums to offer humans a medical remedy or other material assistance.

While I was being raised in Protestant Minneapolis, my chum next door went off every day to a parochial high school, and from comparing textbooks I knew that the Vatican viewed spiritism with active hostility. I didn't see how Catholicism had come to merge so comfortably in Brazil with voodoo.

Gilberto Freyre explained it to me. Freyre is Brazil's native-born de Tocqueville, invaluable for explaining his countrymen to themselves, and he had pointed out that neither the Yoruba, nor the Ashanti, the Bantu, Angola, or Dahomey, docilely accepted the religion of their Catholic owners. In Virginia and Carolina slaves were likely to become Protestant converts, but the slaves of the great Brazilian plantations paid token obeisance to European saints and godheads, while they kept alive, in private, the traditions they had brought with them.

A fête for Saint George? The field hands would gladly leave their chores to worship São Jorge in the pasture behind a mansion. But once assembled there, it was the African god Oxóssi to whom they sent their prayers. If the master had misgivings when he heard the fourth-century knight being celebrated with wailing and screams, he was no theologian and disinclined to investigate.

Nor were the Portuguese settlers apt to be puritanical. From Goa to Formosa and the Spice Islands, Portuguese explorers and settlers had joined enthusiastically with the women who came their way. When they got to Brazil, Portuguese men found Tupi girls waiting naked on the beaches to welcome them, and later they expected no more resistance from their slaves.

Like their North American counterparts, the Brazilian settlers worked the splendid black women in their kitchens and their nurseries, and they sauntered out at night to exercise their right of property in the slave quarters. But when a Portuguese planter became a widower or permanently estranged, he often took a black woman as his wife, if not in the eyes of God, in full view of his neighbors. The result was that former slaves were installed as the reigning ladies of their Bahian Taras, and their mulatta daughters were courted for wealth and position as well as for beauty.

For the first two centuries African ritual was held clandestinely in Brazil. Then, in 1830, eight years after the nation's independence from

Portugal but fifty-eight years before slavery was finally abolished, the first public black spiritist meeting took place on the outskirts of Salvador. The center, or terreiro, took its name from its site, Engenho Velho, or the Old Mill. The ritual itself was called Candomblé, though no one can be sure why.

It was not an African name. Perhaps it was a variation on the name of the dance that slaves did on their plantations and called candombe. It may have been a name they called their drums.

By now, a scholar of Candomblé can distinguish among fourteen African nations that contributed to the rites and their subtle variations in procedure. Playing the drums with the bare hand is a sign that the musician comes from the Angola nation or at least follows its practices. Playing with a brick or stone is pure Alaketú.

The early Candomblés were condemned by the Catholic hierarchy and harassed by the police, and the membership was entirely black. But children with European parents and those of mixed blood heard about the orixás from an early age, and even when they didn't take part in the ceremonies, they grew up more than half persuaded that spirits could return to earth and control the bodies of living men and women.

That conditioning helped to explain why Brazilians seized with such eagerness on *The Book of Spirits*, published in Paris in 1857, by a Frenchman, Hippolyte Leon Denizard Ravail under the pen name Allan Kardec.

In his own country, Kardec's book took a modest place in the ranks of occult literature. But in the social circles of Brazil, Kardec and what he termed "spiritism" became a way to reconcile the ancient African beliefs with European theosophy.

Kardec said his teachings had been revealed to him by spirit rappings and later through automatic writing. His system was based on a concept of reincarnation: some spirits managed to return after discarnation and make contact with living beings. But for all of his acceptance of the supernatural, Kardec rejected the idea of miracles and did not hold that Jesus had been the Son of God.

At a Kardec center prominent doctors of past ages might be summoned to give a patient their expert diagnosis, and other educated gentlemen returned to deliver scholarly lectures. Kardec's followers could count on an evening that would be edifying and genteel, and even Pedro McGregor, who wrote the best introduction to Brazilian religious magic, *Jesus of the Spirits,* could hardly disguise his relief when it came time to turn from inchoate Candomblé and take up the restrained teachings of Kardecism.

For many other Brazilians, however, Kardec was altogether too austere, and when a young man named Zélio de Moraes received an Indian spirit in 1920, he opened the way for new spiritist practices that came to be called Umbanda.

As a form of worship, Umbanda was both voracious and accommodating in its approach to older faiths; its name may have come from the Sanskrit word Aum-Bandha, "the limit of the unlimited." Or it may have been an African way of saying "the art of healing." I was finding that very little about the Brazilian spirits was unarguable.

McGregor described Moraes as a "blondish, six-foot simpleton," but he granted that the man was modest and sincere. Under the tutelage of a spirit named the Caboclo of the Seven Crossroads, Moraes merged Catholicism, Candomblé, and Indian lore into an amalgam that achieved wide popularity. Even the Kardecists, though considering the new movement somewhat uncouth and misguided, and certainly at a lower level of spiritual evolvement than Kardecism, did not find Umbanda entirely uncongenial.

From its start, Umbanda was dedicated exclusively to the white line of magic. It called on the gods only for good works and charity. In time, men whose motives were less pure turned to an offshoot, Quimbanda, the worship of the African god Exú and his legion of devils. The word seems to have been derived from Bantu, Ki-Mbanda, much as "voodoo," the name African lore assumed in Haiti and the West Indies, was a misrendering of the Dahomey word for God, Vodun. In Brazil, macumba gained usage as a vague name that could mean almost any ceremony that courted the spirits.

In the effort to get the distinctions clear, I remembered that the ritual in Encantado had been described as Umbanda, and I resolved to start with only white magic. If later I had a chance to watch Exú at work I wouldn't resist. But for the present, the good spirits were awesome enough.

MIDWAY THROUGH MY READING, I saw that if I didn't stir myself to act, I'd soon be back in Los Angeles trying to write my novel from second-hand impressions of Candomblé or Umbanda. It was comforting to have Pedro McGregor or Gilberto Freyre making sense of the phenomenon, at least historically, and in their pages the idea of possession became more acceptable, less threatening.

But the same Brazilians who had been garrulous about the spirits were not urging me to investigate in person. "You can go to the dances they have for tourists," a girl named Gina told me. "I do not think you should go anywhere else." Jayme, who had been educated in Switzerland, said, "Frankly, Jack, that macumba business is something I don't care to get involved with." Other friends made dates and broke them with excuses I wasn't meant to believe.

At last Armando volunteered to lead me to a ceremony if I'd make up the four dollars in wages he would lose by taking the night off. He was the bouncer at a boisterous nightclub in town and since I had seen him lift a troublemaker by the shoulders and rush him out before a punch was thrown, I wasn't surprised that he showed up Saturday night as he had promised and only forty minutes late. He was slicked up for the occasion and dressed in a tight white outfit that he thought emphasized his resemblance to Elvis Presley. To me, it looked as though the singer and two bodyguards were traveling in one pair of pants.

For all his size and sulky lower lip, Armando turned out to be a good-humored fellow who amused me during the long bus ride with an account of his five worst automobile accidents. Now, unaccountably, his driver's license had been suspended, and so instead of chauffeuring visiting French actresses around Rio, he was reduced to keeping peace at a bar. "I am paid to be a wild beast," he lamented. "It is not a good job for me."

We were headed for Caxias, a suburb of Rio with a reputation for gangsters and unreconstructed gunslinging. Several friends advised me not to go, but it was the site of the only terreiro Armando knew. Also, it was Easter weekend, and I counted on the prevailing piety to have settled the town down.

From the bus station we took a cab, but the place was hard to find and when we got to the unlighted street, the driver wouldn't go any farther. We got out to walk.

Armando went a few paces ahead and located a house built of pink cement and trimmed with green. It was protected by a high wall as well as by three young black men standing guard in the inner court. I hung back while Armando spoke quietly to them and then to an arrogant woman who appeared from the back. She kept shaking her head no, no, but he persisted until she gave one disdainful nod and Armando waved for me to pass through the gate.

But at the first step one of the guards stopped me. He drew a cup of water from a bucket and spilled a portion to the ground on either side of me. Pulling me roughly to his chest, he splashed the rest over my shoulder and onto the road.

Armando knew his way down a dirt trail along the side of the house to the hall at the back. Inside, a gallery for women ran along the left wall, that for men along the right. Armando had told me that the Easter celebration had begun Friday night and now twenty women were still dancing. The songs were being called by a brown man wearing a turban with his white satin suit.

There was one stool, which Armando insisted I take, and I had barely brushed a cockroach off the top and sat down when a supple man in a loincloth of white feathers and warbonnet sprang to the center of the room, pointing his arm at the door we had just come in. Every head turned in time to see a ten-foot snake sliding over the palm leaves spread over the floor.

From behind me Armando whispered, "Cobra." It was the Portuguese word for all snakes. "A giboia," he added, "but very small."

Whenever the snake paused, a small boy pushed it forward with his bare foot until, shifting his bow and arrow, the Indian could scoop it up and let it twine the muscles of his arm. "Akk! Akk!" the Indian cried, dancing with the snake as it coiled around his body.

The snake seemed to be the signal for the spirits to appear. Armando could recognize many of them, and from my reading I knew a little of their histories. Oxóssi, god of hunting, came into the hall in the person of an intense youth seated behind me in the gallery. He shook, spun, and was led away. Iemanjá, queen of waters, was there but not Oxalá, the African god who became identified in Brazil with Jesus.

When a young man received Preto Velho, the black man of Africa, he immediately bent double with the pains of age and was helped hobbling to the courtyard to recover. The woman who had permitted me inside was whirling now and the other dancers caught her up in her own green shawl and sang a hymn to her spirit, Ogum.

> "Ogum não devia beber,
> Ogum não devia fumar.
> A fumaça representa
> As nuvens, a cerveja
> A espuma do mar."

(Ogum should not drink, Ogum should not smoke. Smoke represents the clouds, beer, the foam of the sea.)

As the song ended, the Indian took up a vigil at the door. He brandished his bow and pointed the snake's head until its eyes faced the darkness. With a cry, he dared the devil god Exú to come and do battle. Again we strained to see, but the doorway was empty. Snorting in triumph, the Indian leapt back to the center of the dancers.

A scowling woman of forty had approached an old man next to me at the gallery's railing. He seemed to be the only other white-skinned man in the hall and he accepted her embrace and held out his hands to her. The woman was in the grip of a god who was handling a thick cigar in a bold, even sexual way.

With the hot red tip of the cigar, the spirit crossed each white palm. The man met the challenge, not flinching, but when the spirit had passed on, I saw him rubbing his hands together between his legs.

The woman—the spirit—moved along the rail and stopped in front of me. I ignored the peremptory nod of head and kept my hands stubbornly at my side.

The spirit stared into my eyes with his own empty white ones. Then he looked up, above my head, and fell back with a cry of revulsion. Urgently the spirit caused the woman's hands to raise and snap its fingers in a circle before my eyes. There seemed to be more fear on the spirit's part than mine, but I did look around for Armando and was sorry to see that he had disappeared.

The woman's mouth was gulping now as the spirit called, "Hup! Hup!" and snapped the fingers closer to my face. The noise brought the man in the white turban hurrying to our side.

Nervously he asked, "You are not a brasileiro?"

"Norte-americano." The panic on all sides was affecting me and I stumbled on the word.

"Ah." At once he relaxed and spoke soothingly to the spirit, who moved the woman's head up and down and dropped her hands. "The spirit could not read your thoughts and so he believed that you had come here to make confusion. I explained that you had been thinking in inglês."

Pacified, the spirit took the stub of cigar from the woman's mouth and handed it to me. I bent to take a puff.

"No!" the man cried. "The spirit wants you to take the cigar back to your country as a gift from the orixás of Brazil."

I snuffed it out on the railing and dropped it in my pocket. The woman's body was still shuddering and her strong arms embraced me by the shoulders. "Hup!" boomed the bass voice. "Hup!"

Armando came back smelling of beer and stood against the wall. The encounter had left my head throbbing dully, like a toothache but behind the eyes. "I am ready to go," I said.

"Not now," said Armando. "There will be too many bandits on the road. We must wait now for daylight."

ALONG COPACABANA THE NEXT DAY I was informed with disdain that the presence of such theatrical props as a snake, cigars, and a feathered warbonnet indicated that Armando had taken me to a "low" Umbanda terreiro, whereas the lighter skins and better incomes in Encantado spoke of "high" Umbanda. I had been in Brazil long enough to know that the myth of an open society with no racial or class prejudices was one of the country's more appealing self-delusions.

But if I had been exposed to a range of the social levels involved with the spirits, I hadn't yet watched the gods either counseling or healing. I wanted a test of this divine interjection into everyday life, a wish that was granted when Cristina suffered an emotional breakdown.

Tall and tanned, at twenty-seven not so young and not really lovely but proportioned for a bikini, Cristina had large anxious eyes and, like many Brazilian girls, an overbite that disqualified her mouth as classic but left it sweetly vulnerable. "Cristina is not beautiful," according to Nesio, the man she lived with. "But she suits me."

Nesio could judge unsparingly because in him nature had fashioned a perfect product, not forgetting either the green eyes or the masses of coal-blue hair. In Rome or Cannes, he would surely have become a gigolo, but in Rio rich women were less inclined to cap their decor with a work of art for the bedroom.

Not that Nesio wasn't as likely to amuse himself with an older woman as with a sixteen-year-old. But except for the instance when he was presented with a cowhide briefcase—of limited use to the maître d' at a discotheque—the ripe body had to be its own reward. When Cristina sometimes whispered to me that she suspected Nesio of taking money for sex, I was able to reassure her since most of his assignations took place at my apartment.

Perhaps, as with Jane Gregory, I should have refused when he appeared at my door, exhilarated afresh after—how many conquests? a thousand?—with his latest quarry cowering behind his shoulders. "You are not occupying your bedroom, Jack? We will only be a minute."

Otherwise, Nesio shared Cristina's apartment near Lido Square in the older quarter of Copacabana. Her six-year-old son from her first marriage lived with them, but Nesio's own boy lived miles away in the suburbs. There being no divorce in Brazil, only legal separation, Nesio's short-lived marriage had inoculated him against further danger. He and Cristina lived as man and wife, but I was inclined to blame her growing tensions on the absence of a legal document. As April's autumn days grew cool and short, a listlessness filmed over Cristina's eyes and the blue patches deepening beneath them weren't mascara.

Near the first of May, I spotted Nesio coming out of the pink church abutting the traffic tunnel to Copacabana Beach. He was exuding the air of high purpose that usually preceded a visit to his tailor.

"Church?" I said. "You?"

"The macumbeira recommended it, Jack. Tomorrow Cristina goes for her abortion. After I did the ceremony with the spirits this afternoon, the woman told me I must also come here to pray."

"You have been praying in a Catholic church for the success of her abortion?"

"Not for long," he said placatingly. The anomaly hadn't struck him but he remembered that I was without faith. "One candle only."

Cristina survived that operation but she never really rallied afterward. A few weeks later, Nesio showed up at my door, alone. "Cristina has gone to a hospital for her nerves," he said. "The doctor says she must stay three months. It is not my fault."

"No?"

"Her mother told me that even as a little girl Cristina was nervous." He held out his manicured hand and trembled the fingertips. "The macumbeira is not sure she can help, but she will try. You said you wanted to know more about the spirits. If you like you can come with me now."

I was living in a building on Avenida Barata Ribeiro notorious for its popularity with prostitutes and petty thieves, and we went down in the battered elevator and walked south a few doors to a far more respectable building faced with modernistic swirls of pink concrete. On the seventh floor Nesio knocked at a door. A buxom blonde woman in her late forties opened it warily, then beamed at the sight of him.

By this time I knew that the proper name for the female leader of a spiritist center was mãe do santo or, for convenience, macumbeira, as Nesio said. But since I was still less than committed to the whole subject, it pleased me to think of these women as witches.

This particular witch, as it turned out, was no stranger to me. I had seen her before on the avenue, a handsome, corseted woman in dark tailored suits, clutching always, like a fluttering dove, her pair of white gloves.

Nesio made an appointment for the next afternoon, a Tuesday, which was the day she reserved for her good works. My command of Portuguese was adequate to get me an omelet when I wanted eggs, and Nesio spoke no English. But between us we conveyed that I would like to talk a bit now and she showed us into a living room with a few widely spaced pieces of brown plastic furniture.

I explained that she was the first mãe do santo I had met and if she had a minute or two, I would like to hear her story. She gave me the same shy, flattered smile that had greeted Nesio and over the next hour told how the gods had come to single her out. To me it was as though we were speaking across a broad valley and I caught only an outline of what she said. But sketchily here was what she told us:

My parents emigrated to Brazil from Switzerland in the early twenties and I was born a year after their arrival. In Zurich, they had been Methodists, but in Rio they dropped away from church entirely.

My childhood had been lighthearted, but at the onset of adolescence I started to behave strangely. I don't remember much about it now. First I had headaches, which they told me were due to the changes in my body. But when I fell into states that were more asleep than awake, they heard me speaking unintelligible words in a voice they did not recognize.

They took me to doctors who tested me and found me normal. At that period, psychoanalysis was not well known in Brazil, but my parents had kept in touch with intellectual trends in Europe and they found an analyst and took me to him.

He was Brazilian, the psychiatrist. After hearing my symptoms, he advised us to go at once to an Umbanda center.

I am sure that my parents were more dismayed by his remedy than by my symptoms. To them, Umbanda was a superstition for poor people and black servants. They suspected our maid of slipping off to ceremonies, and once we had found candles, cigars, and bottles of beer set up by our kitchen door. What could voodoo have to do with their daughter?

The psychiatrist held firm. Take your girl to a terreiro, he said.

You understand that this happened twenty-five years ago and I was in a sluggish state much of the time. I do know that we went several times before a babalôrixá, a woman priest, persuaded my spirit to speak its name. My spirit was male, which embarrassed me. I did not understand that there is no connection between the gender of the medium and that of the spirit. It took me many weeks to learn to summon my spirit at will and hold him off when the time was bad for me.

Now I have teen-age daughters of my own, but thanks be to God, so far they show no signs of receiving spirits. It is not an easy life, and if they are spared, I will not be sorry.

She stopped talking. We thanked her and left. Probably because the surroundings had been so ordinary, the cheap furniture I knew from a dozen apartments, the traffic noises off Barata Ribeiro, the woman's story had sounded entirely plausible. It wasn't that I had suspended disbelief, more that she spoke so sanely and with a trace of humor about those first puzzled doctors that I was carried along unresisting. If anything, it had been like those tales of women who go to their doctor for a routine physical and find out that they are four months pregnant. This woman too had learned that there was an alien being in her body, which proved to be rather a nuisance but not insupportable once she learned to live with her condition.

It was only back on the street that the complete unacceptability of her story struck me, and even then I didn't doubt her sincerity or wonder why my usual warning signals weren't flashing "Fraud."

THE NEXT AFTERNOON, Nesio was already waiting in the living room of the macumbeira's apartment when I arrived. Since he had arranged for a full consultation, we waited while six or seven housewives from nearby buildings were escorted away for briefer conferences by a dark woman with a blunt Indian face.

Nesio had found a Donald Duck comic book on the coffee table and was lost in that. The women looked at me curiously as we waited together; some Brazilian men are blond-haired and tall, but something, perhaps the length of my trousers, established me as a foreigner. When

I crossed my legs, the woman next to me said politely that the spirits would prefer I didn't.

It was an hour before Nesio and I were taken to an alcove off the kitchen, he directed to one stool and I to another. I thought there had been a mistake and protested.

"It is necessary, Jack," Nesio said. "She must purify you before my reading."

The dark woman put her palms over my outstretched hands and began to vibrate. Pulling back, she snapped her fingers several times, not before my eyes but in a wide arc over my head. Next she locked our foreheads together for a few seconds until, with an immense shudder, she pulled free and snapped her fingers, this time across my heart.

"She found the spirit of an old man trying to use you," Nesio told me. "But she has driven him away."

The blonde macumbeira had slipped in and was seated at a right angle to us. Both women were smoking pipes, the darker woman a man's pipe with a plain brown bowl, the blonde one with an ivory stem. They lighted the pipes every few minutes and spit just as often into wicker baskets lined with newspaper.

When they were ready for Nesio's consultation, the dark woman shook more violently until her half-dozen silver bracelets were clanging around her wrist. Dropping to the floor, she groveled there, grunting and giving snorts of rude laughter. One brusque word from the macumbeira brought her around, and she recovered and stood up.

Around her own feet, the macumbeira had assembled the items Nesio bought from a list she had given him the day before. After we had left her, he had gone up and down Copacabana, touring the musty spiritist shops to find exactly the charms and notions she required.

There were small, garishly painted statues of three spirits—Ogum, Ôxun, and Nanã Burukê—and these the woman marked on their bottoms with a white chalk triangle, all the while puffing smoke over them from her pipe. The marking was leisurely and she paused to refill her pipe from a green and white can marked HALF AND HALF.

(Afterward I asked Nesio, "Only tobacco? No marijuana? No special herbs?" "Only tobacco," he insisted.)

Murmuring Nesio's full name, she placed the three figures around a straw basket, opened his bottle of cheap whiskey, and poured out a mouthful for him in a black cup. After he had swallowed, she uncorked a bottle of perfume, cheaper even than the whiskey, and unwrapped his bar of soap. These she put on the bottom of the basket.

Nesio had bought four spools of thread and now, picking up the royal blue, she showed Nesio how to hold it bobbing in his cupped hands while she unraveled the entire roll. She unwound, repeating Nesio's name along with appeals to the spirits on his behalf. When she finished, a heap of tangled thread lay on the floor outside the basket.

She lifted this mass into her hand and cut crosswise with scissors until the thread was separated into twelve smaller piles, which she scooped together and deposited in the basket.

The ritual was repeated with the red spool, the purple, the white. Nesio would cage a reel and with each tug she gave, it fluttered behind his fingers like a bright moth.

All this took half an hour and was hard work for the macumbeira. More than once I saw her glancing up to see how near she was to the end of the spool. At last each pile was sheared and set into the basket. Later that evening I asked Nesio what the spools had signified.

We were at his bar, and I noticed that he delayed answering until the waiter had left my table. "They represented the confusion in my mind," he said. "That is what she cut through with the scissors."

With the thread cut, the macumbeira asked Nesio for six white roses. She snapped them off at half stem and scraped their upper stalks clean with a paring knife before she laid the blossoms across the basket, covering the statues and the heaps of thread.

From ribbons Nesio had brought she made large flowing bows of the same color as the thread and these she draped over the roses. The red and purple ribbons made a lid for the basket and now there were only glimpses of the white petals.

Chanting softly, she made the sign of the cross over the basket and drew Nesio close to whisper with him. He nodded and stood. At the door he gave the dark woman twenty-seven cruzeiros, four dollars and fifty cents.

In the elevator, I stamped my right leg, which had gone to sleep. My eyes smarted from pipe smoke and I was getting a headache. Nesio seemed let down and more depressed than before the ceremony began. I asked what the money had been for.

"A virgin must take the basket out to the beach tonight and carry it into the ocean. The money is for her." He pronounced the word "virgin" without a leer, another proof of his preoccupation.

"Are you permitted to tell me what the macumbeira said at the end?"

"Yes." His sigh was nearer a groan. I didn't know what else had been present in the alcove, but there had been silence there and hope. Now we were back on the street with the bus fumes and the incessant honking horns.

"She said there is a good chance for Cristina. It will depend on the sacrifice I must make tonight. But if Cristina gets better now and then later she has trouble again, the macumbeira says we must separate. This is our last chance."

Half an hour before midnight, Nesio stopped for me in a taxi. We circled Botafogo bay and headed out to a district called Grajau. Nesio's mood was still somber and the night was offering no relief. The sky was black; there was no moon. It was up to Nesio to choose the corner for his sacrifice and he was slow to decide. We drove past several crossroads that looked desolate enough to me without his telling the driver to stop.

In Copacabana I had seen offerings in the street but they never seemed genuine to me, more as though the tourist association had paid to have them set out each night or they had been the work of children in a spirit of Halloween.

At a particularly dark corner, Nesio spotted a vase with three red roses standing in the gutter with candles and bottles to either side. He motioned to the driver, and when we got out, the cab pulled into the shadows to wait.

The two of us were alone on the street. To our backs, a corrugated iron door had been pulled down over a store front. The one streetlight was broken. The only sound, a dog barking, came from far away. Nesio knelt at the curb and dug into a brown paper bag. I stood over him and then crouched, ready to help if he needed me.

He lighted a white candle and held the match to melt the bottom. But when he went to stick it to the pavement, it fell over. Several times he tried, each time it fell. He may have been nervous. I know I felt uneasy, as though what we were doing was against the law.

After another minute he gave up and propped the candle against the curb. He lighted a small brown cigar, took one puff, then laid it on a box of matches that was slightly open.

He repeated the process until seven burning cigars were laid at the same angle on their matchboxes. They formed seven miniature altars along the curb, each with a lighted candle behind it.

Opening a bottle of white cachaça, the liquor made from fermented sugarcane, he spilled it generously on all four sides of his row of candles and cigars. When he clinked the bottle down, its echo escaped and ran down the street. Under his breath Nesio had begun to pray.

It was a short prayer, only a few seconds before he rose and gestured toward the cab. As we got in, the overhead light went on and I saw Nesio's eyes full of tears.

For me the ritual had been anticlimactic. Nothing he did was as eerie as the night itself.

On Saturday, when Nesio went to visit Cristina, her doctor reported that she was improving beyond all expectation. If her progress continued, she could expect to go home within a week.

Telling me, Nesio was elated, and I was happy for them both. But I said, "She did know that you were making the sacrifice for her?"

"Yes."

"Don't you think that the offering proved that you cared for her? It made her determined to leave the hospital and come home to you. Doesn't that seem right?"

"Yes," Nesio said.

"So you don't think that the spirits heard your prayer and cured her because of it?"

I have found it very hard to get an argument from a Brazilian. Almost always they agree but with their reservations written over their faces. Or they shrug. Or they say, as Nesio said, "I am not sure."

I HAVE ALWAYS BEEN VERY CONSCIOUS of calendar years, to the point that I cut into the reminiscing of my friends with, "Yes, I remember that. It was nineteen sixty-seven."

Most often the interruption throws them off stride and they ask what possible difference the year makes, while on my side I'm surprised that they wouldn't know the landmark dates of their own lives—when they bought a house, divorced a wife—and that they aren't grateful that someone remembers for them.

That same quirk probably accounts for my classifying life like a vintner, by its good years and bad. The first year I went to Europe, 1955, qualified as excellent, along with 1968, which was considerably more pleasurable for me than for the country as a whole. Most of 1965 I passed as a reporter in South Vietnam, and it left a sour taste for years afterward. Nothing will be worse, I thought, and then came 1972, my thirty-ninth year.

Leaving Rio for Los Angeles that June I'd already had forebodings that a novel about the spirits might be beyond my powers. But I found an apartment in Hollywood, shut the drapes against the anemic sunshine off the boulevard, and set to work.

The first chapter I wrote and tore up a dozen times. That took a month, then two, until it became clear that however much I might want to write about Brazilian magic I had no idea how to start.

As I blundered along, I uncovered at least one curious problem: in print the rituals I had seen were sounding too healthy and unfrightening —too commonplace—for fiction. It was as though by introducing the spirits at all I had contracted with the reader to deliver a horror story.

One Sunday I took the afternoon off and drove out Pacific Coast Highway for lunch with two writers, husband and wife, whom I knew casually. They were a compatible pair, for each was a master of the alchemy that transmutes every slight anxiety or neurosis into a bestseller. I found them surprisingly stable and good-humored, and if they had a fault it was their tendency to treat Weltschmerz a bit proprietorially.

This day I barely ventured a word about my hesitation over the novel when the husband or the wife reassured me with a vivid account of his or her latest breakdown. It far overshadowed any mild depression of mine and it was forming the foundation for his or her new book of fiction or reportage.

When I had finished with the commiseration and congratulations, I tried again. "I can't show an Umbanda ceremony as scarifying," I said, "because the Brazilians don't see them that way. When they ask a god, or even a devil, to enter their bodies, it's only to bring them assistance. My problem is that I don't want to misrepresent that attitude."

"Your problem," the husband corrected me languidly, "is that you don't want to make a million dollars."

The next week I kept that rebuke in mind but I was still writing the kind of novel I wouldn't want to read. David Segal had died of a heart attack eighteen months before and I had missed him badly—and miss him still—but never more than during the fall of 1972.

Thrashing about, I arranged to study Portuguese two nights a week with Antonio, a bearded and unfrivolous instructor at UCLA. Tony was a carioca—the Brazilians' word for anyone born in Rio de Janeiro—but he had come to the United States at the age of eighteen and had never gone back.

I didn't tell him about my dabbling with the spirits, either because I thought that after spending nearly twenty years out of Brazil he would be unsympathetic. Or because it could seem presumptuous for a norte-americano to undertake a book about Afro-Brazilian gods. Or—my best guess—because I still wasn't willingly giving much away.

But about our twelfth lesson together, he made a reference to macumba and I allowed that I was not entirely uninterested in the spirits. It was signal enough. We put away our textbooks and he told me about the pressures he felt on his skull whenever a spiritist he knew was trying to contact him from Washington, D.C.

"I have another friend, also a Brazilian, who used to teach literature here in Los Angeles," he said. "Four months ago he started receiving the spirits himself. Would you like to visit him tonight?"

Usually I would stall for a day or two, the better to dredge up my meager store of sociability. But even so far from home, a Brazilian probably never lost his impulsiveness, and if I suggested waiting until next week, I might never meet this fledgling medium.

At ten P.M. we were prowling the quiet streets of West Los Angeles, parking in front of an apartment house with a staircase running up its side like a fire escape.

Husky, short, and smiling, the professor steered us into the kitchen, and looking faintly conspiratorial we took chairs around the table.

"Tony has told you, I suppose," the professor began, "about the terreiro in Long Beach?"

"No," Antonio confessed, "not yet."

"Long Beach, California?" A nondescript port south of Los Angeles, Long Beach had lately spent millions of dollars to purchase itself an identity in the form of a British ocean liner.

The professor said, "Why don't you call Vonda and ask whether you can bring Jack some Sunday?"

My tutor looked torn. Brazilians live to oblige, sometimes to the point of making promises they know they can't keep. But Tony had lived in the United States long enough to know the American contempt for failed expectations. "I will try," he said.

I asked the professor to tell me how the spirits had forced themselves into his life, and as I listened, it sounded as though his experiences were not very different from those of the macumbeira in Rio. The striking variations were that he was telling his story in fluent if quaintly accented English and he was telling it in West Los Angeles.

For the first forty-five years of his life he had rejected spiritism, he said. During the years he taught in Brazil he had even published books to demonstrate that the phenomenon was a harmless form of folklore.

After Brazil's bloodless coup d'état in 1964, the professor realized that his political sympathies had shut most doors to him at home. He took teaching posts elsewhere in South America, and when he wound up in Los Angeles he expected to live out his life there.

Then only last semester he had learned that department politics at a state university could be more punishing than anything he had fled at home. The chairman called him in to say that his contract would not be renewed. For the second time in eight years he was banished, and he was stunned.

26

He thought of suicide. But by chance he heard of an Umbanda terreiro in Long Beach and he and his wife went to investigate. He stayed all Sunday afternoon, and while nothing happened to him, he found the atmosphere calming and liked being among his countrymen again. The Indian spirit who headed the terreiro gave him permission to come back.

Several months passed until, on a Sunday no different from the others, with the dozen mediums joining hands and chanting softly, the professor was lifted off his chair and hurled to the floor. The Indian spirit sent that unruly presence away, out of the professor's body, and over the last four months had been trying to teach him to control the spirits and let only those of a higher development use him.

The experience had left the professor oblivious to his material troubles. "I will go on welfare if I must. It doesn't matter."

He skipped away from the table and came back with a thick manuscript, which he spread over the kitchen table.

"This describes everything that has happened to me," he said. "But how can I publish it? It would cause every colleague I have ever had to break with me. It would be an immense step. I can't let it out until I am sure. I must be sure."

He had described his manhandling by the spirits with excitement that sounded both proud and frightened. I said, "After what has happened to you, you're not sure?"

"How can I be? It is impossible, what happens to me."

To Tony I said, "I hope that I'll be allowed to see the terreiro."

"It is up to Pai Ubiraja," he replied. "Once before I asked on behalf of a girl in one of my classes. She was an American girl whc heard about the spirits and was eager to go with me. They asked Ubiraja and he said she was not ready. She was very pretty."

"But you will try for me?"

"What do you want?" Antonio asked earnestly.

"I don't understand."

"I must tell the spirits in advance what you want."

"Nothing," I said. "There is nothing I want."

"Everybody wants something." He said it reproachfully.

"Tell them that I want to learn. Learn more about the spirits. Would that be enough?"

"I can try," Tony said.

WHEN TONY PUT THE QUESTION, I had been mildly annoyed. What did I want? By the very asking, he was lumping me with the widows in a clairvoyant's parlor demanding messages from beyond the grave. What did I want? It could even be insulting. How did he miss seeing that I had everything a man might need.

But in bed that night I wondered whether his question didn't explain my lame progress on the novel. After six months I still had nothing to say about the spirits and yet I couldn't let the subject loose. Was there something I hoped the spirits would say to me?

What could it be? Except for this recent stumbling with the novel, I was not unhappy. Approaching forty, I wasn't married, but that was by choice. For a dozen years I had enjoyed the company of a woman who had never bored me and who, if she couldn't say the same of me, at least had never said differently.

Philip Gregory had passed through Los Angeles, newly divorced from Jane, who immediately married her lover and was now sending her secret letters to Gregory. Philip was subdued but not so dispirited that he couldn't twit me. "Don't you worry that you're missing something by never marrying?"

I forwent the easy answers; it was a question that hadn't occurred to me for a decade or better.

Metaphysically I considered my life equally well based. Traveling through Europe on a fellowship at the age of twenty-two, I had come across a wide empty beach in Torremolinos at the same time someone put into my hand *The Myth of Sisyphus.* I accepted its stern view of life with no quibble, although I sensed even at the time that however much sunshine I found to warm myself, the inside of my head would be remaining cold and gray.

As the years passed it turned out that with his bleak statement Camus had given me first a comfort and later a faith, to be defended. When

I pressed Nesio to admit that the supernatural had played no part in curing Cristina, I was fighting to protect a vision of the universe that had become very congenial.

Camus was long dead, the accident at Villeblevin chaining him forever to the precepts of *The Fall.* But had he lived, would the Camus of sixty be living by rules he had promulgated at thirty? And if he were, what had that to do with me? I remembered a news story about a man who walked through life looking only at the sidewalk. By the day of his death, he had found sixty-seven dollars. Was I he? And if I resolved henceforth to look up, would there be sufficient rewards in the sky? Or would I merely miss the next five-dollar bill in the gutter?

In the morning I put in a call for Lynn Nesbit, my agent in New York, and by the time Antonio informed me that Pai had countenanced my visiting Long Beach, I had signed a contract to return to Brazil for a factual book about the spirits.

With the contract came a covering letter to Lynn from Frances McCullough at Harper & Row. From Brazilians in New York, she wrote, she knew something about the orixás and for some time she had wanted to publish a book about them. All that held her back was the assurances of her friends that no non-Brazilian could do the research and live.

Melodrama could still make me smile, though I had reached an age when I should know better. Almost ten years had passed since I had gone to Jackson, Mississippi, for an interview with a civil rights leader. He could see me only after his rally, so it was midnight before we met in his office.

When I took a chair near the window he motioned at me to move across the room. "We don't like to have shadows on the shade. It makes too good a target."

Then, excusing himself, he dialed his home number. "It's me," he said, the receiver close to his lips. "Everything's all right. Keep the lights on. Don't answer the door. I'll be home in one hour."

I listened, admiring him for the show he had rehearsed for us northern reporters. But I was wrong, and ten days later Medgar Evers was shot dead.

So in my mind's lumber room, I knew that Brazilians shot and clubbed and knifed each other to death. But where the brain screened its vivid pictures, I couldn't see them doing any of those things to me.

The day I drove to Long Beach the spring sun was strong enough to turn the ocean gold. Along the beach I found the address Tony had given me, an immense apartment building with a lobby wallpapered with flocked velvet. I crowded into an elevator feeling conspicuous in the new white trousers Tony had recommended I buy for the day.

At his doorway the host was waiting to meet me and my self-consciousness faded away in the face of his transparent goodwill. An American in his middle forties, he gave the impression of a man who had survived a cataclysm and wouldn't ever be troubled again. Reformed drunks sometimes have the quality.

He introduced me, first names only, to the forty people who had already gathered in the apartment. Their terreiro could accept fifty members, he said, because that was as many as his living room accommodated. Another fifty had signed a waiting list.

Furniture had been pushed to the side leaving the room bare, and curtains shut out the distraction of Long Beach Bay. But since the panels were lightweight and the sun was persistent, the room had hardly darkened. Rugs and ceiling were white, the walls cerulean, the Brazilians beautiful enough to sit for Raphael, and when the sweet chanting started the scene would have overcome almost anyone's prejudice against heaven.

The sight of the stunning dancers had caused me to overlook the professor, who was sitting on the floor across the room, his stolid wife at his knee. When our eyes did meet, he waved and grinned. I remembered his saying that he was not yet advanced enough as a medium to be allowed to join the others. They were now circling slowly to their right as they sang about Preto Velho:

> "Preto Velho pequenino vem de Angola
> "Na terra preto velho vem trabalhar
> "Para os filhos ele traz na sua sacola
> "Paz e luz os bênçãos de Oxalá."

(Little old black man comes from Angola. Here on earth, old black man comes to work for his children. He brings in his sack peace, light, and the blessings of Oxalá.)

As I watched, the professor confirmed the wisdom of the other mediums in isolating him, for as the song ended, he was brought to his feet by an invisible hand that seized him by the nape. A moment later he was thrown to his knees as though the same hand had pushed him roughly down. With a roar, he raised up again and charged the length of the room and butted his head on the far wall. Two mediums quickly detached themselves from the circle and led him whimpering to his wife. She took his hand firmly and kept him by her side until the convulsions running through his body slowed and finally stopped.

In the meantime, Vonda, the hostess, had received the spirit of Pai Ubiraja, and her possession was followed in rapid order by other spirits taking over the rest of the dancers. I remarked on the speed of the transformation to an elderly Brazilian sitting at my side.

"Yes," he agreed. "It goes smoothly here. But please do not say 'possession.' We use that word only when a bad spirit has come and cannot be dislodged. In those very rare cases it becomes a permanent condition, which is 'possession.' We prefer to speak of 'receiving the spirits' or being 'mounted' by them. You have heard that expression? It is the reason we sometimes call our mediums 'horses.' "

Around me, most of the horses looked dazed, but each man and woman had a helper at hand to steer him around the room so that the spirit could bless those of us on the sidelines. Two men stopped by me and, holding me by the shoulders, assured me that a trip I was planning to Brazil would go smoothly.

At the first chance I checked with the host and found that Tony had reported I would soon be leaving for Rio.

At a lull the host then put a few gentle questions to me. Learning that I was a writer, he asked that I never use his name and, that agreed, he traced his own history with the spirits. By this time I wasn't surprised that his introduction should have also been born of misery.

He had been an aerospace technician, he said, caught in the industry's recession of the late sixties. Laid off at his plant, he tried to keep

31

optimistic but after a year and a half of watching his savings ebb away, his confidence had vanished as well. Scores of résumés went out; not one company sent back so much as an acknowledgment. He too was asking why he should go on living.

It was a story being told in barrooms from Torrance to Van Nuys, except that this man's wife was Brazilian, met and married in Rio when he was a young sailor. Their married life had been spent in California and he sometimes forgot how different her upbringing had been from his own.

One particularly downcast day she said, "I want to do something that might help you. But I'm afraid you'll think I am crazy."

"Anything," the husband said. "I want you to do anything that will help."

The next evening she invited in another Brazilian woman living in Long Beach. Both of them were dressed in white. After a short prayer, they began to chant. As the engineer watched and disbelieved, his wife's face grew flushed. The corners of her mouth twisted down. With an effort she dragged herself up from the couch, hobbled lamely across the room, and demanded her husband give her a cigar.

"Now," a deep male voice demanded in Portuguese, "what is it you want from me?"

As the host told it, by Thursday of the next week two companies offered him work. They were responding to résumés he had sent out months before. A week after that he accepted a job with a third company, where he had worked ever since.

After Ubiraja released his wife, he asked her how they could have been married twenty years without her mentioning that she was a medium, and she confessed that she had been receiving spirits from the time she was a young girl but that when she met the young American naval officer, she was afraid that the presence of Ubiraja in her body would frighten him away. She had always found the receiving of spirits taxing and so she resolved to live in America as an American wife. Had he not been in trouble, she would never have returned to her Indian spirit.

While the host was speaking, across the floor a teen-age boy named Claudio had begun to act even more strangely than the others. Hands stretched straight out, eyes glazed over, he was shaking as though his lips were blue with cold. Watching him shiver, I wondered how long anyone could endure that jolting. Two older mediums on either side were murmuring encouragement in Portuguese.

His shaking went on for ten minutes, twenty. Thirty. To me it seemed that now his sentries were looking distraught and I thought, My God, they can't get him out of it. What will they do next? Strike him? Pack him down with blankets? Give him a hypodermic?

This time I wouldn't look away. The current seemed to start above his head, run in waves down his skinny body, and short out on the floor. Limping on his left leg, Pai Ubiraja passed in front of me and followed my eyes to the spot where Claudio stood shuddering. The spirit was screwing Vonda's delicate features into a grimace that verged on contempt and in Portuguese he said to me:

"You must not worry about Claudio." (The host translated what I missed.) "He is learning to develop as a medium, and what is happening to him now is doing him only good. There is nothing to be afraid of. But the waves of apprehension you are casting into this room are making it more difficult for the spirits to work properly."

I nodded and for distraction I looked once more to the professor, who was in the midst of four young women, none of them receiving a spirit although all were talking at once. When Pai Ubiraja joined their circle, the host beckoned me over to hear what counsel the spirit was dispensing.

One girl had been complaining in Portuguese but as I joined them the spirit cut her short and told her to speak English.

"A spirit understands all languages," Vonda's husband explained to me. "Although Pai Ubiraja prefers to use Portuguese, he thinks it will be easier for you if they ask their questions in your tongue."

"Thank you." I said it in the direction of Ubiraja, which caused Vonda's face to cloud over as the spirit frowned.

"One does not thank the spirits," the host explained. "One says, 'Thanks to God' or a similar phrase. But nothing so personal as 'Thank you.'"

"Why does the spirit limp?"

"He injured his leg in the forest shortly before his death four hundred or more years ago. We have asked him for more details but he gets impatient."

The Brazilian girl resumed her questioning of the pai. "Sometimes it is not convenient to receive my spirit. It is the wrong time for me. But I do not want to give offense. What should I do?"

The old Indian limped back and forth, puffing on a thick brown cigar. "The spirit guides want to help you," he said, "not to cause you difficulties."

I was looking for traces of Vonda that might have survived the turning over of her body to the spirit but every gesture looked masculine. Now the Indian was clapping himself roughly across the chest.

"Do this," he said and hugged himself tightly, "while you say, 'Forgive me!' That way you can hold off your spirit until a time that suits you better."

"What about me?" the professor asked. He had seemed subdued and despondent since his disruptive spirit had been dispatched. "Is there no way to receive the spirits that would be less embarrassing?"

"When one achieves perfect harmony between spirit and horse, there is none of that commotion." Ubiraja was stumping the circle, speaking from over his shoulder. When he wheeled and faced the professor, he was wearing a sardonic grin. "But why are you ashamed? Why must you always be dignified? This is not your classroom. Maybe the spirit is helping you by making you wild."

The rest of the afternoon was given over to individual consultation. At one point I saw Ubiraja examine a tumor the size of an apricot on the back of a woman's neck, and I heard the spirit of a Dutch clergyman giving advice in nineteenth-century English to a Brazilian diemaker. I only know that several hours had passed when there was no light beyond the white curtains and the host said it was nearly time for the spirits to depart.

Ubiraja was the last to go, and before he left he accosted me a final time. "Do you believe?" he demanded.

"I want to know more."

The spirit nodded brusquely, as though I had given the only sensible answer. "When you return to Brazil," he went on, "you will be able to learn. You are a medium yourself, but of the intuitive kind. As you know, every living person has spirit guides. Yours I do not think you will receive directly."

The Indian turned to go, then hobbled back. "In Brazil you will be invited to visit the Candomblé. I could tell you to stay away, to go only to Umbanda, the white line. But you would not heed me. Out of curiosity, you will go to the Candomblé. When you do, remember what I am telling you now:

"Use only your eyes and your ears. For if you should speak, you could permit uncontrollable spirits to enter through your open mouth and take command of your body."

I forgot my lesson and thanked him.

Ubiraja turned away. After a moment of chanting by the other mediums, he vanished from the apartment. Vonda, left behind, looked disoriented for an instant. Then she smiled faintly and disappeared into her kitchen to lay out a buffet supper for the other hungry horses.

ONCE IN RIO I caught myself delaying my investigation with any excuse I could make remotely plausible. In the tiny occult shops I bought more books about Umbanda and called that a day's work. At night I consulted with Brazilian layabouts and barflies on likely places for my research. Catching one head cold in the chilly May sun, I nursed it into a second, but when that cleared up and the time had come I must set off, I stalled another week.

"I am worried for your safety," said the same Jayme, whose own spirit of adventure had not extended to risking a visit to a terreiro in Copacabana. "If you go up to Bahia, it may help a little that you are American. The French, like the English, have a manner that the plain people of Brazil do not like."

"I'm not worried about them harming me," I said. "I worry about being ignored. My Portuguese is not perfect—"

"No."

"—and they could refuse to talk with me. I'll be entirely alone and I can picture myself going from village to village and no one telling me anything."

"Yes," Jayme agreed. "That is another possibility."

At about that same time Miss Betty weighed in with a number of warnings, though her concern was less for a cracked skull than irreparable damage to my soul. An American astrologist with some thirty-five birthdays behind her, Betty was one of my happiest chance acquaintances in Rio. Her weight waxed and waned in lunar fashion and when we met she was at her fullness, some three hundred pounds of revealed wisdom.

Betty had flown down to Brazil from Mexico City, where the film colony had taken her up, making her the toast of the Zona Rosa and creating a heavy demand for her fifty-dollar astrological readings. In Rio, she found the market in soothsayers already glutted and the shortage of customers was not only daunting her good nature but starving her back to a crescent.

Betty in her turn had found nothing to admire about Rio except, possibly, the unabashed way that Brazilian men fondled their genitals in public. "If they ever get tired of doing that," she would say, "I'll be happy to take over for a while."

(Later I discovered what a gallery of castration ogres the Brazilian male had inherited from his Indian and African forebears. One authority cited twenty-seven different monsters, including the papão [bogeyman], lobisomen [werewolf], Maria de Manta [Devilish Mary], saci-pererê [one-legged Negro boy], and homem-de-pés-as-avessar [man with his feet on backward]. In those circumstances, it seemed only prudent for a man to take frequent inventory. But at the time, I had accepted Miss Betty's view that the gesture indicated a perpetual heat.)

A bawdy spiritist, then, Betty, one who feared nothing on earth and very little on the next nine astral planes. Yet even she cautioned me.

"You had better stay away from this macumba or whatever they call it here. Your chart shows that you are distinctly deficient in spiritual development. You can't handle much exposure to their kind of magic."

Betty's warning I could dismiss as the result of her anti-Brazilian prejudices but it did amount to one more discouraging word.

Nesio at least came up with a practical suggestion. Since there was no single authoritative voice that spoke for either Candomblé or Umbanda, he said, instead of going into the bush why didn't I make the next several months more agreeable by writing about a center near Rio? During my absence Cristina's nerves had snapped again, and Nesio had moved in with a young woman from the suburbs; it was she who would introduce me to her family's pai do santo.

"No. I must go to Bahia," I told him. "That's where Candomblé began and it will be purer there."

"You do not know where to go," he argued. "Salvador is only another large city. You are better off staying in Rio."

"I am collecting the names of towns in the forest that have a terreiro." The sheet of paper in my pocket made me feel that these weeks in Rio hadn't been wasted. Reading the names aloud warmed my blood and satisfied any urge to travel north. "Ituberá, Acaraí, Marau, Itacare, the isle of Limoeiro."

"I have never heard of those places," Nesio said. "Sex will be harder in a small town."

"I am not going for the sex," I said. "I am going for the magic."

Nesio shook his glossy mane and I too wondered whether I was insisting on a distinction that didn't exist.

"Have you decided on a town?" Dimitri asked a week later. He was an artist, pale and brooding, but initiated from childhood into a Candomblé, where he had reached the rank of ogan, or overseer, of his terreiro.

"I am going to a place called Camamu," I told him. "It is seven hours by bus from Salvador and there are supposed to be several mães do santo there."

"Camamu? I never heard of it. Why Camamu?" Dimitri was another of those who thought my research could be accomplished near Rio.

"I like the name," I said. "I'm leaving at the end of next week."

"No!" Dimitri protested. "That would be too disappointing to Tauá. She is holding her Candomblé that Saturday night and you must stay for that. It will be an initiation of two new filhos do santo. You may never have the chance to see another one."

Tauá was Dimitri's younger sister, a twenty-one-year-old mannequin in a Copacabana boutique. Six feet tall, tawny and lean, no one's idea of a genuine witch, Tauá had all the same established a terreiro with herself as the mãe do santo. Her rite would be the first valid reason in a month to put off my trip a little longer.

Tauá and Dimitri lived with their mother, grandmother, and twelve-year-old half-sister Wilsa in the suburb of Deodoro, two hours away by bus. Since it was impossible to find without a guide, Tauá came by for me in the late afternoon. She had already stopped on the island of Niteroi for twelve bottles of batida, the sweet liquor made from fermented sugarcane and fruit juice, and huffing from the load she was also sniffling and red-nosed from a bad case of grippe. Nonetheless, she fell on my neck with a whoop that echoed down the apartment halls and collected a kiss on each powdered cheek.

The bus ride took us first along miles of industrial detritus—smokestacks, oil refineries, water towers—and then past wooden shacks with naked black children playing on their stoops. I had not visited the family before and at their house Dimitri was waiting at the gate to prepare me. "Oh, Jack," he sighed, "please do not look too closely. We are so poor."

A small house had been built to the back of a deep lot, and now in front of its open porch two bare-chested men were raising a green canvas tent roof. "It is for the spirits," Dimitri explained. "They will not come unless we have a covering for them."

Their mother came to welcome me, a sweet, distracted widow who, when she went plump in another year or two, might stop dyeing her hair straw blonde. She held a clerical job with the government and apparently managed her money well for without a husband she had sent Tauá through modeling school and she was putting Dimitri through teachers college, though he intended to paint and never teach.

As he had warned, their house was cramped and poorly furnished, but at the back two rooms had been given over to the Candomblé. In one of them the two young male initiates had been sequestered for twenty-one days. Tauá had shaved their heads five nights ago, and I suspected that at some point the rites would include a blood sacrifice.

But to raise that subject so early in the day smacked of sensation mongering and instead I asked Dimitri how a child of European stock had become involved with Candomblé.

"We were living then in Salvador," he said. "I was a baby, an infant. My mother had taken me for a blessing by a pai do santo. You know the words? A father of the saint. This pai was receiving Inhasã, the goddess of winds and storms."

"I still find it strange that a man may receive a female spirit."

"It often happens. Inhasã came forward and took me out of my mother's arms. She showed me to the congregation and told them that I had been chosen by the orixás, the African gods."

"You have never received a spirit yourself?"

"No," he said, without regret. "I was taught every secret of the Candomblé but I do not receive."

He rolled up the sleeve on his left arm and showed me a figure pricked out on his biceps.

"That was put on me when I was ten years old. The crossbar is a sort of—in English do you say irony? For Candomblé, the lines pointing down and up mean that man digs the hole, but it is God who kills."

"Man digs the grave?"

"So." Dimitri often said "so" for "yes," a habit acquired during his four years of English lessons.

I saw two skins hung to dry above the outdoor sink. "What are those?"

"I do not know your word for them, Jack," he apologized. "We call them cabritos. You understand?" I shook my head. "It says so: Baa, baa."

39

"Lamb."

"No, I think not lamb." Without a bilingual dictionary at hand, we let the matter slide. Later, after I had gnawed at the bone from the cabrito, someone explained that it was goat.

Dimitri led me back to the front yard to see his shrine to the devil, a four-foot cement box near the front porch. "This is my home for Legbara."

"Is that the same as Exú?"

"We say Legbara." Dimitri did not pronounce the g. "Or Leba. Or Exú. He is something like your devil."

He drew a key and opened the door. From inside, a round head glared at us. The fat cheeks and razor-thin mouth made it look like a malevolent Buddha. "I made him myself from clay," Dimitri said. "I could have put horns on him but they would only have been for shock."

"How often do you come to worship here?"

"You can see. It is not clean in there. I think, eight months since last time. Because I have been busy with my school. But Tauá fed her Leba yesterday."

Next to Dimitri's concrete bunker stood a wooden lean-to. There was no lock and when Dimitri pulled the door open, the body of a white hen tumbled out. Its neck had been slit and white feathers were scattered over the ground.

"Where is the Leba?"

"That is he." Dimitri pointed to a pile of rock. Perched at the top was a piece of metal twisted into a shape like a swastika, and given its associations it suggested evil more effectively than Dimitri's round-cheeked idol.

"No face?"

"It does not have to be a representation. Iron and rock are enough."

"Tauá killed the chicken herself?"

"Yes. And the cabritos."

"Slit their throats?"

A shrug. "Yes."

"Do you ask your Leba for favors?"

"Not for a long time."

"He will do bad things if you ask him?"

"Sometimes."

"Would he kill someone?"

I had noticed before that for all their usual doe's softness, Dimitri's eyes could glint like a stag's. "Yes. Yes, Jack."

"Has he ever killed anyone for you?"

He hesitated a long time. I was ready to change the subject when he said, "It is not good to do. I do not like to do it."

"But you have?"

"Oh, three years ago." He spoke as though it were a folly of his youth. He would have been twenty-one at the time.

"Who? Who was it?"

"A bad man."

"Bad how? What had he done?"

We were speaking English, which made his answers as halting as my questions. "A friend of mine came to see me and said someone had done a work against him."

"Put a hex on him?" He did not seem to approve of my paraphrase but he nodded. "And you could not take off this hex?"

"It was very strong. It was necessary—"

"That the bad man die?"

"The other was my friend, Jack."

"How did you know Legbara would help you?"

Dimitri pulled from his pocket a black necklace with two lighter stones at one end. "Coral," he said. "In Brazil, more expensive than gold. I draw squares in the earth and cast the coral beads in front of my Leba. He tells me if he will help."

"He agreed that the bad man should die?"

"He agreed."

"And the man did die?"

"Yes."

"Soon after?"

"A month. More or less."

We had started back toward the house. I might get one last answer before Tauá swooped down on us. "How did he die?"

"A car hit him." He had picked up something I hadn't intended my expression to reveal for he added, "I would not do it now. It was very hard work. Very hard for me. But then I had to do it, Jack, for my friend."

AT TEN O'CLOCK THAT NIGHT, Tauá danced out from the roncó, the room at the back of the house where the initiates had been living for three weeks. She was followed by her six daughters of the saint, one of whom was a young man dressed in starched skirts. I had noticed him earlier when he was still wearing a shirt and trousers, an Italianate boy with his long fingernails painted pink. "Why?" I asked Dimitri.

"He likes to dress up as a woman."

"That must be very hard for him." I had in mind the social stigma.

Again Dimitri was amused. "No, I think for him it is very easy."

Two of the girls were gorgeous mulattas with curried black lashes and skin that changed from red to yellow under the lamplight. One heavy white woman looked already winded from the short trot to the front yard.

Along the fence, two black drummers were rolling out steady thunderclaps while twelve-year-old Wilsa slapped haphazardly at a smaller drum. From the house next door I could hear faint voices raised in song and I asked Dimitri's mother whether it was another Candomblé.

"Protestants," she said negligently. "They do not like us."

The early ritual was informal, the mediums dancing and resting at their own pace. When Tauá went to sit, she was challenged by her layers of billowing petticoats and she had to thrust them up and then plop quickly down before the ruffles and lace beat her to the chair. She won the race and nested there, trapped by underskirts, as though she were decorating a five-foot meringue.

The yard was filling with onlookers, whom Dimitri viewed with disdain. Tradition demanded that no one be turned away from a Candomblé, he explained. But he kept checking the front door to be sure the house was locked.

42

In the midst of a dance there was a stir at the gates and Tauá burst into applause and cued the drummers to a song of welcome. A squat fellow, looking Hawaiian in his floral shirt and checkered pants, made his way through the crowd.

He was the pai do santo from a nearby Candomblé and as such he was entitled to a kitchen chair next to Tauá's own. Several men detached themselves from the crowd and came to kneel and kiss his hand.

Within an hour, that drumroll and chant was repeated five times for other dignitaries as they arrived. One mãe do santo, a stout woman I would have expected to see at a bingo parlor, strode in with a flip of her blue shawl, took Tauá in her arms coldly, then commandeered a chair and studied the proceedings through tinted glasses.

The next time Tauá returned from the roncó she was carrying a bell, a leper's bell with a dire dull clapper, which she swung over the heads of the drummers. To me her dancing looked intentionally stiff and ungainly, but she flung her thin arms wide, lifted the puffy mass of skirts and spun and shook her meatless shanks. Not a religion of us inhibited Midwesterners, I thought. For that matter, how many seminarians would survive Union Theological if they were required to inspire a congregation each Sunday by rising in the pulpit and waggling their buttocks?

A clutch of young men had come to lean against the fence not far from my chair. Most of them were wearing bib overalls, the fashion in Rio at the moment, and they could duplicate the steps of the Candomblé dances as they jostled and nudged each other.

Dimitri looked annoyed with them and he whispered to me, "Entendidos. They always know where there is a Candomblé." Entendido, which means "one who understands," had been settled upon as the word Brazilian homosexuals preferred for themselves.

Tauá launched into an athletic can-can, with a pecking forward dive that sent her skirts flying up in the back. But so trussed in linen was she that only more skirts showed. She had tucked her many necklaces into her blouse to stop their flapping when she spun, and in this dervish spinning before me I saw no trace of the yawning, runny-nosed girl who kept falling asleep on the bus.

The middle-aged mãe with tinted glasses now rose deliberately and tied her shawl over her housedress. Taking the floor, she did a slower, stylized version of Tauá's steps.

Perhaps to confound her, Tauá called for an outright samba, and twenty or more onlookers, including a band of entendidos, joined in with the relief I remembered from boyhood when, after several lagging and seldom-sung hymns, a Lutheran congregation turned to "Onward Christian Soldiers."

This was the traditional Brazilian sound with a beat that allowed for "hey! hey!" and "ai! ai! ai!" Even the mãe in the housedress unlimbered and shook her shoulders with the others. It was now one o'clock in the morning.

Tauá passed among us with a pan heaped with white rose petals. I took a handful, which went limp in my palm while I was looking around to see what I should do with them. At a shout from the back, I turned to see two young men, heads shaved and covered with lace skullcaps, being driven toward us like mules.

Their eyes were closed and they were shivering. One boy's hairy chest looked incongruous with the short white skirts they were both wearing. Pushed forward, they were made to bow to the drums while the dancers tapped their hands over their mouths and gave a child's Indian war cry, "Whoo! Whoo! Whoo!"

On their way back to the roncó, the initiates passed among us and we pelted them with our white rose petals.

After another half-hour of dancing, the candidates appeared again, now wearing colored skirts and with red petals woven into their lace caps. As they were driven away, the rest of us were threatened with a dousing from an unsmiling brown girl who came by scattering blood from a porcelain basin. I wondered whether it had been bled from the goat. Too thick for chicken's blood, I decided, before I recalled that I had never seen a chicken bleed.

Whatever the substance was, the girl scooped it up with her fingers and flung it across the ground.

Most dancers jumped out of her path, but one boy got bloodstains on his jeans, and several more retreated to wipe the red beads off their shoes.

The dirt was saturated with blood by the time the boys were brought out for the third and last time. This, Dimitri alerted me, would be the climax of the evening.

The caps had been plucked off the novices' heads and their shaved male skulls looked feminine, as in the old newsreels French girls who had their heads shaved for sleeping with German soldiers always looked mannish.

Tauá pulled the hairy boy to the center of the terreiro and spun him, still bent forward like a dumb animal, until he looked dizzy. Whirling him faster, she called on the spirit mounting him to reveal itself. "Speak your name!" she cried.

As though a mute had encountered a miracle, the boy leaped high in the air and with a rusty croak gave out a single word.

"I didn't understand," I said to Dimitri. "What is the spirit's name?"

"No one ever understands the names the first time they are spoken," he assured me. "We will have to wait."

While the ritual was repeated for the second young man, the first stood upright, still quivering with his eyes pressed shut. The speaking of the second name seemed to be the signal for mass hysteria, for suddenly Tauá was bent double, emitting hideous caws, and a small dark boy was shaking and grunting like a pig. The plump girl from Tauá's circle had slipped under and was mewing piteously.

Above the barnyard noise, women were wailing like sirens and stumbling blindly until they were taken to the roncó at the back. Most of the men receiving a spirit were instantly set upon by the others, who rolled their trouser legs several inches off the ground. That, according to Dimitri, indicated that the spirit was masculine. Men taken by a female spirit had their cuffs left down to suggest skirts.

Even as the howling went on I could notice distinctions being drawn. One black man made a good show of receiving his spirit, staggering about with the rest, but he was pointedly ignored. Apparently someone had determined that his trance was not genuine.

Along the fence the entendidos were feigning sudden seizures and doing it remarkably well, capturing the absent stare and the lurch that never quite sent them tumbling.

Through the din Tauá remained the most striking figure, emerging from the room at the back as purposeful as a queen and then, when she reached the dancers, doubling over again and beginning her infernal squawking. In her natural state the girl was birdlike enough, with something of the crane or stork about her, and now ruffled and flapping, with any hint of human intelligence extinguished in her eyes, I saw her as a threat, a bird that could cut deep with her talons and bite with hidden teeth. Those claws of hers could handle a knife.

Watching her warily, I had a clue as to why I didn't like birds or animals: one couldn't reason with them.

It was nearly three A.M. when the new filhos do santo, sons of the saint, came out in costumes appropriate to their spirits. One boy was wearing a green skirt and a sash, but he was crowned by a helmet spiked with red and white plumes. The hairy boy was more demurely dressed, and from his pink sash and silver tiara, it seemed his spirit had been feminine. But then a pasteboard sword, also painted silver, was swinging at his side.

"That is Inhasã," Dimitri said. "Her sword should be bronze but it was not ready in time."

The dancing struck up afresh and Dimitri unlocked his front door and urged me inside for a glass of the peach batida. That was how it happened that I was gone from the yard, wincing at the brandy, when the shouts outside took on a different tone. They were coherent, and angry, and I could make out curses in the foulest Portuguese slang. I left my glass and hurried out to see.

All drumming and dancing had stopped. The middle-aged mother of the saint, with her shawl pulled back to a more seemly position on her shoulders, was occupying center stage and she seemed to be castigating Tauá, her Candomblé, the entendidos and other onlookers; me.

On the sidelines stood a figure so heavily hung with hemp from crown to ankle that no feature or suggestion of its sex penetrated the grass disguise. From the books I recognized him as Obaluaé, whose appearance marked the end of a ritual. Instead, this inflamed woman was shouting him down.

She was erupting at such speed that I missed her best vituperation. But I caught the thrust, that Tauá's Candomblé had been a ludicrous

46

failure, ruined by outsiders, strangers who could never appreciate the mysteries, even foreigners come to gape. And over there, those half-men with ridicule in their hearts.

Anyone who believed that the spirits would appear at such a carnival knew nothing of the Candomblé, she shouted. There was only one fit meeting place for the ancient gods and that was two blocks down the street, at her house. There the spirits were assured that they always would be received with respect.

Tauá was equal to the challenge and sprang toward the woman, checking herself a fist's length away. "Go take it up the ass!" she hollered, although in Portuguese the phrase lacked force since its key word was "bunda"—drawn out: boonda—the soft and comfortable sound of an overstuffed cushion.

Dimitri steered Tauá by the shoulders back to the roncó to regain her composure. The other woman was still standing with her hands on her hips, calling on the crowd to uphold her. "Am I not right?" she demanded. They regarded her tepidly, as though the interruption was only another scheduled event.

Which indeed it proved to be. Dimitri loped to my side to report that the woman did the same thing at every Candomblé. "She always disrupts the ceremony and says it is a fraud and only hers are authentic. Tonight it was worse for her because you were here. She has what we call olho grande, do you understand?"

"The big eye? She is jealous?"

"So."

Dimitri left me to stroll over and yell at the woman for a while.

But she had played her scene too long and the crowd was breaking up. With an imperious fling of her shawl, she invited the stragglers to go with her from this contaminated area. No one followed and she swept out alone.

I caught up with Dimitri again, arguing with one of the young drummers. "My friend says we should not have spoken to her so," Dimitri said. "She is his mother."

"Then I can understand his feeling."

"Oh, Jack, he has said much worse about her."

The boy went on fretting but he made no attempt to run after his mother, who could be heard a block away, crying to the heavens for vindication.

Tauá had pulled off her turquoise skirt and was marching about in white petticoats. The entendidos were gone, the boy dressed as a filha had unwound his turban. "I will be heading back to Copacabana," I said.

I had barely spoken when one of the lovely mulattas sank to her knees in the middle of the yard and started to bark like a dog.

"Quick!" Dimitri said, eager that I miss nothing. "She is receiving Exú."

By the time we reached her, Tauá had pulled a white scarf into a huge bow and pinned it to the girl's hair. "No, tonight it is not Exú," Dimitri corrected himself. "It is one of his daughters."

The girl edged forward on her bare knees. Even with a disagreeable smile pulling at the corners of her mouth, she seemed to me as beautiful a girl as I had seen anywhere. Her voice was harsh; holding out her hand, she looked like one of the legendary jazz singers wheedling for a fix.

"Please, senhor," she said. "Have pity."

"She wants money?"

"A little only," Dimitri said. "One cruzeiro, no more. It is Exú who makes her beg."

I put the small green bill in her hand. Her empty eyes ignored it while her fingers clasped it tight. In a monotone, she said to the air, "I am the daughter of a whore. The daughter of a whore, and my father is the devil."

When I looked back from the gate, she was still on her knees. The white bow had come undone from her hair and was trailing on the ground as she tried to coax money from the trunk of a broad-leafed tree.

IN **"Self-Reliance,"** Emerson chides those of us who find adventure in setting off on a journey. You cannot escape yourself, he warns us, but he overlooks the changes in ourselves that an improvement in latitude usually brings. I still had misgivings about the reception awaiting me in the forest, but I boarded the overnight bus for Salvador stimulated by not knowing when I'd be coming back or how I might be changed when I did. I might return doubting that self-reliance was a goal worth pursuing.

Emerson's essay had struck me as peculiarly American, and at the edge of forty, I felt just as American and—who's to call it a tautology?—a little foolish to be expecting an upheaval in my life.

The bus trip to Salvador would take twenty-five hours but as soon as we climbed to the mountains around Petropolis I knew I had done right not to fly. The forest there was a tangle of green in shades from black to yellow, and then two hours later we were out of those wilds, rolling past rich farmland laid out in patches, like a quilt.

The design of the farmhouses never varied, nor did their expression. Each had two windows thrown open as wide as a raised eye, and doors ajar between them to make a pucker of surprise. At every curve we rounded I caught another house spying us with the same look of amazement.

The bus seat reclined into a passable bed, and after a stop for dinner the steward brought pillows and plaid wool blankets. I slept the night and woke up on a rainy morning a few hours out of Salvador.

From its perimeters, the city seemed to be Brazil's San Francisco, built on hills that gave a steep pitch to the streets and provided sudden, sweeping views of the bay. "You will love Salvador. All estrangeiros do." I had heard that prediction regularly in Rio but in the steady rain the city looked dismal and I booked a ticket for the next morning's bus to Camamu.

That bus left its station at five-thirty A.M. Our start through the blackness was promising, quiet and smooth, but at dawn we turned off on a muddy road pitted with holes where the rain had collected. Over the next seven jarring hours we passed through a score of villages, towns, hamlets, of which one was attractive. And Valença qualified only because of a wide square with slightly more green grass than red mud.

Along the road, the small houses were shuttered against the rain, and I took them to be all painted red. But it was mud, splattering them from the road. Their sides were white or pink or pastel blue.

After an hour of preliminary smiles and throat clearing, the fellow in the next seat introduced himself as Manuel. A mulatto with finely cast features, Manuel was wearing a jaunty black beret, possibly to cover his hairline as it moved back from his brow. Helter-skelter gaps among his teeth made his open grin raffish, but usually he smiled with his lips tightly pursed, which gave him a prim, even smug, look.

He worked as the steward at a yacht club near Rio and went nights to hotel school. From dealing with foreigners at the club he could make sense out of my answers, and since I hadn't expected to find anyone in Bahia who spoke English, it was a relief that someone understood my Portuguese.

Manuel was returning home for his holidays. At Camamu he would rent a horse for five dollars and cover the last eight-hour lap to his house.

Before emigrating to Rio, Manuel had spent the first twelve years of his life in Camamu and he was torn between affection and contempt for the town I had chosen. "Muita primitiva," he said judiciously. "Mas tranquila e calma." But even granting the peacefulness, he couldn't understand why I should be going there.

"For the Candomblé," I said.

"Oh, yes. Many Candomblés around Camamu and Ituberá. Many, many."

"You attend the Candomblé then?"

"No," he said, offended. "My family is Seventh-Day Adventists."

He was even more unsettled to hear that I would know no one in Camamu. "Until I arrange for my horse, I will try to help you," he promised. "The people are very simple. They are very pleasant. But most of them have never seen a gringo."

For the rest of the trip, Manuel pointed past the curtain of rain to dendê palms, imported from Africa at the insistence of the early slaves. To acres of green cacau, which Americans called cocoa. To waxy white flowers, like giant lilies of the valley, with a girl's name: Angélica.

"Bonita," I responded and speaking truthfully; everything was strange enough to be lovely. But I would have said "linda" and "bacana" even if I had felt reservations. In coming to Bahia I was pledged not to rate and analyze each novelty.

"Oh," Manuel said finally. "Senhor Jacks thinks everything is beautiful." He pronounced the last word in English and got five derisive syllables out of it.

"Yes. Tudo. All."

"It is not *very* beautiful here," he corrected me. "But I like it."

By the time we reached Camamu it was still raining, and as we drove into town I finally saw something in Bahia that was not remotely beautiful. Camamu seemed to be one cobblestone street of faded houses with rain streaming off their stained tile roofs. There was no one in the road and no faces showed at the windows. "Linda, yes?" Manuel asked sarcastically.

"Tudo," I persisted. "All."

Children were lurking in the doorway of an abandoned church and as we got off the bus, two of them grabbed our suitcases and dashed off, balancing them on their heads. I was still getting my tape recorder off the overhead rack and I shouted, "Wait! You do not know which hotel."

"There is only one," Manuel said.

We sprinted after them along the wet cobblestones. Every building we passed was charred outside and I said, "There has been a fire."

"No, it is dirt."

I saw that Manuel was right. Some roofs had collapsed, and on those upper stories the black beams were exposed, but the dark filth that covered everything was only dirt, not ashes. Manuel felt obliged to say, in extenuation, "The buildings are very old."

But they had the dates of construction chiseled over their doorways: 1952, 1967, 1963.

Except for its painted wood sign, the hotel was one more frame house but its second floor had been divided into four sleeping cubicles. From the bowels of the interior, a harried, fat, pretty woman came out to see what the bus had brought her.

We filed into a dark sala with a cracked mirror and one red plastic chair. Manuel and the woman insisted together that I sit down while they established terms. The parlor was nearer the kitchen than the toilet but it was not the kitchen I smelled.

After some rapid bargaining, Manuel said to me, "There is only one room."

"But two beds?"

He put the question to the senhora. "Three," she said.

My previsions of Camamu hadn't included a roommate, but the town looked so barricaded against outsiders by the rain that I wasn't sorry for Manuel's presence. "All right."

A torrent was hammering at the roof as we went upstairs to inspect our lodgings. The senhora ran ahead to close a broken shutter but the rain had already soaked the mattress beneath the window. I set my bag out of reach of the water sweeping in and looked around us.

A dusty bulb hung by a cord from the ceiling. The walls had once been powder blue, which had later been overlaid with tan paint, except where the painters had skimped or the bedsteads were scraping down to the original white plaster. Those few places where the blue and white showed through might have been sky, except that I had a feeling skies in Camamu were always gray.

Manuel was smiling with his lips closed. "Beautiful?"

It had become a test of will. "Perfeito."

The senhora had bowed herself out, and I sat on a dry bed. "How much?"

"With three meals," Manuel said, satisfied with his haggling, "twenty-five cruzeiros apiece." A little more than four dollars.

The senhora, whose name was Dona Bela, came back with chunks of cardboard to patch the shutter and to bolster some shortcomings in Manuel's bedspring. I looked away, hoping the suspension of critical faculties didn't require offering to trade beds with him.

It would not be the worst place I had slept. Once, reporting from Cambodia, I had spent a night on a Vietnamese mess table and, after Tet, on a bloody stretcher in Hue. But that was for a night or two, and usually with an Australian cameraman along to grumble for both of us and the prospect of a hot bath in Saigon or Bangkok.

Manuel was self-pleased but not insensitive. "I think you should go back to Valença," he said. "It is a bigger town and a few people speak English there. They also have a cinema."

"I did not expect a cinema."

"But Camamu has no restaurant either, and no laundry, no hospital, no telephones, no hot water, no—"

Simpler to break in and assure myself what Camamu had. "But there are Candomblés here?"

"Claro," he said; of course. "My mother is a comadre of a mãe do santo. Tomorrow I will take you to see her."

"Then I will stay in Camamu."

It was nearly four P.M. when the rain let up and Manuel suggested walking to the street's end and looking down at cidade baixa, the lower part of town that ran along the river. At the base of the cliff, a few small skiffs lay at anchor around a fishing launch. The river to the north was intersected by thickly wooded islands, and past them I had only a sense of the ocean beyond. Otherwise, a forest surrounded us and closed the view along the horizon. On the islands the overlay of brush looked hostile to human life, and a current scarcely showed across the surface of the brown river.

"What is the lower town like?"

"We will go down another time. You would not like to live in the baixa. As a gringo, you would feel very isolated there."

Manuel set off to renew acquaintances around town and I went back to the hotel. Dona Bela had made our beds with sheets that were damp but clean and I had barely stretched out when I was asleep. It must have been an hour later that Manuel came in and sank onto his cot. He was sobbing quietly.

"What is it?" I was thick with sleep. "What's the matter?"

When he didn't answer, I reached out and turned on the dim bulb. "Tell me. What's wrong?"

"My mother," Manuel said. "She is dead."

"You just heard now?"

"They thought I knew. They thought that was why I had come home. It was very sudden. Her heart. She was only fifty. Oh, God."

"You are sure? There is no mistake?" Impossible that accurate news could penetrate a forest like this.

"I am sure. Oh, God, why? Why?"

He cried and said she had been a good mother. I said that I was sorry. He blew his nose and said he would miss her with all his heart. I said that I was sorry.

When dinnertime came, he would not eat and I didn't want to leave him alone. At seven o'clock, bells chimed and he looked up from his pillow and asked whether I would like to see the main church.

It was raining again. As we ran down the street, I noticed that each doorway had been daubed with a number and the initials C.E.M. "What does that mean?"

"It proves that the house was sprayed by the Campaign to Eradicate Malaria," Manuel said. "There was a problem some years ago with the river."

The church fronted a square near the same hill that led to the lower city. As we dashed up the steps, three old women followed after, headed for their evening prayers.

We sat in a pew near the front. From a loft behind us, I heard fingers strumming absently across an organ keyboard. Some youngsters climbed the stairs and started to sing softly.

The plain glass windows were covered with dirt outside and in, but by the harsh lights overhead I could make out garish statues of saints and virgins across the altar and a bunch of plastic flowers. Upstairs the soprano voices were midway through another chorus.

Manuel had stopped weeping and was looking around the church, to the altar, up to the darkened loft. "Beautiful, yes?" he asked me with no irony.

"Linda," I said. "Tudo."

HE DENIED IT THE NEXT DAY but Manuel slept soundly until cocks crowed in the yard behind the hotel, and by breakfast he was almost cheerful.

It was I who was downcast. All night the rain hadn't let up. Shaving with cold water was no hardship but the shower was a single nozzle in the wall of the toilet and forty seconds under that had only rearranged the dirt beneath my clothes.

"I will stay here today to show you the town," Manuel said. "Tomorrow I will hire a horse and see my sister. Then I will come back again on my way to Rio."

Surely he would rather be on his way at once and was staying only because he had promised me introductions. But the more I protested, the more adamant he became. "They say my mother has been buried already so there is no hurry, and showing you Camamu will take my mind off my sorrow."

Breakfast was tapioca cake, slices of buttered mata, or bread, and a thermos filled with strong black coffee. Manuel was too distracted to notice when I took the coffee black, and we avoided the argument I could usually anticipate in Rio, where popular taste ran to filling half the cup with sugar. Once I'd had a waiter warn me, "Drink our coffee plain and you will surely die."

But I got past that obstacle with Manuel only to mortify him with a show of bad manners. When Bela came to our table to ask, "How did the senhor sleep?" I replied, "Very well, thank you. And you?"

When we were alone, Manuel hissed, "One does not say 'Você'—you —to the lady of the house. It is always 'the senhora.' You should have said, 'And the lady?' "

"I was taught something like that," I said. "But in Rio, everybody says 'Você.' "

"In Rio. Not here."

When his head-shaking subsided, Manuel proposed that we launch our tour at the town's high school. Schools in Brazil often taught English, he said, urging me up the main street toward a dirt trail. Along the way, we ran into a flock of schoolgirls in white blouses and blue skirts. "Who teaches you English?" Manuel demanded.

"Professora Marlene."

"Who will take us to her?"

The entire brood reversed itself and climbed the slope to the school, which turned out to be a large, low, clean structure, something like a dairy barn. Hearing the excitement, Professora Marlene came out and Manuel accosted her abruptly.

"The professora speaks English?"

"No," Marlene replied with good humor. Round-faced, brown-skinned, she looked no older than her students. "I teach English," she went on, "I do not speak it. When I was studying, the emphasis was always on grammar."

Manuel was aghast and wanted to depart until I assured him that I hadn't come to Camamu to find English speakers. "But in an emergency," he persisted, "if you have a pain you will not be able to tell the doctor where you hurt."

"I will point," I said. "It is all we do in the United States."

He relented and explained rather loftily to Marlene that I was in Camamu to study Candomblé. I was intelligent, he promised her, and I meant well. But the professora must bear in mind that I was an American and that every American said Você, Você, Você, in even the least appropriate circumstance. Americans intended no offense by it, and he hoped the professora would understand.

"Oh, please do not say the professora," Marlene answered, blinking in my direction. "Use Você."

On the walk back to the hotel, Manuel was still chagrined about not uncovering someone to converse with me in English. I said I'd found the professora charming and that at some later time I might invite her to dinner at the hotel.

"It would not be proper now," he snapped.

"Not now. Later."

"Maybe later. Her mother could come with her."

By afternoon the sun was showing itself for the first time in two days and Camamu improved under the yellow light but it still looked worn and smudged. The few people in the street stared frankly at me and I looked sidelong back at them, admiring the result of the zestful intermingling in Bahia—the middle-aged brown man with dusty blond hair, the blue eyes with which several of the blackest children regarded us.

Along our haphazard route, Manuel found a child who knew the house of the mãe do santo who had been his mother's dearest friend. When the boy ran ahead, I tried to keep up and instead I slipped in the mud and got up encrusted with red muck.

"I should go back to the hotel and change my pants before we call on the mãe," I suggested. "I would not want her to think I was showing disrespect."

"No," Manuel said, "everyone will see you and say, 'The gringo tatu.'" An armadillo, he meant, that burrows in the ground. "They will like you better."

The mother of the saint, Dona Luzia, lived off the road and down a steep hill. At the bottom we found her door ajar and Manuel walked in without knocking. Three men were squatting in the parlor on benches while a muscular black man in a T-shirt lounged against a wall. From the back, I had an impression of women rustling in a kitchen. Two black children darted in to have a look at us and ran to hide behind the knees of the older men.

"Dona Luzia?" Manuel asked. He didn't identify himself but the men understood that strangers might come to the door looking for the mãe.

"She is preparing herself," one man said as the others made room for us. Except for their benches, a table was the only other furniture in the room, plus an old Kelvinator painted green.

We had waited several minutes in silence when a curtain over the bedroom door was drawn back and a light-skinned woman, tiny but stiff and commanding, stood before us.

Manuel rushed to her and hugged her around the waist. She submitted to his embrace with reserve but no sign of surprise.

Releasing her, he said roguishly, "You do not remember me?"

Apparently a mãe do santo had human failings with faces and names but a good deal more poise in meeting the problem. Dona Luzia studied him with interest and said nothing.

"Manuel," he said, as a broad hint.

She went on looking at him placidly. To me it seemed an unfair test from a boy who had been gone since the age of twelve.

"Son of Pedro Francisco," Manuel said at last, and then the room exploded in shouts. Men jumped up to shake hands and Dona Luzia returned to his arms and patted his back.

One of the young men was Luzia's son, Antonio. Years ago he had been Manuel's playmate; now he was married and a father, although whether his child was the bold Sebastião or shyer, blacker José or the baby Raimundo or the infant Maria Angélica or all of them, I couldn't sort out.

Antonio took us next door where he was building an addition, three rooms nearly as large as the house itself, that would serve as his mother's terreiro. While we were alone for a moment, Manuel suggested that if

I wanted to give Dona Luzia ten cruzeiros she would not take it amiss.

Giving alms always left me flushed and awkward. I took out the bill to hand to Manuel. "No," he said. "It must be from you."

Back in the house, he explained more circumspectly than to Marlene what it was that had brought me to Camamu. Doctor Jacks does not wish to perform a work against anyone, he said. He wishes only to learn more about the Candomblé. The family accepted that as a natural desire and Luzia volunteered that she would be holding a Candomblé for Ogum in twelve days' time and if I wished to come I would be most welcome. Meantime, would I care to see her shrine?

We went to the back of the house, past a trio of women busy around the stove and into a room large enough to have given this crowded household an extra bedroom.

The room was bare except for an altar built to accommodate a towering female statue and the clusters of flowers and candles in front of lesser figurines. On a clothesline skirts and lace petticoats had been hung to keep them uncrumpled, and in a corner a large Candomblé drum was draped with green cloth.

By the altar I saw a small pile of one-cruzeiro notes and could lay my bill on top.

When we were at the door, Manuel asked, "What other Candomblés are there here?"

"Dona Maria, down the road, is a mãe do santo," Luzia said. "There are others in Valença."

"This Maria, she is a friend of yours?"

"Yes, she is my comadre."

"Then," Manuel promised me, "when I come back to Camamu we will call on her."

"Sometimes," he confided, after we had bid the household goodbye and were on our way back to the hotel, "there are bad feelings between two mães do santo. When that happens, one must be very careful."

Remembering the virago at Tauá's Candomblé I could agree that even without a threat of retribution from the spirits, there were women I wouldn't choose to cross.

THE DAY MANUEL LEFT TO CONSOLE HIS SISTER, I found the room where I would live for the duration of my time in Camamu. Or rather, Ailton, a born procurer, found it for me.

We met when he came to the hotel to sell lottery tickets for the next Sunday's futebol matches. Two cruzeiros or thirty-four cents—plus another fifty centavos as his commission—and he promised with hand on heart that I would win two million American dollars.

Ailton was only a boy, scrawny, shabby but ferociously clean, with skin the color of Cordoban leather, button nose, and a rakish wave of black hair. By my guess, twelve years old at the most. But when he fanned out documents to establish his respectability I saw that he had lately turned fifteen. And that his name was Ailton and not a proclamation: I, Hilton.

I bought a ticket and asked the boy to mark his choices between competing teams. With furrows of concentration, he made Xs down the card. "When we win on Sunday," I said, "we will split fifty-fifty."

Ailton held up his thumb approvingly. "We will go to São Paulo," he said grandly. I learned afterward that he had never been so far as Salvador.

"We will *buy* São Paulo," I said.

The next morning, a little before seven, he slipped upstairs at the hotel and rapped on my door. "You want a casa?" he asked. "I have a casa."

I pulled on a pair of pants and followed him into the street. Directly across from the hotel stood a gray post office building, and Ailton pointed to the second floor where a sign read SINDICATO RURAL DOS AGRICULTORES DO CAMAMU.

"There? What about the syndicate?"

"It has moved. Here comes my friend Zeca. His family owns the building."

A handsome young man with a prominent jaw, long yellow hair, and anxious brown eyes was approaching warily. "The little man says you want to see the apartment. It may not be suitable."

He took us up the stairs to a large room with three windows overlooking the main street. Beyond a ridge of red tile roofs, I could see the river and its islands. At the side, another window framed the church's towers against a sky that was momentarily blue. I was looking out those windows and not at the room itself when I said, "I will take it."

"There are problems," Zeca cautioned me. "No lights, as you see. No furniture. There is also the problem of sanitation." He drew me down a long corridor to a dank chamber where the floor beams had rotted and fallen through to the post office downstairs.

"No bathroom," I said.

Zeca shook his head sadly. "No bathroom."

"Then I am afraid that—"

Ailton had been bobbing around us and now he dragged Zeca away and pulled his shoulder down to whisper in his ear.

Zeca returned to say, "If you will pay three months rent now, I will put in a bathroom. Meanwhile you can use one in an empty house my family owns down the street. Then if you will pay for installing the lights, I will find a bed for you and a table and a chair."

"How much?"

He bunched up his lips in a frown and ran his fingers through his gold hair. First he looked to the ceiling, but near the roof there was an ugly blotch of brown mold over the pale blue paint and instead he inspected the floor's rough planking.

Since I couldn't be sure my Portuguese was understood, I waited a minute and repeated, "How many cruzeiros for one month?"

He sighed and drew from his pocket a piece of paper with the letterhead of Coelba, the light company. Ailton told me later that Zeca collected its bills. Furtively he scribbled a figure and passed the slip to me.

"One hundred and twenty cruzeiros a month?" Zeca winced at hearing the sum spoken aloud. It was twenty dollars. "All right," I said.

Zeca smiled with relief and Ailton capered about us with pleasure. "Will you speak to the electrician?" He nodded. "I would like to have light by Saturday."

"No! Before! Before! Tomorrow!"

When, one week later and at a cost of fifty dollars, the wiring had been completed but for inexplicable reasons a final connection to the main power line had not been made, I borrowed a kerosene lamp from Dona Bela and moved in anyway.

During that week Ailton had supervised the wiring, the moving of furniture, and the transfer of my suitcase across the road. When Manuel returned, the two of us went in search of more mães and pais do santo, and Ailton continued to guard my new loft. In return he asked only that I let him use my portable radio.

On the afternoon we came back from Valença, Zeca was waiting for me at the hotel. By that time I knew that his reassuring smile meant that Zeca bore ill tidings.

"Boa tarde, senhor," he began. "Como vai? Everything goes well with me, thank you. I have come only to inform you that the little man has been seen dancing in the street with the senhor's radio. Was that the senhor's intention?"

"No, it was not."

"Here he comes again."

We got to the door in time to see Ailton, my radio clapped passionately to his heart, executing a samba step along the curb.

I called his name and he ran up, elaborately contrite.

"Perhaps it is better that my radio does not leave the apartment."

"I have only gone to tell my sister that she must be ready to do the senhor's laundry," the boy said. "For a friend of mine, naturally, there will be no charge."

MANUEL HAD INSPECTED MY ROOM WITH A SCOWL, letting me know that only a gringo would have paid more than ten dollars a month for it. But since he had returned to Camamu, he was bringing a daily burst of enthusiasm to tracking down more terreiros and he had me out of bed at dawn.

We went first to call on Dona Maria, stopping en route at Luzia's for directions. "Let me change my dress and I will come with you," she said, joining us a few minutes later in a fresh white blouse and patterned skirt. In better days, according to Manuel, Luzia had presided over her father's considerable fazenda, or plantation, and from her bearing and assurance I might have guessed as much.

We had hired a Land-Rover for the trip and Luzia took a place in the back. It had not rained tumultuously for two days and the jeep was churning up dust. We pulled off the road and jolted over the half mile of meadow to the cluster of wooden huts and shelters where Maria lived. The girls sitting on the porch of the biggest house assured us that Dona Maria was at home, and we walked past them into a large chamber. Its rafters were hung with brown crepe paper, benches ran three sides, and along the back wall the place of honor was given to a large tinted picture of Inhasã, goddess of storms.

In Rio, Dimitri had assured me that while the Umbandists called her Santa Barbara, in Candomblé no one ever did. But Luzia, pointing to the picture, said plainly, "Barbara."

Other hangings were grouped over the walls in no clear pattern. Two painted plaster hands made the good luck sign called the figa, which has the thumb protruding between the first two fingers. A photograph of a black woman I took to be Maria had been pressed into a mahogany frame with silver curlicues at the corners. In a shelf one burning lamp was flanked by a miniature plastic fir tree but also a china vase with two real roses.

I counted three crosses: a red one in a bottle; a simple green one; and a crucifix, the shoulders of its silver Jesus cloaked with dirt. A painted plate implored "God, Protect Our Home." Below it, advertising a dry goods store in the lower city, hung a calendar with a blonde wearing only black mesh stockings and an overlay of the pervasive dust.

At the rear door the photograph came to life, smaller and less haughty, and Luzia fell delightedly on the woman's neck. "God be with you," she told Maria. "Thanks be to God," Maria replied.

With the highest seriousness he had yet achieved, Manuel explained why we had come. Maria heard him out with the same formality but at a reference to me as Doctor Jacks I pulled a face that made her chuckle.

When he had finished, Dona Maria took us to her kitchen at the back and served an acrid green tea. Then she led us out to her garden to show us the leaves she had brewed it from.

"Erva cideira," she said. "Good for disorders of the intestine."

Maria's house was on a rise that overlooked a sweep of low gray grasses, and we could hear leaves and grasses strumming across the valley floor. She broke off a sword-shaped stalk for Manuel and me from a mottled plant.

"This is Espada do Ogum." Did it reflect cultural differences that I poked mine into Manuel's ribs while he was using his to pretend to shave?

Dona Maria cut more herbs and flowers and dropped them into a plastic bag for me to take back to Camamu. "Alecrim de Caboclo," Luzia said, pointing to one sprig. "It is a remedy of the saints."

I asked Maria whether she used herbs for most of the ailments she treated.

"Sim," she said; yes. She handed me a thin stalk as rough as sandpaper. "This is Capim da Lapa. Sometimes it is called Capim Santo. It is excellent for the liver."

A wide leaf of a faded Florentine green she identified as "canela." I knew the word from the title of a novel by Jorge Amado. "In English we call it cinnamon."

"It is used for disorders of the stomach." Maria squashed up another reed and held its minty pulp for me to smell. "Milesia," she said. "For a tea that is calming."

"You calm people, too?"

"Several plants are good for that. Laranja da terra is very calming."

These plants invested with healing powers had been brought from Africa more than two hundred years ago, Luzia said. Plantation owners had sought them out and ordered them shipped to Bahia to placate their slaves. Most herbs were green, but there was a pink bud with a sticky yellow center, as though a bee had been trapped inside and left to molder. There were red roses, too, also medicinal.

"Some years ago," Dona Luzia said, "a child of my terreiro died and his spirit came to lodge in my throat. I felt it choking me and I could not breathe. Finally I drank much rose water and succeeded in making it go away."

"My first cure," Dona Maria countered, "was a bath made with the essence of white roses. I was eighteen and very sick. Sick, sick, sick, sick. Near to death. My parents had already spent more money than they had on medicine and still the doctors did not know what more to do.

"A coffin had been bought and one time I was even placed inside it. Until my mother came and made them stop. She said, 'You cannot bury my child. Her heart is still beating.'

"But I had been sick a long time and other members of my family would come to the bed and say, 'Why do you cause this trouble? Why do you not die?'

"My mother brought a pai do santo to visit me but I took fright at the sight of him. When he said that I was receiving a spirit, I cried and would not eat. He told my mother, 'Be careful where you take this girl. Pick the terreiro wisely for she is going to be a mãe do santo.'

"It was he who told them to bathe me in the oil of white roses and right away I began to get better. But my soul was suffering. Ave Maria! I did not want to give in to this power. If it was really a spirit, I said that it would have to kill me to take my body. I would not accept it. I would not have faith in anything I was afraid of. Only in God."

Maria had been speaking excitedly. Now she paused, her round black face bunched into a smile of complicity. "I have learned much since then about the Candomblé," she said. "But I still know that there are no real healers, only God."

Between themselves the two mães arranged my itinerary for next week's festa for Ogum, or Saint Anthony. Tuesday night I would spend at Luzia's terreiro, Wednesday at Maria's.

"Terça-feira," Dona Luzia promised me, "we will have the drums." In case I did not understand, she beat her delicate hands along her thighs and cried, "Boom, boom, boom, boom."

"I like the drums."

"Remember Tuesday," she repeated. "Boom, boom."

DOUBLING BACK BY BUS TO VALENÇA, the slightly larger town I had admired during our ride from Salvador, took three cold gray morning hours. We were in search of Dona Mira, a famous figure throughout Bahia, and the first taxi driver in the main square knew her well.

Mira's house was light, airy, and freshly painted, the proper setting for the sleek and knowing woman who came to greet us in white blouse and slacks. I was sure she was Mira's daughter and I said, "Dona Mira, por favor."

"I am she."

Manuel was equally surprised. "Mãe do santo?"

She spread her fingers deprecatingly and looked up from under her thick lashes. "Sim."

We had to believe her, and as Manuel launched into his recital, I examined the woman's expressive face. At second look she was older, closer to forty; as with many Bahian women her hips were more than ample. But neither age nor breadth interfered with Mira's being a very desirable woman.

"I do folklore," she was saying, "and also Umbanda, as pageantry at festivals or for the television stations. But my Candomblé, I am afraid, is very simple."

"That is what I am looking for," I said. "An authentic Candomblé. Nothing rich or grand."

"Oh!" Mira said to Manuel. "He speaks Portuguese! Are not Americans clever? They come here and right away they learn our language. How many of us ever learn theirs?"

I looked to see if she was mocking me but Mira teased in everything she said and I couldn't be sure.

Her hall across the road from the house was the biggest yet, and in a side chamber Mira drew out from trunks the sumptuous robes she wore for her paid appearances. They were laced with gold and silver, and one skirt glittered in the sun with shades of rose and lavender. She shook it and the colors ran together mauve.

Manuel had drifted to the front of the hall when Mira sat on a bench and patted the place next to her. "You ask what the difference is between Umbanda and Candomblé," she said. "I simply do not know.

For me, Candomblé is a mystic thing, the spirits that come are real. They are the sons of Iemanjá. I have much faith in the orixás, and I try to lead a good life in order to please them."

Mira was speaking naturally, smiling at herself for being so serious. "Would you like me to sing?"

"Very much."

As simply as though she were talking, Mira sang:

"I am going to throw flowers in the sea,

"A promise I made to the goddess of the sea.

"This promise I made,

"And now this promise I am going to fulfill."

When she had finished, I said, "It does not sound like music for a Candomblé. It is lighter. Sweeter."

Mira was pleased enough to frown. "Of course," she said, "if you want African rhythm:

"My father comes from Aruanda." She was making her alto voice more guttural.

"And my mother is Inhasā.

"O gira de gira gira

"O gira de gira gira.

"That song came from a terreiro in Salvador that is a mixture of two nations, Angola and Kêto. They also sing this:

"Oxóssi rides on his horse

"And his sword shines."

Her voice was like sunlight in the shadows of the hall.

"Oxóssi, King of Kêto

"His flag covers the sons of Jesus."

"There you are," said Manuel. "Ready to go?"

On the threshold, Mira apologized that she would be leaving Valença in a day or two to appear on a television station in Rio, and her next small Candomblé could not be until mid-August. Would I stay in Bahia for it?

"I will stay," I said.

"Listen to him." Mira nudged Manuel. "He even knows the future tense."

Manuel had heard about one last terreiro, this time headed by a man named Senhor Valter, and we stopped off on the way back to Camamu in the town of Ituberá. Manuel asked about the square for a taxi but there was none and we climbed the winding dirt trail that was supposed to lead to his house.

At the open door of a two-story house Manuel poked his head inside and then clapped his hands until a teen-age girl peered out as tentatively as he had looked in and ran to tell her father that guests were waiting.

Senhor Valter walked to the porch on stiff legs and shook our hands as he waved us to chairs. Valter's hair was going gray and his black face was deeply lined, and even so the halting movements didn't suit him. He seemed like a young man impersonating an old one, and not very skillfully. Unlike Mira, he was probably younger than he looked, closer to fifty than to seventy. But whatever his age, Senhor Valter was a tired man.

He was granting to Manuel that for simplicity's sake he might be termed a pai do santo, though that term came from Candomblé and his was an Umbanda terreiro. He had been its leader for thirty-two years and during that time had initiated 3,873 filhos do santo and filhas do santo, sons and daughters of the saint. Valter assured us the number, though it sounded implausible, was accurate; he had kept records.

The spirits he himself received included Ogum, the god of iron, and an Indian chieftain from the forest. Valter practiced only the white line of magic. There was no room for the worship of Exú in his terreiro, although a young black man named André sometimes held Quimbanda sessions a few kilometers away.

Valter's hall was also across the road from his house, and we found it set up as a schoolroom, with desks, benches, and a Brazilian flag painted across the ceiling. "I made this building myself," he said. "When there are no ceremonies, the children study here." Classes consisted of the younger of his own eleven children, plus any other youngsters from the settlement.

Locked away in an airless chamber at the rear, Valter's Umbanda altar looked no different from the Candomblé shrines I had been seeing. He might call Ogum by the Christian name of Saint George rather than

Saint Anthony—it was a significant difference between the cults—but the same spirits were on hand, with a central place for Iemanjá.

Valter sent an older child to bring out his old photographs and he passed around faded formal studies of himself, a sinewy, imposing figure in his loincloth and white feathers. At one time or another, the older daughters had each been fitted with a spangled fish tail to represent the mermaid Sereia. In all the pictures I saw what I had noticed first at Maria's: when photographers in Bahia tinted their work they lightened their subjects' skin by several tones.

Over the hour it took to get back to Camamu, I wasn't saying much, and when we got to my room and Manuel saw that I had kept Maria's flowers spread over my table, he began an uneasy, indirect line of questioning. "You did not like Senhor Valter?"

"Very much. I have been thinking about him since we left Ituberá."

"Jacks," he said, "you do not believe in the spirits?"

"Do you?"

"No," he said positively. "No, Jacks. I know about them. I used to make jokes about the mãe do santo in our village."

"Dona Luzia?" I was surprised.

"No, she was my mother's good friend. This was after we had moved from Camamu, when I was seventeen. The woman lived at the end of our street, and as I went past her house I would shout that she was a fake. She would come rushing out to curse at me.

"Every day it was the same and it only made me laugh. But one afternoon she shouted, 'I am going to have Exú put a curse on you. Tomorrow you will not be able to move your leg.' I asked her which leg. 'The left leg,' she said.

"The next morning I got up and ran to her house and kicked my left leg high in the air. 'Fake!' I shouted. 'Come and see my leg!' But she would not come out.

"From that time on, whenever I passed her house, even if I could not see her watching, I would wave my left leg in the air. How can anyone believe in Exú or the others?"

"But you believe in the Bible?"

"Yes, Jacks. God sent the spirit to Moses and to the others to write His words."

He saw his bind too late and I tightened it for him. "Then it may be that God now sends spirits to Dona Maria and to Senhor Valter."

"Oh, no." His smile was almost coy. "You do not believe that? You do not believe in Candomblé?"

I felt that anything less than a denunciation of the spirits would be letting him down. For Manuel, fighting his way clear of the superstitions of his village, my country was a repository of science and progress. Could I suggest to him that the mythology he had rejected was sounding more attractive these days than any dogma we had ready for export? Did I even believe it? I stuck with what I could defend.

"I liked Senhor Valter very much. I would not want to say that he was a fool or a liar."

"He is a fine man. But, Jacks, every religion has its good men. In America, Billy Graham—"

"He is a good man, certainly. For playing golf with presidents."

Dismay tightened the smug set to Manuel's lips, but he seemed sure that in another minute I'd laugh and admit I was baiting him.

"All right, Jacks, yes, Valter is a good man. But you do not believe that his body is taken over by the spirit of a dead Indian?"

"I do not know what I believe," I said. "I will stay in Camamu until I find out."

I COULD HEAR THE DRUMS even before I passed Marlene's ginásio, and her school was a quarter mile from Luzia's terreiro. The rain had stopped after dinner and I sauntered along the dirt road though the drumbeat was advising me to run. Ahead, crowds of children were galloping down the path toward Luzia's, glad of the diversion on a June's winter night.

Along a hillside above her house, the timid and the staunchest Catholics had gathered to look through the windows from the safety of the road. Clambering down the hill, I was sorry Manuel had left for Rio without seeing me through one ceremony.

It was barely nine o'clock and already the terreiro was jammed with people. Judging from the scraps on plates, pork and popcorn had been passed around and now the crowd was ready to welcome the spirits.

Luzia had not yet been mounted by her guide, Rei das Neves, King of the Snows, and with a light touch on the surging backs and arms around us, she cleared a path to me and gestured with pleasure around her new hall.

For Santo Antonio, the terreiro had been hung with fresh red, blue, and yellow streamers, and the shrine had been brought in from the house next door. Luzia took me over to admire her flowers made from red and silver tinfoil. They were intermingled with real yellow blossoms large as grapefruit but it was the metallic petals that caught glints from the candles and sent off fiery sparks.

Shyly Luzia asked whether the result was not beautiful, and the artful clutter across the altar was more attractive than I could have imagined. "Wednesday you will go to Maria's," she said. "Then you will come back and say which altar is more beautiful."

"I already know."

At the back door Dona Luzia's sons were throwing firecrackers to greet the gods but just then the congregation inside started to clap hands and the rocket blasts were lost in the louder explosion.

Near the door I saw José, the carpenter Zeca had commissioned to build my bathroom. José's baby face was hot and pink, and he saluted me before he went back to pounding his palms together as though they were hammer and nails.

The music was wild tonight, the drums and the license they were issuing for abandon. Three black men beat at them with a sure sense of their power, and the crowd jammed together heel to toe, clapped along, and gave its amen to the sermon the drums were preaching. The ring of dancers stamped to the beat but they could move only inch by inch through the throng.

At the center of their circle, a light-brown boy was bent forward at the waist, shivering a dozen times for every fast clap on the drums. His feet were negotiating the same steps as the other dancers but he moved so fast he put the rest into slow motion. If I was looking for a mindless joy it was here, in a dance with the brain turned off and the body taking its orders straight from the drums.

Most of the time the boy was whirling on his heels, a trick that looked

70

harder than balancing on the toes. Sometimes he lost balance and smashed sideways. Once he fell.

The faster the boy spun, the more feverish the clapping grew around him. José the carpenter lifted his hands over his head and then everyone did, as they shook their bodies at the hips. The singing passed over to shouts. The room shimmered with sound. I did not clap or call out, but I focused on the boy's spinning body and tried to let his motion and the noise lift me away.

Then everything stopped. I hadn't seen the gesture that cut off the drums and neither had one dancer, who had begun another chorus. She laughed self-consciously in the silence, and the mulatto boy straightened up and threw out his arms. Waiting for the next chant, he rocked to and fro on his heels. Head sunk down, arms outstretched, he looked as though he had been hung out to dry.

When the drums picked up a different beat, the boy rocked slowly into its rhythm. Then he was gone again, his whole body vibrating and his feet flying in triple time. But the interval didn't seem to have refreshed the crowd. Along the walls, its individual parts were sagging or listless. But the older women sang faster, to drive the drummers forward, and the crowd sprang back to life.

They danced and sang that way for five hours. Once or twice the boy disappeared into the private shrine to have his spirit lifted off him. Ten minutes later he was back and mounted again. A few other dancers received spirits and gyrated at his side, but most of the girls, looking virginal in pink bodices and long white skirts, glided delicately around their circle, foot forward, foot back.

The men took themselves away by twos and threes to drink in a back room, and a young man I recognized as Zeca's brother, Joaquim, touched my shoulder. Blond and shovel-jawed, an improbably Irish face among the tans and blacks, he turned up a thumb to his mouth amid the noise to suggest I join him for a batida.

In the back a dozen men were unsteady from cachaça and they welcomed me warmly. "We are all your friends," one lurching fisherman assured me. "We watch you tonight and we like you because you are simple." He threw back the cloth on the table and rapped the unvarnished wood. "Simple. You understand?"

"I think so."

I gulped down the colorless Jacaré whiskey. To breathe again I took a glass of beer. "Am I right?" I asked the room at large. "I have counted three Catholic churches in Camamu but they are closed and people tell me there is no priest. Yet there are at least two mães do santo here. Does that mean the people care more for Candomblé than for the church?"

I was joking. They listened with reserve and didn't smile back. "Camamu is very poor," one man said. "We cannot afford to pay a priest."

We turned the talk to safer things—futebol, the rain, Los Angeles. When they passed me the cachaça again, I waved it away with thanks. I felt I had nothing to learn about the way liquor affected my brain.

As for drugs, I had sat with friends in California until their visions subsided. Once in Laos I had smoked enough opium to bend my reality for a few hours. An amiable evening; nothing to repeat. Nothing to compare with receiving into my body, with no stimulant beyond the beating of a drum, a spirit from another realm.

THE NEXT NIGHT IT WAS A BONFIRE, not drums, that pointed the way to Dona Maria's terreiro. Her Candomblé had entered its third and final day, and the terreiro was dark except for three candles on the far wall. My eyes were still filled with color and smoke from the fire outside so I wasn't prepared for the figure that dashed out of the shadows and threw itself on the floor across the doorsill.

I bent over and gave Dona Maria my hand. She looked almost round in her wide skirts and formless black jacket, but she jumped up neatly, hugged me while I kissed her hand, and called on the gods to protect me. I recalled my lesson from Long Beach and said, "Graças a Deus." In a foreign language the words came easier.

Each dancer stopped long enough to repeat Maria's greeting. Several were men, and with them I was at a loss. Instead of kissing their hands, I took each man in the loose embrace I had seen at Luzia's, heads to one side, then the other.

But it was very dark, and one young man mistook my direction and we cracked skulls painfully. For an hour afterward, the right side of my head stung.

The mood inside the room was somber. Dona Maria lived four miles from Camamu, and since there were only a half-dozen cars in the town, her crowd was small, thirty people at the most. Even by candlelight they looked darker than the dancers at Luzia's and, in a way hard to define, poorer. Ailton had come with me and we shared the corner of a bench.

The music struck me at once. The songs were in an African dialect, the melodies were simple and less lively than those of the night before. But the accompaniment was far more complex, made up of two drums, a pair of maracas, and a tall oblong box that looked like a vegetable shredder. It was played with a stick run across its notched surfaces, and its rasping tone, with the muted drums and the maracas played on the off beat, gave out a dissonance that sounded electronic. With the grunts and the high-pitched squeals from the dancers for punctuation, it might have been a Stockhausen tape.

Not that either music or dancing lagged. Yet I felt more awe here and less joy. When Maria went to brew a pot of her bitter green tea, the cuing of the musicians was taken over by an enormous woman, three hundred pounds or more, who sang out a line and paused. The music scarcely answered her and she went to the next line and sang it louder. Then the drums spoke up, joined by a few of the other dancers. By the third line, they were shrieking at each other, drums and voices, the drums bound to win.

Ailton had never seen a Candomblé and in the flickering light I could see his whole eyes, both their whites and their brown yolks. "Do you like it?" I asked.

"I like." But his eyes didn't blink and he wasn't smiling.

A young black man broke free from the circle, grabbed up a long braided straw spear, and began to thrust blindly with it. Along the wall we shrank back from him.

"Porrah!" Ailton exclaimed. It is the commonest of Brazilian oaths, and if a people swear only by what they value, it's worth noting that "porrah" is the male sperm.

With a shout the warrior ran from the house. Through a window we could see him dancing around the bonfire and finally hurling his weapon into the flames.

"Oh," said Ailton, much relieved, "brincando, yes? A joke?" I didn't answer and he turned to an old black fellow on the other side of him. "He was only joking?" But the man stared straight ahead.

I drank Maria's tea in the kitchen and watched the dancers reeling across the hall. By three A.M., when my eyes started to close, Ailton was already curled up asleep on the bench. Dona Maria saw me nodding and, bearing a stack of sheets across the floor as though they figured in the ritual, she made up a bed for us in a small side room. I felt abashed. The Brazilians had been dancing for three nights but it was the American, worn out with watching, who had to rest. But I was glad for the bed and pulled a blanket over me while Ailton hunched down by my feet.

An hour later I woke up. For an instant I couldn't remember where I was, except that I thought I was being held prisoner. I eased off the mattress so that I wouldn't wake Ailton and slipped back to the hall.

The candles had guttered down to three small points of light. The room was like a cave carved out of the earth. Dancing was continuing, though only seven women were forming the circle. Through a slit in the door of the shrine room I saw Maria shut up inside with a man kneeling before her.

Half asleep, I had been sitting for twenty or thirty minutes when the fat woman called for a faster and more powerful chant. The others had barely taken it up when she bawled out a single word and bent forward and shook her head as though she was trying to snap it off her neck.

Lowering that way, not dancing but tossing her head like an animal bitten by ticks, her figure looked huge and inhuman. She bayed and shook her mane, like a beast from the swamp, and when the others approached her, she was too violent to handle. A girl ran for Dona Maria.

Maria shuffled out unalarmed and as she approached the woman, she traced the sign of the cross over the hugeness of her shoulders. That failed. The convulsions not abating, Maria seized those shoulders and steered the woman backward, patiently but firmly, through the door and into her shrine.

Remembering Ubirajara's rebuke, I tried not to flood the room with concern. But I couldn't stop going to look into the nook and assure myself that the daughter of the saint, flat on the ground now, was still breathing. As the immense body shook, Maria crooned and laid her hands over the woman's head. Behind me, subdued dancing had resumed, and the woman on the floor grunted at the sound. Then gradually the spasms came less often and she was quiet.

When she was absolutely still, Maria pressed her heavy head to a straw mat and, with a whimper, she went to sleep.

I was bone cold and went back to bed more to get warm than because I needed the sleep. Ailton was balled up, his one good shirt riding up and crumpling under his arms. I drew the blanket over both of us, closed my eyes, and imagined that the sound of the drums through the wall was the familiar noise of rain on the roof.

AT COLLEGE IN MASSACHUSETTS, fellow students from Boston and New York had found my Midwestern upbringing a reliable source of amusement, insisting on stories about the cows and chickens, the town cracker barrel, the potbellied stove. And if Minneapolis had been the village they imagined, I would have been better braced for life in Camamu. As it was, even a close reading of *Winesburg, Ohio* wasn't preparation for the hypocrisy and gossip that were the staples of small-town life.

Being Brazil, the surface was all brotherhood. "A good heart," any resident said loudly of another. "A fine person." The distrust, the resentments, came after. Even then, being Brazilian, the criticism had a mild sound to it.

As he had boarded the bus for Rio, Manuel warned me against my landlord: "Now that Zeca has your rent money, I do not think he will be persistent about getting your lights connected. I do not have confiança in him."

Zeca, it was true, kept his distance for the week I was fumbling with Dona Bela's kerosene lamp. But then one morning he burst up the stairs so fast I was sure it was Ailton. "The lights!" he shouted.

Outside my window a man in sandals was perched midway up the lamppost, holding a long hooked stick. In a minute I had light, one bulb, and Zeca was cavorting around the room, flicking the switch and accepting congratulations like a new father.

A few days later, he was back to warn me against José the carpenter. "I saw you in the bar," he said, "drinking a beer with José. I will find more suitable companions for you. I do not have confiança in José."

At the hotel Dona Bela asked why I hadn't brought my laundry for her maids to wash. I told her about Ailton's sister; after his grand gesture, he was accepting money on her behalf, but the work was fast and neat. Dona Bela raised troubled eyes.

"I do not have confiança in the sister of Ailton," she said, leaving me to speculate how a laundress forfeited one's confidence.

For his revelation, Bela's self-effacing husband waited for a day that I was in the hotel kitchen drinking coffee. Then he confided to the room at large that he had no confiança in Ailton himself.

I realized that in each case I was being told whom not to trust. But the phrase, não ten confiança, was too bland to be alarming, too much on the order of not having confidence in the stability of the franc.

At that, though, I couldn't deny that Ailton had become something of a trial. His mother was gone—dead, I assumed. His father, a bus driver, had brought a new woman into the house who didn't care very much for either of his children.

"My father doesn't like me, either," Ailton said. "If you do not believe me, ask Zeca. Ask Zeca if my father likes me."

Ailton was looking not only for a more satisfactory father but for a best friend and a wealthy patron, and I had to resist being cast in any of those roles.

"Who do you like better," he would ask, "Zeca or me? Urbano or me? Joaquim or me?"

He lighted each cigarette with the look of a man who had found his place among men, and if the bar owner would have permitted it, he would have poured himself a glass of my beer.

Once he asked me who among the people I had met in Camamu I liked and who I didn't. "I like them all," I said disingenuously.

"But who?" he demanded, and as I ran down the roll, to tease him I left out his name.

"You do not like me?"

"No," I said.

"Why not? Why do you not like me?" It wasn't a game anymore; I suppose it never had been. I gave him an impersonal reason. "Because you smoke cigarettes."

"That is all?"

"All."

He took the cigarette out of his mouth and tossed it out the window. There was only one more left in the pack, and that he crumbled in his palm. "Now do you like me?"

It was more responsibility than I wanted to assume. "Brincando," I said. "It was a joke. I like you whether you smoke or not."

But from that day, I never saw him with a cigarette. I had no confidence that he didn't light up at the snooker parlor or when he was out of sight in cidade baixa; in fact, I hoped he did.

SENHOR VALTER'S CLASSROOM, its desks pushed to the walls, was full of black youngsters waiting while their mothers withdrew behind a partition to change to long skirts for the ceremony. For nearly an hour the children had waited on the benches with remarkably little fidgeting, and the scene reminded me of basements in the African-Methodist-Baptist churches of the American South ten years ago, when parents left their youngest behind and went out to march for the right to sit downstairs in a movie theater.

Later those adults who hadn't gone to jail or to a hospital came back and sang hymns and it was then that I wanted to go from bench to bench, apologizing.

At the Umbanda ceremony tonight mine was the only white face and yet I wasn't feeling constrained. Except that the U.S. government was abetting the Brazilian military junta inexcusably, I was guiltless, and even that political guilt was only intermittent, nothing compared with walking through an American city feeling like an accessory to the slave trade.

The terreiro grew hushed, and with a cry the chief priest burst through the center door. I had to look again to be sure it was Senhor Valter. This man pounced around the room like a lion cub, crouching and springing on rubber legs.

From a door to his right, twenty black women in bulky white dresses issued out in a line, white bandanas over their heads. I had been thinking about slavery and here came a parade of women directly from the kitchen of an eighteenth-century plantation.

Valter—the priest was he—was clad in a lime-green outfit with beads hung around his neck. But the men filing out from a door to the left were wearing ordinary shirts and slacks.

The opening ritual took more than an hour, and Valter conducted it fastidiously. An offering of cornmeal had been set out in the middle of the floor, and the dancers circled it, singing a chorus about Exú.

I knew that Umbanda terreiros differed over the wisdom of alluding to the devil-god. In Long Beach, they hadn't placated him with so much as these dishes of grain. But Valter apparently believed in starting the night with a cleansing and he directed two men to carry the plates out the front door. Exú would follow; the hall would be purged.

Until the men came back, the open door was an invitation to evil and the threshold couldn't be crossed. That was so basic to the ceremony that I was surprised when a girl of ten or twelve, old enough to know better, made a move to go out.

Valter rushed at her as though she were walking in front of a truck. Just short of the door he seized her arm and propelled her roughly back to her seat.

All litanies are dull. Once, aged fourteen, I said as much to our Lutheran minister and got back a sermon on the beauty and comfort that ritual lent to a service. But litanies are dull, and Valter's individual blessing of the three dozen filhos and filhas do santo went on long after my interest flagged.

Also, the drumming tonight was utilitarian. The three men leaned against a wall and thumped only to keep time. Valter was the soloist, they were modest backing.

When the preliminaries were finally done, Valter was mounted by his spirit efficiently, proof of the mature partnership between god and horse. As it was used by Ogum, Valter's body seemed younger still, and every movement was lithe and insinuating. Hearing his sly laugh, I guessed that of the 3,873 sons and daughters he had brought to the spirits, a great majority had been daughters.

Dancing to the bench where I sat, Ogum raised his satyr's face to mine and seized my hands. He led me, faintly resisting, to the center of the floor. "Open the doors," he commanded a man standing near the central shrine. "I want to speak to this man."

I remembered that Valter tolerated no shoes inside his altar room and at the door I kicked mine off. The cement was very cold. Still drawing me by my fingertips, Ogum backed into his alcove. Behind us the door swung shut.

He stepped onto a platform with a high-backed chair and carved armrests. The seat was covered with fragments of bright cloth sewn one over the other until they ruffled like parrot feathers. The spirit directed me to a stool at his feet.

"What do you want?"

"I want to watch and listen," I said. "With your permission, I will come back to learn more."

"Certainly," Ogum said impatiently. "But what do you want from me now?"

"Nothing."

"You have no wish?"

"No."

He took a brazier of red coals and wafted its smoke over my hands and past my face. In the small room the sweet incense was suffocating.

"Come back then," he said.

"Yes." I might have added "Graças a Deus," but his mocking eye was on me. His hand slid wearily off its armrest. It might have been a wave of dismissal.

COMING TO KNOW THE COUNTRYSIDE AROUND ME had left me no more comfortable in Camamu than the day I arrived. From my window over the post office I looked out on roofs of tiles curved like stacks of rusted cans, and past the roofs the marshy land along the river seemed to float on the water like green scum.

The face of the river never moved, and the islands themselves were a drab green except the one that had been stripped by an American mining company looking for ore. With the foliage gone, a plucked red mound faced the town, its baldness the one proof of human life on the horizon.

But for all its deadness on the surface, the country wasn't peaceful, and beneath the earth a roiling never stopped. The very forest seemed to pulse. Even with my heavy shutters pulled, the cricket noises shut out, I felt I heard a movement under the ground, and it was less disturbing to concentrate on the rats gnawing behind the walls or to turn over on my bed and make the straw mattress crackle like breakfast food.

Camamu had been given birds to match its landscape. The first time I said, "I do not like the urubus," people took it for a joke. It was as though I had said I didn't like air or grass. The urubus, being everywhere, weren't worth having an opinion about.

They belonged to the condor family but crossbred with another species, vultures or eagles. Possibly bats. Certainly turkeys. Chests swelled and waddling across a roof, they carried their necks in the neurotic manner of turkeys and their beaks trembled as though they were gabbling.

They were black except for white wing tips that showed when they fanned themselves or pecked at their bodies. They could perch anywhere, even on the cross of the deserted church. Six or eight of them would line up on the ridge of a roof across from my room and lower their heads to stare at me.

In the air they were more graceful than seagulls. They never crashed out of the sky in the clumsy way of a gull diving for fish. They circled like buzzards, sat in judgment like ravens. They should have figured, but did not, in the Candomblé lore as sacred to Exú.

One day I dropped by to see Dona Luzia, but at her door her thin and crafty sister welcomed me with an air that made every word conspiratorial. "Luzia is resting," she said and paused significantly. "I will come back." "No!" She called, "Luzia!" and willed me into a chair.

Dona Luzia emerged from her bedroom, blinking in the sunlight but smiling and taking my hand in both of her small tan ones. The first thing she asked about was Maria's Candomblé.

"It was very different from yours." She and her sister both nodded, pleased that I had detected the difference. "Hers was very beautiful, too. But there was less—light."

More nods to confirm my insight; I wasn't asked which ceremony I had preferred.

"It is too bad you were not here the next night," Luzia said. "Exú appeared and also Oxóssi."

"My friends in Rio have built a house," I said, "about this size, for their Exú, their Leba."

"I do not have such a house," Luzia said. "I practice here only the white line of Candomblé. Sometimes when it is necessary that I consult Exú for a work, I go there." She pointed up the road.

"To Dona Maria? She has a house for Leba?"

"She has. I do not have to go very often. Most of my works—thanks to God—can be done without it."

"You do many works?"

"Many, many."

"What do people ask?"

"To cure their pains. To have success. To end a work that someone else has done against them."

"Do they ask for love?" An idea was taking shape.

"For love, too."

"The first time you received your spirit, do you remember? Were you afraid? How old were you?"

"I remember very well. I was thirty-two. Yes, I was very afraid. I was very sick at the time, very worried—"

The spirits seemed drawn to the deathly ill and the suicidal, and I thought of what Manuel had said about Luzia's family once being prosperous. Was it when the money melted away that the spirits had arrived to console her?

IT WAS INEVITABLE that in a town with so few amusements I would find myself an ongoing entertainment. Until I learned to lock the door, children would drift upstairs on their way home from school, fingering my clothes, trying on my dark glasses, picking over the litter on my table.

Zeca stopped by routinely to exercise his droit de seigneur by cutting his toenails with my manicure scissors and thumbing through any letters I had left about.

A girl who ran a dingy government office down the street didn't waste time on anything as peripheral as correspondence. Her conversation came off an official questionnaire:

"How old are you?" As she asked, she was snapping on my radio. "Where do you live? Why are you not married?" She bounced with scientific detachment on my straw mattress. "This stuffing is not fireproof. You must get foam rubber."

"I do not smoke. And I like the noise it makes when I roll over."

She quashed down hard and listened to the chirping of the straw. Smiling, her eyes went off-duty for a moment. "As long as you are sure you do not smoke," she said, "it may be all right."

Against Ailton, no defense of mine was a match for his ingenuity. He showed up with presents—a buttered roll, two large green lemons. A piece of unfamiliar fruit with the pitted skin of a potato.

"Who is it?"

"Ailton! Open the door!"

"Later."

"I have a present for you! Open the door!"

"Thank you. Leave it on the stair."

"It is a bottle of soda. The bar demands the bottle back right away."

Once inside he would run to the window and holler down to his friends. In Bahia street calls had a musical lilt. "Fernando! Hey, Fernando! Fernando! Hey, Fernando!" Ailton only wanted the street to know that he had slipped past my barriers.

That accomplished, he ran downstairs with a casual, "Até logo." And was back in twenty minutes with a newspaper, a thermos of coffee, my laundry.

In spite of this attention, I was more defeated by the language than I had expected. Bahians began each sentence with a gulp of air, as though they were loading a musket, and at the end they spewed out a random scatter of words. It consoled me a little that even among themselves they were forever saying, "Eh?"

Then, too, I was boring myself witless using a few kindergarten phrases and freezing my face into a smile whenever I wasn't quite sure what had been said. I sought out Professora Marlene for relief, and we arranged that three afternoons a week we would read Portuguese together in her family's front parlor.

Besides the lesson, I could depend on Marlene to clear up the day's confusions. "I think Dona Bela told me that today is the feast of Our Lord Jesus of the Pencil. Can that be right?"

"Lapa," Marlene corrected me. "Not lapis. It is the day of Lord Jesus of the Grotto."

After almost forty years, I was looking forward to going to a class. Most days we simply talked until Marlene used a word I didn't know. Then I would write it on my pad and make phrases with it.

The single drawback was that throughout our early lessons Marlene sat at my side, adhering to the theory that a foreigner was more likely to be deaf than stupid. Whatever I didn't understand she leaned over and shouted in my ear. But as the weeks went by, I was able to measure my progress by the way her voice was dropping. I hoped that by the time I left Camamu she might be whispering.

At the corner bar the town's eight-year-olds congregated each evening around my chair to hear a few English words. Particularly they loved to ask me what a garde-chuva was called in my country. "We say 'umbrella,' " I would reply.

"Umbrella!" they exclaimed, as rapturous on Thursday as they had been on Wednesday and Tuesday, until I began to wonder whether the word might not have a pornographic meaning in Portuguese.

As our "okay" gesture did. In Brazil a circle of thumb and forefinger stood for "cu," or anus, and an audience could be convulsed by the sight of a clean-cut GI in a Hollywood war movie giving the sign to another soldier; better, to a nurse.

"Umbrella!" What might it mean?

Other puzzles were easier solved. Since I took my meals at the hotel, I found I could classify visitors to Camamu by their geography. If they came from Salvador, they rapped for service on their water glasses, picked disdainfully through the platters of rice and beans, and called for shrimp when there were none.

But any man from a hamlet even smaller than Camamu would gorge himself on the sticky heaps of rice, spit his fish bones on the floor, and grab at the breasts of the serving girls.

These girls, Railda and Alda, worked from six each morning to ten at night, seven days a week, in return for their room, meals, and twenty-five dollars a month. Whenever they could save the money for cloth, Dona Bela's youngest daughter ran them up a blouse on the hotel sewing machine.

At first look, Alda was the prettier, with a lush, unflawed brown skin and pale eyes that never refused any man outright. Railda was darker and rougher textured, her eyes distant, mouth discouraged. But when Railda smiled, she showed long, white, hopeful teeth. And when she strutted in, holding a tray of beans as though it were a prophet's head, every book salesman and dendê merchant tried to run his hand up her sturdy black thigh.

Menus at the hotel varied with the number of guests. If all four rooms were filled, Bela was cooking for twelve, and she had money for shrimp and crab, even lobster, and for the better cuts of ox. When the clientele shrank, we regulars got the bowls of white rice and brown beans, a jug of farinha, and a saucer of a spiny fish broiled in dendê oil.

But Bela's desserts redeemed the rest. Goiabada, a reddish fruit paste, tasted like pressed apricot; the beaten sugar was flavored with maple syrup. Best of all was the marmory—which meant marble—stripes of chocolate pudding alternating with stripes of coconut. Eating marmory was like biting into a sweet zebra.

Júlio, Bela's other steady boarder at the hotel, had arrived in Camamu a month before I did, serving out a one-year contract to learn the banking business. He came from a larger and more urbane town near Salvador, and I began to look for his long face at the dinner table and the bitter laugh that asked what crime he had committed to be sentenced to Camamu.

Besides being a cosmopolite, Júlio was a college graduate and he didn't feel his talents were being nurtured at the bank. When I came by to cash a check, he was staring at an open ledger, and he would pass me a note: "All day long I have done nothing. Do not tell the manager."

For no good reason but boredom I started saying to people that it was sad for a young man Júlio's age to be drinking so heavily. That slander enjoyed an immediate success, and around the hotel I suggested that Júlio probably embezzled.

These rumors were making Júlio something of a personage around town, especially after I gave Railda to understand that his girlfriend was pregnant. By suppertime that news had reached Júlio and for the first time he remonstrated with me.

"My sweetheart is not with child," he said sadly. "And anyway I have given her up." He raised his forefingers and put two resigned horns on his head. "I found out that she had other men."

Saturday night, when the snooker parlor closed at nine, a good share of the town's youth straggled into my room in hopes of cadging a shot of whiskey. Júlio was looking even more desolate than usual and to raise his spirits I taxed him with having an affair with a chicken.

"I have met the chicken," I told the other young men, "and I admit that she is pretty. But it is not becoming to a young banker to be seen everywhere with a little brown hen."

Júlio was ready with a fervent rejoinder. "I will not give her up," he vowed. "I love Ana and Ana loves me."

"Ana?"

"Ana Galinha. The chicken. I have tried women and now I have tried chickens, and chickens are better."

He explained why with such ardor that the others were instantly converted. "I know the chicken for me," one boy said. "Maria Galinha!"

"Mine will be Rita," said another. In Portuguese, the *r* is pronounced as *h*, Heata Galinha.

Zeca's brother Joaquim had come in late, and since Júlio had lately taken a walk with his sister he demanded to know who was this rival named Ana.

"Ana Galinha!" Júlio declaimed. "My love!"

"Sister of Rita Galinha!"

"Sister of Maria Galinha!"

Snobbery had blighted Zeca's entire family, and Joaquim wrinkled his nose. "I do not know these Galinhas," he said. "They must be from the lower city."

The next week Júlio took his revenge for my brincando, or so I thought at the time. He was pacing my room after lunch, waiting for the rain to stop, when he said, "I do not believe it myself, but everyone else in town thinks that you are an espionage agent for your country. You are either with the FBI or the CIA."

"In Camamu? You make a joke."

"They all say it. I know the police think so. They say the Candomblé is just an excuse."

"What would anyone want from Camamu? Photographs of mud? But this is your joke, isn't it? You made this up because of my story about the chicken."

"Ana has nothing to do with this. They even think you pretend to speak Portuguese badly so that you can gather more information."

"Do you believe that?"

"I do not think you pretend."

FOR THE NEXT PAI DO SANTO I MET, I was indebted to Ailton. He overlooked my grouchiness and kept asking around town until he unearthed a black man from Salvador who was living as something of an exile in the lower city.

"His name is Senhor Nelson," Ailton said. "I have told him about you and he can see you right away."

Júlio's bank was located in cidade baixa, as were the grocery and dry goods stores. But going to see Nelson was the first time I had headed down the muddy paths where the fishermen lived.

If cidade alta gave the impression of having suffered a fire, the baixa looked racked by war. Many houses were less than shells—a part of a roof, three walls. Even the better houses looked as though a firebomb had charred their innards; the mood was that of a village after a saturation raid.

But the only enemy here had been neglect. And the people lived stolidly among their ruins. I could see them at the back of long dirty corridors, carding their nets under a patch of roof.

By the standards of the baixa, Senhor Nelson was living well: his house was dark and narrow but intact. We were shown into a gloomy bedroom with a dressing table serving as the shrine. Pictures of Jesus had been cut from magazines and pressed into frames, and a few candles burned on the cement floor.

Senhor Nelson, very black, moved in a choppy, nervous way that had its own authority. His enlarged right eye looked worthless in his head, as though he had popped it out for polishing and pushed it back askew. He wore a short-sleeved shirt over an orange pullover with long sleeves, a combination that made his arms look bleached.

Nelson had been living in Camamu only a year, and he was finding life as a pai do santo difficult here. In Salvador, he said, people had understood the value and significance of the real Candomblé. Here— would I credit it?—there was a woman who professed to run a terreiro and she did not even have a house for Exú.

"Any ceremony that begins without an offering to Exú," Nelson concluded angrily, "is no Candomblé at all. These women who think they are receiving spirits—it is only a fantasy of their imagination."

He regarded me with his good eye. "You have been to meetings here," he said. "Have you ever heard this?" He chanted a line in which I caught only the name of Ogum.

"African?"

"Of course, African! Do they know this one?" He called out another song, its verse filled with harsh monosyllables. "They do not know that! They know nothing!"

I tried to look noncommittal.

"A frango? What do they call it in Africa?" Nelson demanded.

Frango was cock, rooster. "I do not know."

"Akikó! These!" he went on, tapping his shoes. "What do your caboclos and your women who think they are mães do santo, what do they call them?"

"Sapatos?"

"Ha! Anipe!" he cried. "In Nagô, anipe."

"How did you learn Nagô?"

"My grandfather in Salvador taught me when I was a boy. He was Nagô. When he died, he was one hundred and thirty-six years old! Look at this!"

Nelson opened a tough yellow palm creased with deep lines. "My life," he said, pointing to a gully that ran off the map of his hand and down his wrist.

When Ailton announced his find, I had been hopeful. I knew that Luzia's mild benevolence would never have satisfied Dimitri back in Rio that hers was an authentic Candomblé. Even that glorious night of dancing was starting to seem no more occult than a barn dance.

Dona Maria might tell me all she knew. But her method seemed grounded less in tradition than in what had worked for her. I was drawn to Valter, hoped to see him often. Yet, Ituberá was nearly an hour away and the jeeps were not reliable. If Nelson, who lived within walking distance of the post office, had secrets of Candomblé to command, I was ready to apprentice myself to him.

But on this first meeting he wasn't inspiring confidence, and when I asked which spirit he received, Nelson pointed to a painting of Jesus.

"Oxalá," I said dubiously.

"Certainly!"

It was not impossible. I had read that Oxalá did sometimes descend, and at Tauá's Candomblé, Dimitri had indicated an ax-faced boy with no upper teeth who had once received him.

I said, "May I ask you a few questions?"

Nelson leaned back and crossed orange arms on his chest.

"Do you know Exú Manqueira?"

"Of course. I know all the Exús. Seca Pimenta, Sete Facadas, Exú

Corre Linha, Tranca Rua. And I have Exú Caveira."

"You receive Caveira?"

"I receive."

"What do you offer to Exú?"

"Chicken, cock, bode—the male goat. Dendê oil. Farofa. Cachaça of the Jacaré mark. White candles, cigars, matches."

I ran through a list of the gods of Candomblé, checking Nelson's answers against texts like Pedro McGregor's. Nelson identified Obá as one of Xangô's wives. But then he insisted that blue was the color most pleasing to Ogum, not the red the other authorities cited. His answers came prompt and assured, and I tried to avoid the appearance of catechizing him.

Once or twice when he mentioned a new name, I held up my paper for him to check that I was spelling it properly. Each time he hunched forward, squinted, and grunted.

Nelson said he planned no Candomblé until August, six weeks away. But if I cared to come back to the baixa this very night and bring along my tape recorder, he would enlist a drummer and several singers to show me what real Candomblé music sounded like.

"That would be too much trouble for you," I said. "I will wait for your ceremony."

But I saw that Ailton and the pai do santo had settled it between themselves. "Not too much trouble," the boy said in the voice he used when I was to understand that this was not brincando but solemn truth. "Sargento Jaime will take you there."

THAT NIGHT the sergeant swung his Land Rover in front of the post office and honked the horn. I knew that Jaiminho, his wily, pale son, was a great chum of Ailton and that Sargento Jaime himself was round and affable. He was in a sports shirt again tonight; I had never seen him in a police uniform.

Our destination was another house in the baixa, the cramped and clammy home of Zulmira, Nelson's most faithful parishioner. She greeted us in her ceremonial robes, a frail creature with long flowing hair. Her eyes slid easily to heaven, imbuing her with a look of suffering sanctity that might have been due to receiving Iemanjá. Or to being the mother of ten children.

Waiting with Zulmira was a black woman with a face flattened as though it were pressed against a window. She was Nelson's wife, and the paler girl with small thrusting breasts was their teen-age daughter.

Zulmira's husband was working in Rio; her older boys were also normally gone from home to jobs in Salvador, but they were back tonight: a Frenchified blond fellow with shoulder-length hair and wrap-around dark glasses, and a swarthy crew-cut boy with the bullying air of a Marine corporal. Zulmira's other children also alternated between fair and dark, with a couple of towheads to offset her fifteen-year-old twins Cosme and Damião.

Even with a full house, Zulmira had reserved the choicest room for her shrine, which covered much of the floor and was laden with seashells. The married daughter who led me to the altar outwaited me there until I had left a ten-cruzeiro note.

This mercantile aspect of the ceremony was beginning to unsettle me. I wasn't at all reluctant to part with a little cash but I had no notion of the going rates, and to be bargaining with people who would shortly be surrendering their bodies to Saint Anne or to Jesus would make me a Pharisee as well as a scribe.

Zulmira's living room, except for one white cupboard, was bare but the children brought folding chairs and Sargento Jaime took a seat in the corner.

To me it seemed that despite his stature as a lawman Jaime was looking uncomfortable. Possibly I was projecting my own attitudes onto white Brazilians but they often seemed ill at ease in the presence of families as black as Nelson's. And I had detected the blacker residents of Camamu treating the whites and mulattos with a touch of condescension that might once have been purely defensive.

Nelson waited while I plugged in my microphone and led off with a tribute to Exú. He apparently didn't intend to receive Oxalá that night for he hunched in the chair next to mine and fed song cues to the women. They attempted to dance around the cramped quarters and sing what they remembered of the African words. When they faltered too badly, Nelson cursed under his breath and switched abruptly to an easier song.

Zulmira danced briefly with the others before she received her spirit in a contented daze, staggering a bit and looking even more saintly than before. The thuggish son from Salvador knew the songs for Iemanjá, and when Nelson tired he took over, calling the hymns like cadence.

From my first night at a terreiro, the response of children toward their elders perplexed me. I had imagined that when a familiar face contorted and a voice grew thick or—like Zulmira's now—ascended to an inhuman piping, smaller children would be frightened and the adolescents scarlet with embarrassment.

Wrong, and wrong again. Toddlers did their best to sway the way their parents did and were encouraged with fond pats when they got the rhythms right. At Luzia's festa for Ogum, one of her grown sons from Salvador hadn't been sure that I remembered being introduced to him, and when the small brown woman began clutching at the air while the spirit descended on her, he said, "That is my mother." He spoke quietly so that I wouldn't think he was boasting.

Tonight, eight of Zulmira's children were lined against the walls, singing and shouting encouragement to the goddess mounting their mother. A ninth child, a seven-year-old girl, was dressed in a duplicate of her mother's costume and she was trying to receive a spirit of her own.

Joaquim, Zeca's brother, had heard about the unscheduled Candomblé and had crowded with Zulmira's neighbors into the narrow hallway. Being short, he had to raise his head to see, so that he never seemed to be looking down his nose at the ritual so much as looking up his chin at it.

Next to him stood an unusually tall, bulky man. From his professorial horn-rimmed glasses and his brooding big nose, I decided unelatedly that he was a fellow American.

So far I had met two compatriots in Camamu, both of them middle-aged businessmen. A man who introduced himself as "Bud" claimed to have been cheated out of his share of a Bahian mining company and, he was back to seek reparations in court. "Lived here since 'thirty-nine," he told me over dinner. "Never went to one of those Candomblés. Had the chance. Wasn't much interested."

The American manager of the Firestone rubber plantation near Ituberá had lived eight years in Brazil. The one time our paths crossed he had welcomed me cordially without understanding my enthusiasm for Candomblé. "I went to one of those things," he said. "It was just a lot of people jumping around and acting crazy."

This new arrival, however, wasn't one more American come to scoff but a native-born brasileiro and Zulmira's son-in-law. At a break, he told me how he had come to revere Nelson, who had once cured a wound for him and in the process seemed to have infected him with the same dynamic style of speech.

"How old do you think I am?" The music had stopped and he was shouting over the low conversation around the room. "I am forty-two years old! Yes! That is my wife—that girl there! There! She is eighteen."

He hiked up a pants leg and showed me a faint scar. "Infection had set in here," he said. "An infection! Here. An infection had set in here," he said. "An infection! Here. An infection here in my leg."

"I understand."

"The doctors wanted to cut it off. Wanted to cut off my foot. Told me they would cut off my foot! Because of the infection. Here!"

"In your leg."

"Exactly! I went to Senhor Nelson—him. That man there. Nelson. The pai do santo."

"Nelson."

"Nelson is that man there. You see him? Look here, Nelson! I went to him."

"And he cured you."

"Nelson! That man! The pai do santo. He cured me. The doctors wanted—"

"With herbs?"

"No! With knives! They wanted to cut it off. Because of the infection! Here. In my leg."

"How did Senhor Nelson cure you?"

"With herbs! With Espado do Ogum. It is a plant shaped like this. Espado. E-s-p-a-d-o. Do. D-o. Ogum. O-g-u-m."

"I know the plant. I saw it at Dona Maria's."

"No! Not Dona Maria! Nelson! Nelson. He is sitting there in the orange shirt. Nelson, raise your hand!"

"How long did it take?"

"What?"

"Five months? Six months? Until you were cured?"

"Five months? Six months? Until I was cured?"

"Yes?"

"Who told you that?"

"I am asking you."

He leaned forward and hit my knee smartly. "Three months!"

"That is very good."

"Very good! That is very good! For works, Nelson is the best man in the state of Bahia. The best man!"

"In all of Bahia?"

"In all! Total Bahia! For works, he is the best. But he is poor! He does not even have a terreiro of his own. This"—he gestured around Zulmira's small living room—"is no good."

"Small," I allowed.

"Very small! Too small! Nelson needs a terreiro. But they are very expensive."

"Expensive," I repeated despairingly, hoping to dispose of the subject.

"No! Not expensive! But for him—he is poor."

I moved to head off any pitch before it was beyond deflecting. Already I had wondered whether these cruzeiro notes I was leaving on the various altars weren't reviving a cottage industry. I said, "It is too bad none of us is rich."

"I am out of work. No work! I do not have a job. I worked in Rio. Now I work no place."

"What was your work?"

"Public relations."

"Perhaps there would be more opportunities in Salvador than in Camamu?"

"Yes!" he agreed. "More! More jobs in Salvador."

"Then you are going to Salvador?"

"Now I live here," he said. "Camamu is very calm, yes? Calm! Tranquil! I have been wanting all night to ask you something: Do you play snooker?"

THE NIGHT AT ZULMIRA'S ENDED with no spirit asking me what I wanted. But I was turning over the question. I wanted a spirit to take over my body; if that paramount wish wasn't granted I should have alternatives.

I quickly ruled out asking for money. The unhappiest man I had ever met was a technological wizard who by the age of forty-five had gathered to himself ninety million dollars.

Somewhere around his fortieth million, people had stopped seeing or hearing him. They read his face as they would study the skies, to see whether it would rain gold. The only words they listened for were yes or no.

In a very minor way I was already meeting that fate in Camamu. Without depriving myself I could buy a new dress for a schoolgirl, a few textbooks, an ice cream cone. Or medicine for a sick child, or the bus fare to Salvador. Hardly a day passed that I wasn't asked for these small favors, and I was distressed to find myself as capricious about granting them as the magnate had been in backing a movie or launching a newspaper. I was learning that if one had to be just there was no fun in playing God.

One child got a piglet simply because he asked for it with so little hope. Other times I had to say no, which was hard, but no worse than getting notes under my door after I had said yes:

"Jaques is the friend I had waited for all my life."

"Senhor Jacs is the father of my prayers."

The boy with the pig named it after me.

If not for money, for love? One of the staple requests, according to Luzia, but for me to fall in love in Camamu would be no gift from the spirits.

94

I suspected that the orixás, like Casanova, spoke of love when what they meant was sex. But given the complaisant Brazilian attitude about going to bed, sex was scarcely worth a prayer. Nesio's grisly predictions had proved wholly false, and although protecting local reputations did require stealth, I found that no hardship.

I was on guard, too, because of a story my friends had told me before I left Rio. A foreign engineer, it seemed, got a girl pregnant in Rio Grande do Sul, but when her father came to him, he refused to marry her. "She was no virgin when we met and I made no promises," said the engineer, who was Swiss.

Twice again the father returned. The Swiss was adamant, a stance that Brazilians call inflexível and do not admire.

The final time, the father came back and brought half the men of the town. They marched the foreigner to the gas station, where they pulled down his pants, stuck an airhose in his cu, and pumped him up until his condition matched the girl's.

That was how the cautionary tale had been told to me, and if I had expressed my doubts that the punishment was anatomically possible I would have been proving myself as inflexível as the Swiss.

THE DOOR TO SENHOR VALTER'S TERREIRO stood ajar. A kerosene lamp hanging from the ceiling had been turned low and the large room was dark. But past the threshold of his shrine, I could see Valter seated in profile, hands on the armrests like a pharaoh. One of his young lieutenants beckoned me in.

Valter seemed lost in meditation. I asked the young man whether he had been doing works all day.

"Since eight o'clock this morning. Twelve hours."

Valter's expression disconcerted me. I was expecting to see the gross gargoyle's face of Ogum and instead he was holding his head daintily and his mouth was atwitch with sweet smiles.

"Boa noite," I said as I sat on the stool by his knee. Small talk with a god still came hard to me.

Valter's face regarded me with maternal affection.

"I have come to ask a favor," I said.

The head slowly nodded.

"I would like to know the ritual of Umbanda from beginning to end. The songs. The dances. Not only what happens out in the main room, but what goes on back here in the roncó."

"In Umbanda," the young man corrected me gently, "we call this room the abasé."

"Abasé," I repeated. "I would like to watch while the senhor receives people for healing and other works. Is that possible?"

Again the spirit on the throne nodded comfortably and spoke to the young man, who then turned to me. "I am to help you," he said.

He appeared to be in his late twenties, round-faced, with a downy brown mustache and soft, obliging eyes.

"May I ask your name?"

When he told me, I didn't understand and I offered him my pad. "Deoclides Assis," he wrote, in a fine, faintly Arabic hand.

"Have you been long with Senhor Valter?"

"Seven years."

"I have many questions," I said. "I am afraid it will be much work for you."

"It will be only pleasure. Do you know who it was who told me to help you?"

I glanced through my notebook to be sure of the name. "Ogum of the Seven Swords?"

"No, not now." He pointed to the second tier of the altar with its two-foot statue of a woman dressed in white and blue.

"Iemanjá?"

"Sim. All day it has been Iemanjá."

At the sound of her name, the spirit gave four or five dry gasps and receded into her calm staring.

Deoclides said, "The roncós you asked about are there at the sides, the dressing rooms for the filhos do santo and filhas do santo. They are also the living quarters for the initiates before their confirmation."

"What is the main room called?"

"The ringo of the terreiro. Sometimes the terreiro itself is called the aldeia."

"How long do men and women spend in isolation before their confirmation?"

"Various times," Deoclides answered. "It depends upon what they have to learn. If they wish to master all twenty-one of the signs for making works, they may spend three months. Or more."

"Going out never?"

"They do not leave."

The rooms had looked empty on my other visits and I heard no sound now. "No one is staying at this time?"

"Not now. Closer to the end of the year they will begin to move in."

"And the abasé, this room, is where the works are done?"

Deoclides said, "No, that is a different place called O Templo."

"May I see it?"

"Certainly," he said, but not rising to take me there. "You will see it."

WHEN I WENT BACK THE NEXT MONDAY NIGHT, Valter was not receiving a spirit and he took me hospitably into the terreiro, where Deoclides joined us. By that time I had learned that the younger man lived with a wife and four daughters in an even smaller village six miles from Ituberá. After working ten hours in the fields, he walked to and from the ceremonies at Valter's terreiro.

A large white cloth had been spread over the floor in the main room and white roses set out in vases as a tribute to Omulu. In the abasé Valter took his usual seat, the one that raised him a head above us. I found it less intimidating to speak with Deoclides, letting him appeal to Valter for answers when he was puzzled.

"Many men and women must come here wanting to be sons and daughters of the saint," I began.

"Many," they agreed together.

"How do you separate the sincere ones from those who are not worthy?"

"First, Senhor Valter consults with them."

"I can tell the good from the bad quickly," Valter said.

"Second, they undergo several works for purification. Third, they spend time in the terreiro learning the knowledge of Umbanda."

He paused and I looked down at my notebook. "Fourth—?"

"Fourth, there is the consecration. You say, I think, baptism."

"Can you tell me about your own baptism?"

Deoclides looked to Valter. He was staring off tranquilly at a far point and did not stop him.

"The fluid for my baptism included blood from a white cock I had brought for a sacrifice."

"You drank the blood?"

"I drank," he nodded. "The first day of January I was confirmed at a festa with many other filhos do santo. The ceremony is always on the first day of the new year, between four and five in the morning."

I spoke directly to Valter. "What is the youngest filho do santo you have?"

"I myself started doing works at the age of seven," Valter said. "But that is too young. It was many years before I properly understood Umbanda. I would not accept a child now younger than ten."

"Could we start at the beginning of the ritual and go through it all? First, the opening sacrifice."

"For a true sacrifice," Valter said, "one should have at least a sheep. Custom demands an ox. But it has been three years since we could have an ox."

"For the regular ceremonies, though, a sacrifice to Exú of a bowl of farinha made from the manioc root is enough?"

"It is enough."

"Before that," said Deoclides, "if you wish to begin at the very first, here in the abasé we fill a glass to the brim with water and we light one white candle."

Valter said, "The glass and candle are placed on a straw-colored cloth with a drawing in white chalk that will drive Exú from our midst and close our terreiro to him."

"Could you show me what you draw?"

Valter took my notebook and sketched a sign:

"And then?" I asked Deoclides.

"Then a man carries the glass out and throws the water far into the road, to dispel any bad influences that might have collected here."

"Any man of the terreiro can do that?"

They smiled to each other. "No, it must be a man with a powerful spirit to call upon, so that he can hurl the water a great distance."

"Could a woman do it?"

Their amusement became embarrassed. "No," Valter said reluctantly, "she would not have the power."

"Yet there must be women who receive strong spirits?"

"Very strong. But a man must throw the water. There is a song that goes with it:

"Deus no ceu," Deoclides spoke the words,

"Umbanda na terra,

"Agua e vela

"Retiraram Exú."

I was copying it in English: God in Heaven, Umbanda on Earth. Water and candle will drive out Exú.

"It is no good without the music," Valter said, frowning. "The words alone sound foolish."

"I have a tape recorder in Camamu. I will bring it to the next ritual and record the music too. But then sometimes the words are hard to make out."

"As long as you have the music to go with them, he"—Valter waved a hand toward Deoclides—"can write the words for you. But it is not right to separate them."

"What comes next?"

"Next, two plates of farinha, one red and one white, are placed in the middle of the terreiro beside a candle."

"I saw two men take up the plates when I was here last month. Do they throw the farinha into the road?"

"No!" Deoclides was scandalized. "They put the farinha on a piece of paper outside the terreiro where Exú can come for it."

"In Rio a friend of mine in Candomblé calls Exú by the name Legbara or Leba."

"There are many names," Valter said. "Elegbara is another. Manqueira. Caveira. And there is Lucifer. He is the chief of the Exús."

"The Lucifer from Christianity?"

"The same. And there is Exú of the Closed Road, Exú of the Strong Wind, Exú of the Two Bones—"

"They are all bad?"

"All," Valter said. "The black line—Quimbanda—has seven songs they sing to Exú. Our line has three, to get him away from the door and let us pass through in safety."

"I watched Senhor Valter give a blessing to each filho and filha," I said. "He was receiving Ogum."

"One Ogum," Deoclides qualified. "You said the name the other night. As with Exú, there are many. That was the Ogum Sete Espadas. Six swords at his side, one in his hand."

"Are there any others he receives?"

"The caboclo named Tupinamba who sometimes visits me also comes to Senhor Valter."

"I have a ridiculous question."

They smiled and nodded encouragingly.

"Can you both receive Tupinamba at the same time?"

They continued nodding. "Sometimes he will come to me and then afterward to Valter."

"No, I mean this: Let us say that it is ten o'clock on the night of a ritual. Exactly at ten hours could you receive Tupinamba while Senhor Valter was receiving Tupinamba?"

The idea obviously struck them as indecent. "No, never," Deoclides said. "First one, then the other."

"I thought that if the spirit was large, it might be possible—" Valter interrupted. "Never."

SINCE MUCH OF A MÃE DO SANTO'S WORK INVOLVED HEALING, I wanted to confront Luzia or Maria with an ailment. But I was feeling better than I had in years, perhaps because of Maria's green tea, and the worst affliction in the town seemed to be a rash of chest colds.

Then an opportunity arose: Ailton caught his right hand in my door. I was slamming it in exasperation when he stuck in his fingers and scraped off a bit of skin. After preternatural wailing, he treated me to a look that would have been more effectively reproachful if I hadn't just warned him to stay downstairs.

He disappeared for twenty minutes and returned from the farmácia with a bandage the size of a fielder's mitt. Over the next week he presented me with doctor bills in an illegible scrawl that did not of itself prove that they were legitimate.

"You say that you went today to the medico in Valença," I told the boy on the eighth day after the mishap. "But your friends saw you playing snooker in Acaraí. And your bandage has not been removed."

He gave me a look of pity for my ignorance of technology. "The doctor has a machine that sees through bandages."

From my window I could see him waving and gesticulating with his friends. But by the time he reached my door and knocked with his limp left hand, he had tucked the bandaged fingers into his shirtfront to make a sling. When I pulled his hand free and bent his knuckles to test his recovery, he gave long, soundless screams.

I considered presenting Ailton to the spirits but the abrasions were healing of themselves. And acknowledging to the boy that his wound merited calling on African gods to cure him would have exposed me to another month of resigned shuffling and elderly sighs.

It was time to visit Maria again, though, for corroboration of something Valter had said that perplexed me. Lately I had been seeing her by the light of candles or the moon, and coming now in the afternoon I was reminded how cunning she could look.

She met me on the rise of earth outside her terreiro, patting my shoulder and purring welcome. When we were inside the dark hall, I said, "I have come to ask you a question."

"Calm! Be calm!" she enjoined me. "First you must have your tea."

"I have just had lunch—"

"Oh!" she said reproachfully. "Oh? Oh?"

"—and I am not very—"

"Oooh?" She drew it out to let me understand how foolish my resistance was, how unavailing. Her round, dark face was very nearly flirtatious, so confident was she that I couldn't refuse her for long. "Oooh?"

"I would like some tea," I said.

In the blink of an eye she was gone. Alone by her altar, I saw that even red plastic roses could fade and that their blanched color made them more lifelike. In another vase, real white roses sprung as wide as peonies were shedding their petals over the shrine.

I ducked under the slanting roof to the alcove where Maria did her works. Even stooping I couldn't reach the back wall with its line of painted clay vases. A pan full of fresh popcorn had been set on the floor along with a bowl with a feathered white wing that half covered the decaying head of a dove. The bird's bright eye shone among shards of black meat.

Maria brought the tea. I said, "What I wanted to ask you was—no, first I would like to see your house for Exú."

She took my hand and we went out, around to a side yard hidden from the road. There Maria had built a house five feet square, large enough for children to play in. It was made from sand bricks that were decomposing but its red roof was freshly tiled. Maria reached above the doorsill for her key.

"It is large," I said, as she swung open the door. "Three times the size of the house for Exú that my friend has in Rio."

"You would have to go to Valença to find a larger house for Exú," Maria said.

At the back was a simple arrangement of iron and stone. About half the floor was covered with dried candlewax and what appeared to be caked blood, along with bits of dirty feather and dark rings where bottles had been set. At the center rested a bundle done up in white and blue cloth and looking not much different from the offering Nesio paid a virgin to cast into the Atlantic.

"A sacrifice," Dona Maria said. "From last Monday. I do works on Monday. Sometimes—for Ogum—on Tuesday."

"Do you receive other spirits besides Ogum?"

"Inhasã."

"But I think there are many Ogums. The chief of an Umbanda in Ituberá receives Ogum Sete Espadas."

"Many Ogums," Maria agreed. "The Ogum who comes here is Ogum of the Patrol."

"Here is what I do not understand: If a man comes to Ogum for help —let us say for problems with his liver—is it not possible that Ogum will turn him away?"

"No, the spirits help all."

"That is what they told me in Ituberá. But it is hard for me to understand. Can the whole world get whatever it wants from the gods?"

She snapped her fingers, the Brazilian gesture for many, many. "Everyone can get."

"What if I came and I wanted something bad? Would your Exú help me?"

Maria rolled her eyes as though I were a wayward child. "You could not come here for that. Look at me." She was holding her arms out from her side. "Not one pin that keeps my dress together has been bought with money that came from evil. Ave Maria! I was not born to harm anyone. I cry when I see suffering."

All playfulness was gone. "We stand under the eyes of heaven," she went on. "We must not do evil in those eyes. They have come here and offered me much money"—she snapped her fingers again—"much, much, to do a work against someone but I have told them, 'Heaven sees everything,' and sent them away. Some do not speak to me after that."

"Your Exú is here only to undo evil works that others have done."

Maria patted my arm. "You understand. I hug everyone. When they hug me back, it means they have given me a little of their heart."

"Dona Maria, who instructed you in the use of herbs and plants?"

"My mãe."

"Your real mother?"

"No. Until I became sick, our family did not know about Candomblé. It was a mãe do santo in Valença who helped me to accept that I was receiving a spirit."

"Who was she?"

"Bela Conceição Santo. She comes here often for my Candomblé."

"She must be very old," I said and only realized the tactlessness when Maria dropped my arm.

"One day you will meet her," she said distantly. "Then you can decide for yourself."

I WANTED TO LIKE SENHOR NELSON, all the more because I felt sure my misgivings about him were due to the prevailing American fetish for success. Had I seen Nelson in a flourishing terreiro like Valter's, surrounded by dozens of sons and daughters of the saint, that show of prosperity might have validated his spiritual gifts.

But he greeted me on this cloudy afternoon in baggy white pajamas and a limp broad-brimmed hat, unshaven and looking like a disreputable Uncle Remus. "It has been a long time," he said.

"Two weeks only."

"You have been in Ituberá?"

Nelson knew there was a competing pai do santo there, and I had come to realize that when the mães or pais felt I was neglecting them they were not concerned solely for the small bills I left on their altars. Being a foreigner and not caught up in the town's intrigues, I was becoming an arbiter of local magic. The americano spent all afternoon with Maria and only an hour with Luzia? Then Maria must be better connected with the orixás.

Nelson and I went down a long corridor stacked to the ceiling with green firewood and sat at his table near the kitchen. It was the spot Nelson preferred, possibly so that he could always spit in the same place on the floor.

That epidemic of the grippe was still sweeping Camamu and keeping the villagers hawking. Even Dona Bela's shadowy husband obtruded himself at mealtimes, gliding into the hotel dining room, leaning over the balcony and spitting down to where the chickens shared the yard with a noisy black hog.

To my question, Nelson agreed with Valter and Maria that the gods would never refuse a request, but he could go them one better since he received Exú Caveira and so commanded the black line as well as the white.

"You do harm?"

"I do."

"And healing?"

"Certainly."

"But sometimes a person requires surgery." I had looked up the Portuguese word but to be sure he understood "cirugia" I made a sawing motion across my arm.

"Yes, sometimes cirugia is required."

"You do that as well?"

"I do."

"When other pais do santo have done surgery," I said, "they claimed that they were being guided by doctors who had died. I have read that Arigó, who was so famous in Brazil, took direction from a Doctor Fritz, a German surgeon who was killed in the First World War. Who is your guide for surgery?"

"Oxalá!"

Jesus. I had to sigh or change the subject. "Are there days when one cannot receive his spirit?"

"Women, as you may know, cannot receive during their menses," Nelson said. "And on Good Friday no one receives. We are all completely closed to the spirits on that day."

"Do you have people coming to you who want to be a son or daughter of the saint but cannot be?"

"Yes, they do not possess the force. Their faith is not strong enough."

"Can you help them to receive?"

It was a question with a hook since I knew that both Umbanda and Candomblé were Calvinistic in their insistence on predetermination. A man equipped to receive a spirit might learn to develop and refine his gift; that had happened in Long Beach when young Claudio vibrated for an hour. But if a person lacked the elements that prompted the spirits to use him, he was condemned to watch from the galleries. He could reap the benefit of communing with the gods but he would never be mounted by one. In the world of the spirits, no freer from dissension and heresy than our own world, that was one point on which all sects could agree.

Or almost all. "I can prepare them," Nelson said. "I can strengthen their faith and make them ready to receive."

"How long would it take?"

"Three weeks, more or less."

"THREE WEEKS?" Valter repeated with a sad smile of disbelief.

"That is what the pai do santo told me."

"It is true that we can work with a man who has the capacity but needs instruction," he said. "Perhaps after nine months he will be making progress. But three weeks—" He shook his head.

I had come to Valter's terreiro early on Sunday morning to watch Ogum of the Seven Swords receive supplicants. It had meant catching a ride to Ituberá on Saturday and spending the night in a crowded barracks where beds rented for a dollar. At dawn I got up—I had slept in my clothes—and set out along the dirt road to Valter's house.

The first stretch took me past a hillside cemetery that hung over the town like a tangible sorrow. The crypts were smaller than Dona Maria's house for Exú, the plaster headstones were cracked and grim, and the weeds grew taller than the ornate Greek crosses on the tombs.

Where the hill crested, the road turned and took me past a dozen huts with their doors open, like a row of brothels. Men sat staring at the horizon, women were already at work in their kitchens. In the center of one shack a spindly girl of twelve stood alone, gyrating furiously to American rock from the station in Salvador.

Farther along, the road dipped and there were no houses, only a rutted slope straight downhill that made jeep drivers curse and fear for their transmissions. Picking my way down holding to the shoulder of the hill, I looked across the forest and knew why I felt no peace here. With the sun barely risen, the land looked like an early experiment by a Nature groping its way toward harmony.

First there would be a tree of jade green with its limbs bunched into a fist, and it mocked the squat yellow palms that drooped like willows. Then trees as tall and black as chimneys thrust up through the pale leafy domes around them and ruined their cathedral line.

From dead and barren trees the parasitic vines still clung and rustled like snakes. Across the ground incompatible grasses had been scribbled in at the base of each tree. There were patches of crumbling chartreuse moss next to prickly needles, and at the next trunk ferns like a fine green webbing.

With the profusion came a harshness, a clarity across the forest that allowed for no blending. Every shape and color was pricked out until the leaves were standing against each other with no hope of reconciling them. A disturbing scene, with an aggression that was contagious. Alone in the woods, a man felt not only challenged but ready to hit back.

I rounded a curve and saw the river breaking over its islands of rock. A girl knelt by the bank, scraping a blouse against a crag lathered with soap. The clothes she had laid behind her filled the meadow like distress signals.

I went over the open bridge. A child was clinging to the rocks below with one hand and spreading a tiny brown buttock with the other. The river's current washed his droppings downstream.

Deoclides was waiting for me in a terreiro yellow with sunshine. The dusty paper ruffles that hung from the rafters and gave the ceiling its thatched look had been replaced with fresh white crepe paper. Doves nested above the beams and rustled the paper when they flew in and out. After the forest, it was good to have reached this cheerful sanctuary.

"A girl has come for a work," Deoclides said. "If you would care to watch—"

We went into the abasé and Deoclides closed the door behind us. Except for two candles, it was as dark as night. When my eyes adjusted to their light, I saw slouched against the wall a young mulatta in a blue miniskirt with thin legs that looked cold. From Valter's mouth issued the lordly voice I recognized.

"E-yuh," said Ogum of the Seven Swords. It seemed to be a snort of affirmation. "My father will help you."

Ogum turned in his chair to face the shrine and stretch his arms beseechingly. "Father," he said, "this girl comes to you for assistance."

To Deoclides, I said softly, "Ogum prays to God? To Olódùmarè?"

"Yes. But we call him by the Indian name of Tupã."

At interstices of his prayer Ogum sounded a silver bell. When he resumed speaking, I caught a sharp puffing sound, as involuntary as a cough, from low in his throat. It was as though his breathing apparatus was knocking as a motor sometimes does. Ogum took no note of the gasps, except that after four or five of them he sat straighter in his chair.

A black man entered the abasé, notebook in hand, and went to stand beside the girl. I took him for her husband, but then Ogum addressed him directly. "I want you to write this down for the girl. Are you ready?"

The man bent on one knee and took Ogum's hand in an elaborate handshake. When he arose, he opened his book.

"Primeiro, uma pomba branca," Ogum said.

I raised my eyebrows to Deoclides and made a gesture that I would also like to copy the list. He grinned and scribbled in the palm of his hand the way I had done. "First, a white dove," I wrote.

"Then, a bottle of light beer. A carton of white candles. Mel. It must be silvestre."

Mel was honey. I fished out my pocket dictionary for silvestre: wild.

"And a cock, also white. Return here when you have bought these things. Now you may go."

The girl looked sullen and unimpressed, but she knelt on one knee to allow the spirit to make the sign of the cross on her shoulders.

The next man through the door dropped to his hands and executed a limber salute fully prone across the floor. His agility was the more remarkable since he had come to complain of pains in his legs and upper arms.

Ogum took his hand and, holding it in his own palm, gave it three cracking hard slaps. Then he gestured to the man to turn around. "Breathe deeply."

As the man inhaled, Ogum pressed his ear to the middle back. He moved higher and listened again.

"Come here," the spirit commanded Deoclides.

Deoclides stooped and put his head to the man's chest. "His heart is beating very fast."

Ogum nodded. "He is suffering from arthritis as well. Now this is what he must do. Get the liniment that this man will write for you." The patient rubbed nervously at his pencil mustache. "Apply it according to the directions. Do you understand me?"

"I understand," the man said.

"Come back here in one week."

The man knelt and accepted Ogum's benediction and handclasp. The spirit then turned to me. "What do you want today?"

"To tell the senhor the truth, I have come today to speak with Senhor Valter. Coming here into the senhor's presence intimidates me. It is easier to put my questions to Valter."

"You should not be intimidated," Ogum said. "But I will be sending Valter to you shortly."

He extended his hand. When I took it, he manipulated mine in a grip of three stages that could have been a Black Power handshake from the United States. "Do you know the meaning of that?" the spirit demanded.

I shook my head.

He took my hand again and gave it first a conventional shake. "That is for Tupã."

He slid his palm up mine until our thumbs locked. "That is for Oxalá."

Not letting go, he worked his fingers back into a second regular shake. "For the Holy Spirit," he said.

I left the abasé and introduced myself to the man who had been writing out the sacrifices and prescriptions. "I am José Rocha da Conceição," he said. "I have been working with Senhor Valter for three years and have reached the third stage of development. It is possible that I will be confirmed next January first."

"Where do you work?"

The question was confusing because in a terreiro "work"—trabalho —referred to those deeds the gods performed. Ogum this morning had outlined a "work" for the girl in the miniskirt.

"I am employed at the Firestone plantation," he answered, using the word "empregado" rather than "trabalho." "I live there, too, at Villa Three, with my wife and six children. She"—he jerked a thumb toward the mulatta girl, tottering up the road on high black heels—"works there with me."

"She told you that she wanted to consult with Ogum?"

"Yes. I arranged for today because it is the only day she is free, but the spirits do no works on Sunday."

"What did she ask of Ogum?"

Deoclides left the shrine and joined us in the center of the terreiro, which, in the bright sun, was looking only like a poor country school-house. He drew up benches around a table.

"If you like, we can talk until Senhor Valter joins us. Then we will have coffee."

"I had asked José what it was the girl wanted."

"She is having trouble with her supervisor at Firestone and the trouble is making her nervous. She came here for help."

"What will Ogum do?"

"Since the spirits do only good, the solution must benefit the supervisor or at least not hurt him. One or the other of them might be transferred, for example."

"When will she come back?"

"Sometimes to buy the chicken, buy the dove, is hard for people. They save the money and then come back. Or sometimes their problems go away and a work is not necessary."

Overhead there was a thunderous beating of wings, and Deoclides

110

sent José with a stick to prod the doves into flying outside. They fluttered with a conciliatory cooing but José persisted with the pole. The birds retreated and the fresh paper hangings stirred only from the wind.

Alone, Deoclides was less the dutiful pupil than when Valter was monitoring us, and I went to those questions that might offend the older man.

"When you receive Tupinamba, do you retain your consciousness?"

"No." With Deoclides, an apologetic smile was never far from his lips. "My mind goes entirely black. Afterward, I remember nothing."

"But you do not fall down?"

"No."

"How long do you receive?"

"Since I was six years old."

"Excuse me. I meant, at any one time, for how many minutes? Thirty minutes? More? Less?"

"Various times."

I was finding that any insistence on dates and times was likely to rattle Deoclides. Now he became reluctant to venture any information, for fear it might be wrong.

"But usually?"

"Usually, one hour. More or less."

"And when the spirit leaves you?"

"It is as though that hour has never existed."

"In Umbanda," I asked, "do people believe that the spirit comes back into other bodies?"

Deoclides looked at me as though I were weak in the head. "Yes. Yes."

"I am speaking badly. The soul of one man, I mean to say. When you discarnate, will your soul come back to live in another body?"

"No." He seemed relieved that my question made some sense after all. "One life only. Then the soul ascends to the spiritual realm."

"But one day your spirit could come back as a guide for men on earth?"

"It is possible." But given his modesty, I could tell that he considered it unlikely.

"Does Umbanda believe in life on other planets?"

"Mars? Jupiter? Yes. Not material life but spiritual life."

"Why do the spirits return to help men?"

"Why?"

"Why should they come back to earth to do works for anyone who asks it of them?"

"Oh," he said, still smiling but dismayed by my cynicism. "You would have to ask the spirits to answer that."

Within the shrine the silver bell rang and Deoclides jumped up. "Da licença," he said. Excuse me.

"Pois não." Certainly.

The doves had returned, pleading to stay. Half-heartedly José took up his stick again.

When Valter came out barefoot from the abasé and slipped into his sandals, he looked haggard. He hadn't shaved, and the stubble was growing in white. "I hope you have not been waiting long," he said to me.

"It has all been interesting."

"First we will have café. Then we can have a long bate-papo and then lunch."

"It is enough that you feed my mind," I said, "without having to feed my body too."

"Come."

WE CROSSED THE PATH TO VALTER'S HOUSE, where his brown sparrow of a wife was setting four places at the living room table. The night of a ritual with Valter jumping and twisting, she might have been his mother; this morning they looked the same age.

"Senhora," I said, "it is very kind of you to ask me to breakfast."

She grew flustered and looked away as she gave me her hand. Hospitality was Valter's to dispense. She claimed no credit for it.

We men sat, and Valter's wife and one of his plump older daughters served us biscuits, butter, and coffee. That I took my coffee sem açúcar caused the expected astonishment since Valter heaped three spoonfuls into his cup, until the bottom was a silt of sugar.

"I think brazileiros should admit that they use coffee merely as an excuse to drink sugar," I said. "Look at the mountain in Rio de Janeiro. It is not called Coffee Loaf."

"Sugar is very good for energy," José said.

"You have six children and I have none because of the difference in the way we take our coffee?"

"Claro."

"Between the three Brazilians at this table," I said, "you have twenty-one children."

They calculated on their fingers and laughed shyly. Valter's eleven were surrounding us, the youngest three or four of them naked and bouncing pendulous brown bellies as they ran and fell, laughed and cried, cut themselves on the bread knife and called for their mother. Valter's wife sat apart from the table and pulled a sobbing child into her lap to pet.

On the path in front of the house the older boys were kicking a ball made from newspapers and string. In the kitchen the girls were washing dishes. Through the kitchen door I could see the riverbank, and the forest as it edged its way toward the house.

"Are there snakes in the mata?" I asked.

Each man had a snake story, which, like fish stories, had to be told with the hands: How José had picked up a cord of wood only to find a viper this big beneath it. How Deoclides had walked six kilometers without noticing a snake this long coiled on his backpack.

I told them of the Umbanda meeting in Caxias where the caboclo had danced with a snake.

"No snakes here," Valter said firmly. "No snakes and no cigars."

"Not even cigars for sacrifices?"

"Sometimes then. But we never smoke as part of our ceremony."

"Does it matter what you eat or drink before you receive?"

"Eat, no," said Deoclides. "Drink? No whiskey." He turned uncertainly to Valter. "But a little beer—" Valter nodded indulgently.

Bate-papo means to beat the gullet, the equivalent in American slang to "chinning," and to go on with our session we went back to the terreiro and took our chairs around the teacher's desk.

"I have wondered whether the spirits have any rules about sex," I said. "Most religions do."

Valter wriggled his index finger, the Brazilian gesture that says, No, no! Never! How could you think such a thing? Absolutely not!

"Sex is not important to the spirits," he said. "Only before the baptism is there a short abstinence."

"Otherwise the orixás put no restriction on the sexual activity of men and women?"

"On the contrary." Valter said it with a satisfied laugh and Deoclides and José grinned. "On the contrary."

At my prodding, Valter described his own exposure to Umbanda as a child. His teacher, like Maria's, was still alive, living in a small town not far from Ituberá.

This time I was guarded. "What is his age, more or less?"

"He is very old now," said Valter, "and stooped. He hardly goes out."

"His age in years?"

"Old. Old. He is—oh, sixty-eight." Valter I found out later was twenty years younger.

I had asked which spirits the filhos and filhas do santo received in this terreiro, and the three men called out names as they occurred to them:

"The women first: Oxun, Inhasã, Iemanjá, Janina, Sereia Menina, Nanã Buruké."

I cut in, "I wanted to ask about Nanã Buruké. When a friend of mine in Rio made a sacrifice, he had to bring a statue of her to the macumbeira. Who is she?"

"Another daughter of Iemanjá," Valter said. "She has no name from Christianity."

"Now the men—"

"Besides Ogum and Tupinamba, they are Ave Rei da Caça and Rei Angola"—Bird King of the Hunt and King of Angola—"who are African spirits. Oxóssi you already know, and Xangô. Five preto velhos come here: Manuel Francisco, Manuel do Sacramento, Manuel da Hora, Pai João, and Pai Joaquim."

"There are caboclos too. Boideiro is one. And the Caboclo of the Mines. The Caboclo of the Great Lake.

"We also receive these Indians: Oxóssi of the Forests, the Sultan of the Forests, the King of the Turks. The King of Hungary. Rei do Matinha, King of the Dawn."

"No one receives Tupã?"

Even before they shook their heads, I was sure that the highest god, by whatever name a terreiro might call him, was too remote to be received.

"Or Oxalá?" I asked, thinking of Nelson.

"No," said Deoclides. "No one can receive Oxalá."

Valter overruled him. "It is possible but rare. Here, some years ago, we had a man who received Oxalá."

"In California I know a Brazilian woman who receives the spirit of Ubiraja."

"He sounds like one of the Tupininkuin tribe of the Amazon," Deoclides said.

My mentioning the terreiro in Long Beach set Deoclides speculating. "You told us that in the Estados Unidos you do not have cachaça," he said.

"Other whiskeys and liquors. I have never seen cachaça there."

"When the people of this center in California do their works, what can they use instead?" He sounded genuinely distressed for them.

"They do not do works yet," I said. "That is a source of displeasure to some of their members. But Pai Ubiraja says that since their terreiro is new, only about two years old, they have not yet accumulated the necessary spiritual force."

"That is right," Deoclides said. "It requires patience and the right place. O Templo here is very old."

"I would like to see it. One day."

"One day," he agreed.

I asked Valter how it had happened that the spirits of Brazil's Indian tribes had merged with the African spirits, and he explained that once, when the world was new, all nations and peoples had lived in the forests that connected South America with Africa. That also accounted for the

King of the Turks visiting a terreiro in Bahia.

"In the spirit realm, all spirits know the others?"

"They mingle freely there," Valter said.

"Could a man in modern Turkey receive the King of the Turks?"

"A man anywhere in the world can receive a spirit," Valter said. "But some places make it easier. When you bring together many spirits in one center, as we have done here, it helps the other spirits to descend."

"Does it matter where one constructs a terreiro? You have built this one on a hill."

"What matters is the spiritual force," Valter said. "When a caboclo does a work, he feels that force and knows that is where his terreiro should be."

"Then there are places where he cannot receive his spirit?"

"Places where it is harder. It is like a man in a house. When he is surrounded by his family, he draws strength from them. When he is alone, he has less force. The spirits gather in that same way."

I mentioned a theory I found attractive: The insane in other countries were only mediums who did not know how to handle their gifts. Because their culture didn't understand the spirits, such people were deemed mad.

The three men agreed vigorously. "Many people come here because their families think they are louco and want to lock them up in an asylum," Deoclides said.

"You can always cure them?"

"Always," Valter said promptly. Then he seemed to recollect some failures, and after a pause he said, "They should come here before their families shut them up. We can help them."

"Do you perform surgery too?"

"When they need operations, I send them to a doctor."

"The doctors here are friendly?"

"Many doctors hate Umbanda," Valter granted. "But I know others who believe that we work together as colleagues."

"And the priests? Do they give you trouble?"

In Rio I had read about Padre Boaventura Kloppenburg, a German-born priest who had investigated Brazilian spiritism at the behest of the

Vatican. Summing up his research, Father Kloppenburg had not denied the existence of spirits, only that they interceded in the lives of men.

"It is inconceivable," the priest wrote, "that someone truly loves God and at the same time practices necromancy and magic that has so often and so severely been forbidden by God. For this reason, a Catholic may never be a member of any group, confederation, society, fraternity, center, church, tent, temple, or hut of Umbanda."

"Trouble with the priests?" Valter asked. "Why? We all believe the same."

I asked whether he knew of a Padre Kloppenburg. He did not.

The morning passed. I put aside my pad and we talked more generally. Senhor Valter asked if he might look at a book I was carrying and I passed it across the table. "I thought I might read last night at the hotel," I explained. "But the light was too weak."

"This is the name of the writer?"

"Yes, João-Paulo, and his last name, Sartre. It is a novel about the occupation of Paris by the Germans in the last war. In Portuguese I think the title would be *Sono Perturbado*."

Valter handed it back to me with a shake of the head that passed no judgment on the book or me for reading it. He was merely acknowledging the distance between his terreiro in Bahia and a world where men fought wars.

But it led to talk about our countries. All three men were vague about Vietnam—where it was, why the United States should have sent soldiers there. But they were better informed on their own domestic politics than I expected.

Even if I hadn't been chary about criticizing the Brazilian government, the scandals in Washington had dampened any native American self-righteousness. I did say that I thought the people should be trusted to select their leaders.

They heard me out impassively, and I thought what a hard time Brazilian revolutionaries must have in rallying a nation that uses the same verb for "hope" as for "wait."

When Valter's wife came to call us for lunch, Deoclides was surprised and asked me what time it was.

"Noon. Did you think it was earlier or later?"

"Much earlier." The time had gone equally fast for me.

On the table were bowls of brown beans and orange rice and cold spaghetti. And a platter of small bones and gamy meat that might have been baked dove. Again we four men ate alone.

They were surprised that I refused a beer. "A beer at lunch," I said, "and I sleep all afternoon."

"You speak of sleeping," Valter said. "I wanted to say that when you come next time there is no reason for you to stay at the hotel. We will always have room for you here."

FROM MY FIRST DAYS IN CAMAMU, I had heard about Dona Elza. "You must talk with Elza," Zeca had said. "She is the mãe do santo on our fazenda. Someday I will get horses and we will ride out there."

Soon afterward I learned that one of her many nephews was Ailton's friend Adruba, fifteen years old and bright as a squirrel. One morning Duba came clattering up to my door, shaking his long hair out of his eyes and extending his hand.

As I shook it, he pulled me down the stairs. "Tia Elza is here!" he said. "When the car is repaired she must go back to the farm. But you can talk with her right now."

"I must go to Ituberá at noon."

"Elza will be gone long before that. We must hurry!"

Briskly we walked to the last house on the road before it plunged down to the lower city. Sitting by the river I had sometimes looked up and wondered who lived in the trim house, and it was a surprise that Duba's family did. What he wore around the town was more patches than pants and I had assumed that even by the standards of Camamu his people were poor.

The parlor was plain but highly polished with two wicker peacock chairs and a couch to match. "Sit! Sit! I will get my aunt."

In good time, a massive woman moved deliberately into the room and took a chair. If in his portrait Picasso had colored Gertrude Stein's skin the same shade as her dress, he would have painted Elza. Two young women and a crone followed Elza into the room, and Duba hovered at her side like a page.

After the introductions I began by asking what spirit Dona Elza received.

"The Sultan of the Forests of Oxóssi," Elza replied in a deep and melodious voice.

"Does the senhora remember the first time she received this spirit?"

"The first time," Elza said, "was twenty-five years ago when we were living in Acaraí, and the mayor of the town had gone to Salvador to negotiate for a carnival to come to Acaraí and everyone was very excited since they wanted very much to hear whether the managers of the carnival had accepted what the mayor had offered them, which was three thousand cruzeiros, and as a joke I said that I had received the spirit of a gringo and that we would know at nine o'clock the next Thursday whether the carnival had accepted."

I was writing as fast as I could and barely had time to look up and nod.

"Of course my family did not believe that I had received a spirit but the fact was that although I was joking I had a feeling the telegram would come when I had said it would and at nine hours on Thursday morning everyone was waiting outside the house of the mayor for a telegram but when nothing came they teased me about my gringo spirit. Just as everyone was starting to leave a burro came up the road and the mayor was riding on it and he said The carnival is coming! And everyone began to cheer and they shouted Viva the carnival! and then someone shouted Viva Dona Elza! and pretty soon they were all shouting that and it was a good advertisement for me but that as I said was only joking. The first serious time came when my father died near Christmas and the next month which would be January I was very nervous and I took pills from the pharmacy to calm me but they only made me worse and after four days or five I started to have terrible pains and they took me to the hospital. That was in the middle of February and they gave me every drug cortisone everything but when I was discharged from the hospital I was still not cured and I went to live with a niece of mine in

Ilhéus. I was not eating, nothing but tea and I was cold very cold no matter what I wore and it was impossible for me to sleep."

I was scribbling now, not looking up, so I didn't see the two younger women slip from the room.

"I could only take water and then at one point I fainted and when I came to I was in my bed and I said My God what is this? The doctors came again and they all agreed that it was a problem with my liver but I said I cannot stay here longer or meet these expenses and I must go to my house but when I got to the farm they decided I needed a complete examination and sent me to Doctor Alberto Barhato in Itabuna and I went there by bus sitting in the front and on the way there was an accident and I hit my head on the roof."

The old woman sitting by the window gave a loud yawn, which Elza ignored. It died away in a sigh of resignation.

"I was in shock but when I got to Itabuna I was very hungry and not cold as I had been before and I slept almost continuously for five days but I still had pains and when I went to Doctor Alberto Barhato he said to me jokingly Elza you are a horse and he meant that I was receiving spirits although he was not serious and he gave me another complete examination of blood urine everything and it was all totally normal and I stayed at the hospital for a full day and had lunch in the infirmary where they told me about a grand festa that would be held that night and all at once a terrible feeling came over me and I felt like taking up a knife from the table and plunging it into my heart and I could not speak and I could not move."

This time the old woman reversed the order, sighing first, then yawning so wide that even across the room I could see her back teeth.

"By five in the afternoon I was somewhat better but the doctor was still worried and afraid I might hurt myself so there were to be no knives around me and then the doctor Doctor Alberto Barhato said to me Dona Elza your pain is not for us it is a spiritual pain and a colleague of Doctor Alberto Barhato was there and he said Stop doctors must not say such things and then I stayed at the hospital three more days but one morning I got rebellious and left and dressed all in white I went to a house of Candomblé operated by Dona Cecilia."

Duba poked my arm. "It is time for your taxi to Ituberá."

"I liked the singing and the dancing but I went to other houses as well searching for seven days or more until a caboclo said to me it is only lack of faith that makes you look everywhere and I decided then to proceed to the baptism in Candomblé."

I was on my feet, still writing as Duba tugged me toward the door.

"The baptism required certain materials and I remember going to Salvador and looking everywhere until finally a man he was an engineer told me about a pharmacy on Rua Chile it was called the pharmacy Cauda and I went there and asked for—"

"May I come back another time, senhora?"

Dona Elza's neck turned slightly to where I stood in the doorway but her body stayed planted toward the place where I should have been sitting. At the distraction, the old woman jumped from her seat and skittered out of the room.

"I have more to say," Dona Elza said.

WITHOUT MY REALIZING IT, Camamu had been narrowing around me until after two months I could feel the tightness through my chest. The nights were worst, with a sun that set at five-thirty and a routine that put everyone to bed by nine.

Not that I was usually alone in my room. At dusk, rats ventured out from their holes along the baseboard. I had to lob my copy of *Gravity's Rainbow* across the floor to drive them back again. Baby bats, too lazy or inexperienced to fly, sometimes scuttled out, and them I had to scoop up with a broom and carry to the window while they clung to the straw, unwilling to risk a fall. But when I shook them free they found they could glide as far as the roof next door.

Huge moths, hardly smaller than the bats, flocked around the light bulb, transparent, overly attenuated for their wingspread, so sluggish that whenever I sat I crushed two or three into a moist powder that wouldn't brush off my pants.

If the rain had let up, I would lean out my front window and watch the woman down the street as she paced listlessly in front of her door. She resisted sleep, perhaps until dawn, for when I gave up at midnight and went to bed, she was still drifting along her ten feet of sidewalk.

"That woman is crazy," Júlio told me. "She takes men from the hotel for sexual relations in the shadows."

I looked at her more closely after that. She was not old, not forty, but pressed dry by the years until her body seemed made from old newspapers. Júlio said she had been a widow for three years, but the same even before her husband died. By nine, her teen-age children were in bed, and they never talked about her vigil on the street.

I had brought a book on self-hypnosis which I hadn't yet read. But the way my mind was emptying out for hours some afternoons, I wondered whether I hadn't absorbed the book's secret just from packing it. I lay on my bed, which was so narrow I had to hoist up on knee and elbow to turn over, and I stared at clouds floating dense and gray against the hard winter sky.

By raising higher, I could bring the filthy roofs into view, and the malarial river. Beyond, the ocean's surface looked solid, and desolation I had known as a boy in Minnesota came over me again, the same sense of being crushed in a girdle of land.

Despite some progress in Marlene's class, I was still starting anecdotes and realizing midway through them that I didn't know a key phrase at the end. It meant trailing off or changing the subject, and it gave me a preview of being senile.

Certainly there were pleasant times, and one came regularly at dinner-time when the children from the street arrived to record on my tape machine the latest Brazilian love songs and their curiously passive rock 'n' roll.

After she had finished the dinner dishes at the hotel, Alda crossed the road to sing ballads in a true voice as high and faint as mist, and on other nights the twenty-year-old boys from the high school sat in a circle on the floor beating the boards with their knuckles and shouting sambas.

"Do you like the samba?" one chorus ran, in English.

"I like it too.

"If you love the samba,

"I love you."

As they sang, Júlio was leaning against the wall, sipping his beer slowly. "They are happy," I said.

"Yes," he said morosely, "we are a joyous people."

One afternoon while I was reading on my cot, Ailton and his rascally friend Jaiminho cut a tape. From their smirking when they had finished, I had an idea what to expect, and that night the older boys came by, heard the song, and were appalled.

"Do you know what they did to your tape?"

"I heard the word 'puta,' " I said. "But they were laughing so hard I did not catch the rest."

"It is a terrible song," they said. "Awful! Disgusting! You take this machine to the Candomblé and to your lessons with Professora Marlene, do you not?"

"Sometimes."

"You cannot let those rapazes, those boys, use your machine again. It would be very bad for a woman to hear that song."

That concern was one of the few signs of courtliness I observed among the youth of Camamu. They came to my room in bunches, sprawling over the bed and across the floor, and should five or six girls from their school class venture up, hesitant, poised to flee, the boys greeted them unenthusiastically. Until I insisted, they never thought of surrendering their seat to a girl.

The girls old enough to drink refused when I offered them a Scotch or batida. "It is because they remember the Brazilian formula for a perfect evening," a high school boy explained. "A whiskey before, a cigarette after."

Many younger children couldn't wait for the dinner hour to record and they brought small gifts throughout the day in hopes of being asked inside to sing a few choruses. One six-year-old brought me the last two bites of his raspberry ice and lingered to inspect the mysteries of my room.

He was a strange child; at first I had taken him to be retarded. But he was simply so shy that whenever anyone spoke to him, he hugged himself, shut his eyes, and grinned with anguish.

123

He pointed to a green plastic vial next to my thermos of coffee. He was too timid to ask what it was, but he raised his eyebrows at me.

"Lift your hands," I said.

He threw up his small brown arms and I squirted Tally-Ho deodorant in their hollows. The child wriggled with delight and ran back to the street.

In less than a minute, the stairway was full of bare-chested infants waving their arms above their heads and pleading, "Perfume me! Perfume me!"

Another night the same children brought a book from their school and grouped around it, ready to record every lugubrious verse of the Brazilian national anthem.

They made a courageous sour start but midway through their second chorus, the toothless postman from downstairs came rushing up to protest. The Brazilian hymn was not a fit subject for brincando, he cried. They must stop at once!

Crestfallen, the children filed out with their heads bowed.

When they were gone, I said, "The children were not making fun."

"I heard them," he said sulkily.

"They were serious enough. They just sing badly."

But as a servant of the state he was unappeased. The next day Zeca showed up to say that he did not know about the custom in my country but in Brazil children were brought up to have respect for their anthem.

PUSHING ALONG THE DARK CORRIDOR to where Nelson was waiting at his table, I had to step around a light-skinned Brazilian sitting in the hallway with a black chicken cradled in his arms.

"If you are busy," I told Nelson as we shook hands, "I can come back later."

"That man has come here for a work," Nelson said. "All the way from the city of Nazaré. Do you know where that is?"

"West of Santo Antônio de Jesus? Near Salvador?"

"Exactly. They come from all over Bahia for my works because they know how powerful they are."

"You said I could see your house for Exú."

"Today is a good day because of the work I will be performing. Come along."

Out the back door, a stony hill rose so sharply there was no level place to stand. Midway up the rock, Nelson had hewed a shallow niche, and at the back lay a skull made of clay that he identified as the female Exú. To the front, a foot-high statue of an imp was smoking a real cigarette. The face and outsized hands looked faintly Balinese.

"I made him myself," Nelson said. "He can also smoke cigars."

The man with the chicken had moved to the back door and Nelson called, "This americano comes here because he knows we have the true songs of the Candomblé."

I spread out eight drawings across the table. "Senhor, these are sketches out of books that show the markings used in Africa and Brazil for doing works. I wonder whether you recognize them?"

It was a mistake I should have avoided. Whenever I had mentioned a book to Valter or Maria, I saw that they became cautious. They had learned the rituals entirely by ear from older mães and pais do santo. But they were reluctant to contradict the written word, even when it didn't match what they knew.

My motive in citing authorities had been to prove that my interest was genuine. But now, watching Nelson grow wary and protective, I resolved never again to quote from a printed page.

To our mutual relief he found two of the eight signs familiar. The first was a more ornate version of Dimitri's tattoo.

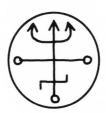

"It is for Exú Lança," Nelson said. "Who is also called Exú Tranca Rua, Exú of the Closed Road. He is the Exù of Santa Barbara."

"I did not know the saints had Exús."

"They have, they have."

"You make this mark on a cloth?"

"On a red cloth," he stipulated.

"A new cloth every time?"

"Naturally it must be new for each new wish," he said. "You cross two candles; they represent the lances. And you sacrifice a black cock."

"Do you need beer or cachaça?"

"Either will do. Whiskey is better."

I pointed to the other sign he had recognized:

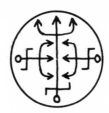

"That is for Exú Pagão," Nelson said. "Exú the Pagan. Dona Zulmira has him."

"She receives him?"

"She receives. He is the god of supplemental loves. Loves outside the marriage."

Nelson called to his sullen teen-age son. "Francisco, write down this prayer in his notebook."

"Sim, pai." The boy appeared and took my pad doubtfully. As his father dictated he wrote four lines of an African chant in an indecipherable hand, then made a Portuguese translation nearly as mysterious.

"Nagô," Nelson said, including the man with the chicken in his explanation. "Pure Nagô. You will not hear that chant anywhere else until you get to Salvador."

Later that afternoon, Marlene inspected the page with good-natured contempt. "Be ou baré um bambi é," she read aloud. "What is this supposed to be? It means nothing."

"It is a phonetic rendering of Nagô. I recognize a few words. A friend in Rio told me that ocossi owô in the fourth line meant 'little money.'

But there is a Portuguese translation across the page."

"Huh!" she said, reading Francisco's version. "There are many mistakes in grammar here. But I will write it correctly and you can put it into your language."

In English, Nelson's prayer read: I am all or nothing. Nothing makes me tremble. I am a child seeking to know my life. This little money is not for buying clothes. Neither is it for buying meat. Nor is it for buying farinha.

But when Francisco handed me back the book I saw only a page of slashes and dots. I said to Nelson, "Am I interrupting a work you were going to do for this man with the chicken?"

"I do not do it now. At dusk."

Nelson looked behind him and saw that the man had tied the leg of the chicken to his stool. "You must cut him free," Nelson said. "He already belongs to Exú. He must not be tied up."

"I would like to come back for your work," I said.

"Six o'clock," Nelson said, looking about for a knife to cut the chicken loose.

I HAD DISCOVERED A SHORTCUT that wound down the cliff to Nelson's house, a grassy path workmen used when their mules were loaded with lumber or cacau. In the dying light I picked my way around heaps of black manure.

Nelson's wife took me to the shrine room, also Francisco's bedroom, where Nelson was sitting on the edge of the mattress, a gray jacket over his striped pajamas. I took a place at his side.

"Where is the man?" I asked.

"He did not need to stay," Nelson said. "Once he brought the materials his job was finished. He has gone back to Nazaré."

"And the chicken?"

"The cock has been fed to Exú."

Spread out at our feet was a tan cloth with bottles of Jacaré to hold down the corners and three more bottles along the border. Two bowls of popcorn were set next to a bowl of red farofa and one of white, and seven cigars were laid in a circle next to seven white candles.

In a jumble in the middle were heaped seven matchboxes, several spools of thread and a stack of colored cloths. On top was some black stuff, like coarse brunette ringlets. "What is that?"

"Fuma da corda. You understand?"

"Burnt rope," I said in English.

"We will begin."

"What has the man asked you for?"

"What do you mean?"

"Does he have a pain? Does he want to be rich? Is he in love?"

"This work is not for him. It is against his enemy."

"He wants you to harm someone else?"

"This man." Nelson lifted up a photograph that was curling at the edges and turning brown: a handsome, pouting mulatto in a suit and tie.

"Is this not your son? It looks like Francisco."

"It is a man named João, the man this work is against. It was taken when he was younger, nine or ten years ago. To get the picture the man you saw had to go to the high school in Nazaré."

"They work together?" I was thinking of the girl from Firestone who had come to Valter in Ituberá.

"This man," Nelson raised the photograph again, "is the boss of the man you saw. Now we begin."

Even at the bedside, Nelson was coughing up thick yellow phlegm and spitting it on the floor. Sometimes he remembered to spread it over the concrete with the toe of his sandal.

He bowed his head and sang a simple African chant. Taking up a roll of black thread, he unrolled half of it until it covered the face in the photograph. When that was done, he reached into a drawer and drew out a doll about twelve inches long.

Seeing the doll, I felt a sense of dread I couldn't explain away. It was as though somewhere I had seen that doll, and though I couldn't remember where, its details were familiar: the fitted jacket of its gray suit; the white protuberance, like a bandaged thumb, where a head should have been.

I don't want to watch this, I thought. More honestly—though I am jeering at myself as I write this—what I thought was: I don't want to watch this again.

But sitting beside Nelson on the bed, I was not jeering. In an impersonal way, a way that didn't involve my own safety, I was afraid.

From the drawer where he had gotten the doll, Nelson pulled out a scrap of white lamb's wool and he wrapped the doll and the photograph in it, but not tenderly or as bunting. In his dark hands, the curls of wool looked like the fumes from dry ice. It seemed then that the doll must either be scalded or freeze to death.

Nelson pulled the thread tight around the wool until the doll was trapped inside. Only its white cloth skull stuck out. With precise gestures he pulled out lengths of thread across his palm and knotted them around the white head.

"One," he counted as he pulled a strand to make another knot. "Two."

He was not in a trance but his breathing had become irregular. By the fourth knot around the cotton head, his voice was cracking, and as he counted he couldn't have sounded more vindictive if he held the victim's head in an iron vise.

"Six!" Nelson said angrily, and he yanked at the knot until the doll's head was deeply creased where its hairline should have been. His malevolence gave the figure life; he couldn't be hating it so much if it weren't living. I had an instant where I felt I should reach across and seize the doll from his hands.

"Seven!" He threw the limp doll down, the spool still dangling from its head, and turned to the pile of cloths. His exertion with the knots had left Nelson breathing hard and I missed his first words as he dropped a silken black square across the small body.

But as he let a red cloth fall, I heard, "This represents the blood upon your black cape."

The white and the purple cloths he threw down together with a phrase about the contrast they made. Then he turned on me so abruptly I drew back. The ceremony was over.

"You have never seen anything like that with your caboclos of the Umbanda."

"No."

"Pure Nagô," Nelson said.

"Now if the man—João—wants to undo this work, he must find another pai do santo and make a sacrifice himself?"

"He can try," Nelson said, his living eye triumphant. "But he will have a hard time finding anyone with the power to remove this curse I have put on him."

"What becomes of the offering?"

"At midnight a driver will take it to Ibirapitanga." It was a town southeast of Camamu, two hours by car.

"Why there?"

"There is a closed street that is good for works of this kind."

"The man need not go along?"

"No. He paid the driver forty-eight cruzeiros to take his offering."

"How much did he leave here with you?"

"Fifteen cruzeiros." A mere two and a half dollars for that outpouring of hate.

"And yet," I said, "the work was expensive for him—the cachaça, the cloth. He must have spent a hundred cruzeiros."

"A hundred? Two hundred and fifty!" Clearly the size of the amount elated Nelson, testified to his effectiveness. "Each of those cloths was a full metro long. The doll had to be specially made. That alone was forty cruzeiros."

I wanted to leave and stood up brusquely. "Thank you for letting me watch."

Nelson stayed seated next to the sacrifice across the floor. "You have never seen anything like it?" he asked again.

"Never. I saw that you tightened thread around the doll's head. I suppose the man who paid you wants this man João to have pains in his head."

"No," said Nelson. "He wants to drive him mad."

THAT NIGHT I INVITED THE YOUNGSTERS of the town to my room. I poured out cachaça for the male students, urged the girls to stay past their usual curfew, suffered the children to punch and maul the tape machine. By ten o'clock I wasn't dropping hints that it was bedtime but imploring everyone to stay another hour or two.

Finally they left. I lay on the bed with the light on and played a tape of old rock songs: "Don't Be Cruel," "Wild One," "Chantilly Lace."

The mood from Nelson's was passing. I wasn't at all frightened. But I was still disturbed. And chagrined that his ritual should have had the power to shake me.

In California I had copied out certain passages, antidotes against future experiences, like the one today. Before turning off the light I got my notebook and read one of them. It was from *Memories, Dreams and Reflections:*

> I can still recall vividly how Freud said to me, "My dear Jung, promise me never to abandon the sexual theory. That is the most essential thing of all. You see, we must make a dogma of it, an unshakable bulwark." He said that to me with great emotion, in the tone of a father saying, "And promise me this one thing, my dear son: that you will go to church every Sunday." In some astonishment I asked him, "A bulwark—against what?" To which he replied, "Against the black tide of mud"—and here he hesitated for a moment, then added, "of occultism."

BY THE NEXT AFTERNOON, I could describe Nelson's work lightly to Marlene, expecting that we would laugh over it together.

When I finished, Marlene asked, "You do not believe that what a man does here in Camamu can injure another man in Nazaré?"

"Of course not."

"Neither do I. I do not think the spirits would do harm in that way."

"Not even," I said, still smiling, "when a man knows the sign for Exú Pagão?" On my open notebook I sketched the circle and three tridents.

"Please do not make signs," Marlene said sharply. "I have a fear of them."

I HAD NEVER WANTED TO BE COUNTED among those who find goodness insipid. Yet I couldn't deny that when I returned to Nelson's house several days later, I went better disposed toward him because of the scare he had given me.

As I headed for the trail to the baixa, a band of children intercepted me. "Jack! Jack!" they clamored. "Gravador a noite?"

"You have seen my staircase," I said. "There can be no more playing with the tape recorder until the stairs are fixed. Now they are too dangerous for children."

The landing had been rotting for years, and the day after my session with Nelson it collapsed. I had been picking my way like a cat burglar up and down the few remaining steps.

Fairly, the children protested, "It has already been three days!"

"Do not talk to me. Talk to Zeca. I have asked him to find a carpenter."

Nelson came from his bedroom in pajamas, spitting more bountifully than usual. I said, "I wondered what you had heard from the man in Nazaré. Whether the work has been successful."

"If you would like to talk with him," Nelson said, "he comes back next Wednesday at four o'clock."

"I remember your telling me that anyone can receive a spirit."

"They can."

"That if it does not come naturally, it can be taught."

"Yes."

The time had come to ask. I couldn't pretend to be worried that Nelson might think I was being flippant. He and Maria, and Luzia, Elza, Mira, and Valter, were all too convinced of their powers to suspect that a man might call up the spirits idly. My reluctance, as I had known for some three years, lay elsewhere.

I said, "Could you teach me to receive a spirit?"

Nelson paused only to let his cough subside and spit yellow at our feet. "Yes."

I am going to pay for this, I thought. With luck, in money.

"This is a good time to start," Nelson said. "My Candomblé will be coming on the twenty-fourth of August. That is, if I can raise the money. They are very expensive."

"In the town of Caxias near Rio," I said, "children passed among the people holding a sheet. Everyone threw in a few cruzeiros."

"Not here," Nelson said. "Here, the people pay for the works but a festa must be free. There must be sheep and goats, all very expensive. A pig, as well."

"How much does a sheep cost?"

"Each one, two hundred cruzeiros," he said. Thirty-four dollars. "And I must have three. Do you have your notebook there? I will give you an idea of what I need.

"First there is the milho, two kinds—branco and vermelho."

I opened the book reluctantly to copy what was sounding like a shopping list. "Maize," I wrote, "white and red."

"Black beans and two other varieties of bean," Nelson said. "A milhaca gorda. Inhame roxo and inhame branco."

I had no idea what a fat milhaca was. Inhame was a crisp edible root rather like a potato.

"Amendoim."

Peanuts.

"Bananas da terra." Bahia grew several species of banana. Da terra were coarse and tasteless.

"Arroz."

Rice.

"Farofa with oil and with milk. How many items is that?"

I counted. "Twelve."

"That is only the fruit, the beans, and the grain. Then I must have three sheep, two goats, a pig, eight ducks, ten chickens and four cágados. Do you know what they are?"

"Similar to what we call turtles."

"They also have the name 'Goats of Xangô.' Then we must have whiskey and fireworks. You see it is not easy."

"Are the goats cheaper than the sheep?" Doing my part didn't rule out looking for a bargain.

"The same."

"How about the pig?"

"More!" said Nelson triumphantly. "Three hundred cruzeiros! Then there is the cost of the dresses and suits. Bring them out!" he commanded his wife.

She had been sitting on a stool, contemplating the vast outlay of money that Nelson's list represented. Now she jumped up and came back with several pair of coarse white linen bloomers and seven lace-trimmed skirts.

"These wear out," Nelson said. "That means more expense."

Thrown across a table was one of those quilts that every mãe and pai do santo seemed to have—bright strips of rag stitched onto burlap to let the remnants ruffle gaily. I pointed at it. "Very nice. What is it called?"

"Singah!" Nelson said.

I wrote the word, making a note to check with Marlene about the final *h.*

"Would you like to look at it?" Nelson asked.

"Very much." The only ones I had seen had either Maria or Valter seated on them.

Nelson crossed the room and threw the handsome cloth across a pile of wood. He pulled at the top of the table and from some hidden compartment a sewing machine emerged.

"Singah!" Nelson repeated.

I opened my pad and drew a heavy black line.

"Make something," Nelson instructed his wife.

"It is not necessary," I said.

He held up a hand. "Wait, she will make something."

From the bedroom Nelson's wife recruited their chunky young daughter. The girl was seated before the machine to work the treadle and run a seam on a blue sash.

When she was finished, Nelson said to his wife, "Come here!"

Obediently she lowered her head while Nelson wound the scarf around her brow with deft fingers. His knot left two points like horns over her forehead. "Bahiana style," he said.

I knew what I had to say before I could leave: "I would like to make a contribution to your Candomblé."

"Good."

"We can talk about it when I come back Wednesday to see the man from Nazaré. And about the way I can receive a spirit."

"We will be expecting you," Nelson said.

VALTER DRAGGED OUT A LARGE GREEN SLATE the teacher used when the terreiro was a classroom and he propped it on the desk.

"Since you are interested in the signs of Umbanda," he said, "it will be easier to draw them than to describe them."

It was late on a hot Saturday afternoon, and I was winded from the climb to his house. I took a chair to one side of the blackboard, across from José, the initiate who worked at Firestone.

Valter had held off a few minutes, waiting for Deoclides to join us. But with no telephones in the town, when a man failed to arrive he was presumed to have a valid excuse and Valter didn't seem annoyed that his lieutenant was missing.

"Here is a sign to bring happiness," Valter began, drawing with care. "It is a sign from the line of Ogum."

"The third line of Umbanda?"

Valter held up a hand to say, All things in good time. Methodically he added heads to the seven arrows he had drawn.

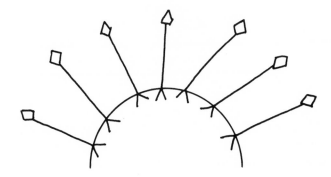

"This sign must be made with white chalk on a cloth of white, pink, and green," he said.

Thinking of Nelson's sacrifice to Exú, I asked, "A metro of cloth?"

"Somewhat more than a metro." Valter looked to see that I had finished copying the sign before he erased it. "Now I will show you two different signs to use when one wishes to reach the spirits of the dead. Both are very ancient, and they serve the same purpose."

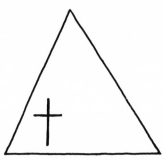

"That is the African sign," he said. "It is to be drawn on black cloth."

"The cross suggests Christianity."

"This sign is much older than that," Valter said. "It is one of the oldest of African signs."

In Rio, I had seen Umbandist books that showed the same drawing in white, as a tribute to Oxalá. But I held to my resolution and kept still.

"This mark is also for the dead. It comes from the Indians of the Amazon." Valter sketched in the hair with short, quick strokes.

"This is the sign when you want to ask the help of Sereia the mermaid. It must be made on pink cloth."

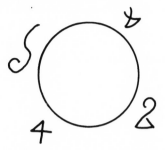

I was copying as exactly as I could, but I had to say, "I do not understand the significance."

Valter pointed to the circle. "This is Sereia's home, the sea. Here" —he started clockwise at the upper right—"is her seat above the water. This is her hollow in the rock. This is her doorway. And this," he touched the symbol at the upper left, "is her bed or couch."

"Do you have to remember all this?" I asked José. He smiled bashfully and nodded without much confidence.

"Different men are needed for different tasks," Valter said. "One man"—he gestured to the place Deoclides sat the last time we were together—"may learn and remember exactly all the signs and the history of Umbanda. Another man may be good at works. It is not necessary that their training be identical.

"This next," he went on, "is drawn on white cloth. It is a sign for Iemanjá." Valter formed a crescent and wrote in block letters next to it:

He hesitated, concentrating ferociously. I wasn't sure that either reading or writing came easily to Valter. When he had looked through my bilingual dictionary he picked out Portuguese words much as I did, with the same bemusement that the black marks across the page actually meant something.

At last he wrote the final two letters and turned his back to the board.

If José noticed, he gave no indication. I said, "Is it part of the sign to write her name next to the moon?"

"In her case, yes. Not with the others."

Next Valter drew a sun with a merry face.

"That is for riches," he said.

"The color of the cloth?"

"Gold."

"That is a key," Valter said. "Do you remember the sign we use to close the terreiro to Exú?"

"A star and a cross."

"This key is the sign to open doors. Not to Exú, but to good things. To let good things come out. The cloth should be green, and in one corner a cup of water and a candle must be placed.

"Now this is a useful sign":

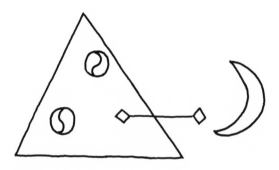

As I was copying, Valter said to José in an undertone, "Soon he will know everything." I shook my head and kept drawing.

"This is the sign when you want to know where someone is. Let us say that you have gone away from this place and I do not know where you are. With this sign I can tell whether you are living or dead. And if you are alive, where you are."

"How is it done?"

"I put a cup of water here," he said, pointing to a place midway between the circles, "and stand by to watch. The information appears in the water."

139

"Special water?"

"Ordinary water."

"Can anyone do this?"

"No, it is the spirit who reads the answer, not a man."

"You are receiving Ogum and it is he who consults the glass?"

"Yes," Valter said. "But remember: should you wish to know the location of more than one person, the water must be changed each time or it becomes clouded and the spirit cannot read the answer."

Before leaving for Ituberá, I had copied a page full of the signs for Exú so they would be in my hand and not Xeroxed from a book. They included the two Nelson had recognized, and now I held them out to Valter.

"These are complicated," he said. "I will give you their names. That is for King Exú—Lucifer."

"Senhor," I said, "I heard something the other day that confused me. Do the saints have Exús at their disposal?"

"It is not simple," he said. "But yes, when a saint wishes to use an Exú as a messenger, he may do so."

"Then the Exús can do good?"

"In those cases they are doing the bidding of the saint and the saint can do only good."

"Different Exús for different saints?"

"Yes," he said. "For Iemanjá, Exú Lalu. That is an African name, as is the one for the Exú of Omulu: he is called Exú Daké. For Xangô, it is Exú Marabô. For Oxóssi, though, the name is Portuguese: Exú Tranca Rua, the Exu of the Closed Road."

Valter drew a breath. "The rest of these signs you show me are for

Ogum. For example, that one"—he pointed to the sign at the bottom right—"is Ogum da Oia."

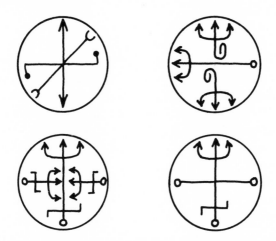

"I thought they might all be for Exú," I said, "since they all have pitchforks."

"What happened is this," Valter explained. "When Quimbanda began, they stole the strongest signs from the gods of Umbanda and gave them all to Exú. Rightfully, these four belong to Ogum."

More likely, I decided later, when Umbanda was born its first practitioners scavenged among the ritual of Candomblé and, trying to lessen the influence of Exú, awarded his signs to Ogum. And still later the Quimbandists repatriated them.

"Now I would like to go over the seven lines of Umbanda with you," I said.

I had copied out Pedro McGregor's list of the seven chieftains of Umbanda as being authoritative. But after half an hour, only four of Valter's seven lines agreed with McGregor, and I understood why everyone who wrote about the spirits added a disclaimer about the final accuracy of his research. There was, after all, no court of appeal. In Ituberá, within Valter's jurisdiction, he awarded the fifth line to Omulu, and whatever his glory might be in Rio de Janeiro, Xangô here was no more than an aide to Ogum.

I picked up my notebook and dictionary and rose from the table. "So soon?" Valter asked.

I was thinking about what Manuel had impressed upon me two months ago, as we were leaving Valter's terreiro after our introduction: "Never come here alone at night," he said.

"Everyone seems friendly."

Manuel snorted. "It takes only one person who is not friendly to hurt you. At night, come in a car. If you must walk, bring Zeca or his brother."

"What if they will not come?"

"Bring Ailton. At least he would know how to call for help."

"All right."

"Remember what I am saying," Manuel said.

"I will remember."

Now, feeling craven and rude, I said, "I would like to walk back to Ituberá while it is still light."

But Valter only nodded approvingly. "Sim."

"When I come back," I said, "when you are not so busy, I was wondering whether it might not be too much trouble for you to—"

Valter waited serenely for me to finish.

"—do a work for me?"

He seemed unastonished by the request and waited for me to go on. "I thought," I said, "that perhaps the work that opens one's paths might be a good one to ask of you."

It was a potent work from the white line of magic. If anything should go amiss at Nelson's—

"He would like the work of caminhos abertos," Valter told José. "He wants it as research for his book."

"Not just for my book," I said. "Truthfully, not just for that."

AFTER LUNCH AT HIS COMFORTABLE HOUSE, Ed Houser, the manager of the Firestone fazenda, drove me around the twenty-six thousand acres he commanded between Camamu and Ituberá. "The largest-producing

142

rubber plantation in South America," he said. "Three tons a day."

His workers began at dawn making incisions in the bark to bleed the white latex. Before noon they had come back to empty out the black tin cups that were strapped like trusses around each trunk. By midafternoon everyone was gone from the fields.

Cleaning and processing the rubber required only two white-tiled troughs and a row of old-fashioned washing machines. After the wash, bales were rolled into sheds the size of a freight car to dry for three days.

Houser's was that forthright amiability of bald men. He lived alone, a bachelor, the only American on the premises and presiding over a community of five thousand workers and their families. Throughout the afternoon I had looked in vain for traces of Senhor Kurtz.

"How much does a man or a woman earn for collecting this rubber?"

"Seven cruzeiros a day," Houser said. A dollar and seventeen cents. "It's the going rate for farm work. But there's one difference: here, they know they'll get paid. Other places a man may work for months and get nothing."

That much was true. Work on my bathroom had come to a halt because, for all the land his family owned, Zeca was short of cash. The workmen wouldn't come back until they were paid for cementing the floor.

The houses that Firestone provided for its workers were neat and freshly whitewashed, and the two schools looked to be the equal of Marlene's in Camamu. Another point of attack occurred to me.

"How much of the plantation do Brazilians own? Either in private capital or through their government?"

"Nothing," Houser said calmly. "It is all American capital."

I told him about a poster I had seen in the market: photographs of a dozen young men and women labeled TERRORISTS.

"Damn fools," Houser said.

"I've been wondering what the people think when they see those pictures," I said. "In Camamu the students are fascinated by Angela Davis. But it's because she's black and good-looking, not because she's a Communist."

"Damn fools," Houser said again.

His adult life had been spent on overseas plantations in the Philippines; Africa; Cuba, where the fields ran down to a cove where Errol Flynn docked his yacht and Hemingway came to fish. The best years of Houser's life.

The previous October he had fallen from a roof and broken his arm. The bone had been badly set and not much strength had returned to it. Coming in sight of his fiftieth birthday, the accident had depressed him. He was even talking nostalgically about the United States. Its comfort. Its ease. "Everything here is so hard," Houser said, and looking across the miles of trees I understood him.

First, crews had fought their way in to clear the forest, felling the trees, digging up stumps, carting them off to burn.

Next, the land had to be scrubbed clean, plucked of rocks and weeds, fertilized, and, finally, planted with seedlings that wouldn't yield rubber for seven years. The day of our tour, one third of Firestone's acreage had been cleared and planted. Before he left Bahia, Houser wanted to double that amount.

He parked his pickup on a hill to let me look out over the miles of rubber trees. Their trunks were mottled ivory, like old piano keys, and where the branches weren't bare, their leaves had gone a lifeless yellow. Still, the plucked and regular rows, threatened on all sides by a predatory forest, spoke of peace and human care. Of victory.

The wrong emotion, I reminded myself. No Brazilian spirit would choose to enter a heart that responded to this sterile patch of order.

But the thought brought back the Sunday morning at Valter's terreiro, and I said to Houser, "I know you're not interested in macumba, but a week or two ago in Ituberá, a girl from your plantation came to the caboclo of the Umbanda to have a work done because she was unhappy with her supervisor."

"My God," he said, "do they still do that?"

"Still."

"I wonder how many hexes have been put on me."

"The day you fell off your roof, how many people smiled and looked sage?"

"I think they leave Americans alone," Houser said. "That's the way it used to be in Africa. They didn't bother with foreigners."

WHEN DONA ELZA CAME BACK TO CAMAMU, Duba rushed once more to alert me. This time I was shown into the dining room at the back of the house and Elza and I were left alone.

I looked at her handsome brown face with its proud mustache and felt remorse at being restive the last time. I wondered whether Duba or the other women had teased her about that monologue, for now Elza was replying almost curtly to my first questions.

No, if she had her life to live over she would not choose to be a mãe do santo. It was difficult work and she did not care much for it.

No, if a man or woman did not receive a spirit naturally, there was no way to cultivate the spiritual force that was needed. And the risk was great. A person might open himself to unruly or malicious spirits from down below.

No, she did not do works concerning love. Her spirits were not interested in the subject. What might please one of the partners could be harmful to the other. There was no way of knowing ahead of time that the work would bring equal benefits to both man and woman.

Yes, she could cure the insane. She had done it on five occasions. "There was the case of Maria Domingus, who was in such a state of rage that her every mood and action was ugly, ugly, ugly."

Soft and uninflected, the repetition lulled me, and my mind drifted out past the window, to green islands floating on a still sea. I heard the bem-ti-vi birds saying, I saw you well, I saw you well.

"She had cut off all her hair—"

The clouds were thick and white. It was a day to find a copse of soft grass and watch the bees make honey. But in exploring paths around the town, I had never seen Bahian men and women sprawled on the grass doing nothing.

"It was necessary for me to concentrate my spiritual qualities and to speak very well. Luckily, the house was surrounded by trees and flowers, which have a calming influence—"

The wind rose, the boughs of the trees answered the birds until they sighed and sang together.

"When I arrived, she either was saying nothing at all or she was singing in a loud—"

Elza's own voice was like mel silvestre pouring over me. I was stuck to my chair, my hands stuck to my knees. My eyes began to close.

"A cup of water—"

My chin sank further on my chest. "Doctor, doctor, doctor," I heard Elza saying, "that was all her family talked about. You do not have the competence to treat this case, they said, but I went right ahead—"

I shook myself awake. "—given up for dead, and truly difficult, then—"

A cloud passed over the face of the sun. Suddenly the air was thick with the threat of rain. If I had been sleeping in the woods, it would have been time to move for cover.

"—in her coma, over and over, Dona Elza, do not go away, do not leave me—"

It had been raining the day I drove my uncle's wife to the state mental hospital. She hadn't cried or begged me to stay with her. She sat beside me in the front seat, wearing a cheerful red wool coat. Her hands were near the door handle, which I was watching, and they picked at the handbag in her lap.

She understood that there was no other choice. The nursing home had done her no good. After two weeks at home, she had sunk again into apathy and despair and this time her doctor insisted on the state ward ten miles out of the city. There was no one else to take her. As I drove, my eyes slid from the road to her hands.

"—came to and she was hungry and she stayed fine from that day afterward. Later she said, In my delirium, Dona Elza, I dreamed of you, and I—"

My aunt was of the generation for which mental illness meant disgrace. In earlier years hers had been a problem of nerves, much like Cristina's. She had been treated in a private hospital not too different from a hotel. Now she was on her way to an asylum.

Remember that you are signing yourself in, I said. You can leave at any time. She began to weep and took her hand away from the door

146

handle to search her bag for a handkerchief.

"Cecelia said it could not even be counted a work since there was no black hen, no dendê oil, but I said to her—"

The ward smelled of linseed oil. Women were sitting on metal chairs. They didn't speak to each other. My aunt was taken to a room with a low bed and a dresser. There was one window and it had bars.

I'll go now, I said. She nodded. Thank you, she said.

"—in Salvador, but I said, I am not interested in money and anything I do—"

"I understand," I said.

The trip to the asylum happened five years before. If my aunt resented my role, she never gave a sign of it. Within a few weeks she signed herself out and never went back.

I got up to leave Elza thinking that a mãe do santo probably could not have helped my aunt. And that driving her to Elza and not an asylum, I might have felt just as helpless. But I doubt I'd be remembering the day with the same remorse.

THE DRUMS WERE RAPPING OUT THE ORDER TO COMMENCE. Dona Maria called impatiently for the doors and windows to be shut. Gray smoke from urns of incense filled my chest and hid half the room. A shiver that began at my ankles was sweeping up my body in waves and puckered my skin.

I put away my notebook. This was the night to give myself to Candomblé.

I had asked Sargento Jaime to come for me early enough that we might see Maria's opening ritual. Now fifteen women were parading out of the inner shrine, five of them with large pans of meal balanced on their heads. They danced slowly but with grand flourishes. Had they been less practiced, their turns would have sent the pans flying.

Leaning back against the wall I could feel music entering my body and throbbing against my chest. The incense was peeling my throat raw, the drumbeat had me shivering.

The women set down their pans so that the edges made five points.

That star they then outlined with fifty white candles. Beside me on the bench, Sargento Jaime gave me a nudge. "Do you not want a photograph of this?"

Not anticipating how susceptible I would be feeling tonight, I had brought my Polaroid to take pictures and hand them out around the terreiro. Now I was trapped. I stood up and focused the lens.

I peered through a sight with a red dot that blotted out Maria's face. Next I would have to push the button that would rip the room apart with white light. I should have sat down and put the camera back on the floor. But Jaime was waiting avidly.

The tourist clenched his teeth and took his picture.

Both the white tab and the longer yellow strip pulled free from the camera without sticking as they sometimes did. I stuffed the camera back in its bag and held the film gingerly, waiting for it to develop.

The people of Camamu knew that such things existed as tape recorders and instant cameras. Their mayor even had a television set that allowed him to receive a scrambled transmission of presidential messages. So when I tore away the picture's protective cover and showed the result to Jaime, I was not competing in magic.

But if my photograph wasn't supernatural, to Maria's congregation it was more fascinating than anything she could summon at the moment. From Jaime's hands, the picture passed along the benches. Men hunched forward to see it better by the light of the sacrificial candles.

Then it made its way to the daughters of the saint. One by one, each woman dropped out of a chorus of "I saw a moon, I saw a candle" to squint and pick out her face in the picture.

It went to Maria last. Since she wasn't receiving a spirit, she could give it her full attention and she studied the surface for a long while, the singing going on without her. Then she hopped up and whispered to Jaime.

"They are going now into the chamber where she does her works," he said to me. "Would you take another photograph there?"

I took pictures of every nuance of the ritual until at last I ran out of flashbulbs. Meantime, the ceremony did go forward but only in the one-minute intervals while we waited for the pictures to develop. I think, without me there, it might have been a beautiful night. The music was different from anything I had heard, simple, sometimes only one line repeated for many stanzas. But every chant was sung with passionate belief.

"I am going away in the balance of the wind," the women sang. And, "Oxóssi plays on the moon, Congo plays on the stars." And, "Sailor, I do not own the sea, but I have come here to save you."

One song haunted me all of the next day. It was an appeal of the women to Ogum:

"Da-me licença, O Senhor.

"Da-me licença, O meu amor."

Permit me, Lord. Permit me, my love.

The singers forced their voices high, the sound was grating and nasal, but it was desperate, and filled with erotic pain.

Jorge Amado had written that the music of American Negroes reflected "the suffering and humiliation of beaten men." Songs inspired by the Candomblé were different, he said. They sounded like carefree laughter.

And when a chant was alive with the samba beat, Jorge Amado was right. But what could he say about this keening? These women wanted to be in the arms of their god. It would never happen; they were bitter at their loss. Yet they were consoled that on this night he might hear their plea and come down to use their bodies, not as women but as his own.

The time was nearing for the women to receive. Maria collected Sargento Jaime and me and took us back to her kitchen. "Beer?" she asked, a bottle in her hand.

"None for me," I said.

"Oh? Oh?"

"Dona Maria, I can get beer at any bar in Brazil. I want some of your green tea."

She poured the tea into a high china cup with a rose decal on its side.

"I would like to ask something of you," I began, sounding smooth to myself. It was getting easier. "Will you do a work for me?"

"Naturally."

"It would be to ask the spirits for help on the book I am writing."

"Whatever you like."

She lifted a basket of cookies and passed it under my nose. "You do not eat these? Oh? Oh?"

Maria went back to the dancing. Obviously I was forgiven my gaffe about her mãe do santo. But I wanted to clear up the matter. "Sargento Jaime?"

"Sim?"

"Do you know Bela Conceição Santo of Valença?"

"Sim."

"How old is she? More or less?"

"About the same age as Maria, more or less," Jaime said. "Perhaps a few years younger."

Back in the hall, Maria had just finished receiving her Ogum, striding the floor and delivering a loud prayer for the assemblage before her body fell back with a shudder. When she straightened, she laughed a high-pitched, defiant laugh and skipped into the shrine room. Around me the black faces were grinning in the candlelight.

"She has received Cosminho," said Jaime. "Saint Cosme, but as a small boy. There will be a lot of fun now."

As though he had overheard, the child using Maria's body bobbed out of the shrine to tug on Jaime's arm. "Come play with me," little Cosme said. "Nobody here ever wants to play."

Jaime answered him with mock severity. "Cosminho, you told us last time you would not come back because we were too dull. Why did you change your mind?"

"Somebody has to help you not to be so boring," the boy said impudently.

Dona Maria's squat body was bouncing at its knees and swinging its arms like a fighter warming up. "Let us play!" its voice piped. And then, "I want wine! Why cannot I have wine? Everybody else has wine!"

"Because you are only a little boy," one of the other women said. "Children must not drink."

"One finger! One finger only!" Cosminho pleaded.

"All right. But remember: only one."

The woman poured out ruby wine in a glass, measuring the amount against the width of her forefinger. The child threw down the drink in one gulp and puckered his face, begging for more.

"You promised," the woman said.

"Then give some to my friends." Cosminho pointed to Jaime as he hugged me around the waist. "You cannot say that they are not old enough."

For me the woman poured out half a hand. I drank the wine straight down as Cosminho had, while the child applauded delightedly.

He spied the Polaroid pictures on a table by the altar and with a naughty look grabbed for them. "Pretty," he said, rifling through the stack. "Except for this old woman. Who is she?" He rubbed his thumb over Maria's face. "She spoils the picture every time."

The boy was still jumping around the room as he spoke, bounding to its corners, swinging his arms with the sheer joy of being eight years old. From the main hall, there was a new commotion and then a mischievous voice called, "Cosminho, get away from all those old people and play with me."

"Little Damião," Jaime said.

I looked into the terreiro. The huge woman who had lowed and moaned at the first Candomblé was now skipping, belly out and hands behind her back, like a little boy in Sunday clothes.

Sidling up to Cosminho, little Damião said, "You have been drinking wine!"

"I have not!"

"I am going to tell. Unless you get a glass for me, I will tell."

Cosminho raced for the bottle and poured out a finger. But before Damião could reach the glass, Cosminho drank it down himself.

"Now I *will* tell!" little Damião whined.

They were skipping around, hands clasped behind them—two boys ready to throw their arms over each other's shoulders or make fists and come out swinging.

"Do not sit!" they called to the filhas do santo on the sidelines. "Play with us!"

At that command, the drums gave a cheerful clap. The girls rose and jerked to the rhythm until a few of them staggered, twisted, and became small children themselves. Unperturbed, those women not receiving a child's spirit resumed their places along the wall.

From some recess in the shrine room, Cosminho had discovered the sort of noisemakers Americans use on New Year's Eve. Now the children were marching around the terreiro giving shrill toots in the faces of their elders and daring them to make them stop.

"Popcorn!" Cosminho demanded, and his playmates ran to plunder the sacrifices from the inner shrine.

They came skipping back with the boxes of corn on their heads, making fun of the procession that had gone before.

"Popcorn, senhor?"

A twenty-year-old girl, voluptuous in a turquoise sweater, was crouched before me as timidly as the town's children when they crept upstairs to offer a bite of dry biscuit.

The popcorn was unbuttered, but mixed among the kernels were thin slices of coconut meat to make it moist and sweet. Across the room, Jaime's cheeks were fat with popcorn, and a woman was filling a plastic bag for him to take home to his children.

Cosminho dashed away into Maria's house. When he came back, he was waving three pink plastic dolls with coarse blond hair. "Do you want a doll, little girl?" he asked the spirit who had fed me the popcorn.

"Thank you, Cosminho," she said, cradling the doll against her breast.

"And you, little one?" Cosminho held out another doll to Damião.

"I do not play with dolls. I want wine!"

Maria's grandchildren came out to see what had become of their toys. In all, she had forty-five grandchildren, but tonight there were only six on hand, solemn as they watched the adults tease and pinch each other and grab for the dolls and whistles. These real children didn't smile or frown, or look puzzled, indulgent, bored, or distressed. They simply watched, and went willingly when their father came, collected their dolls, and sent them to bed.

Sargento Jaime said, "They will go on like this for another three hours." It was already one A.M. "But I must work tomorrow."

"You cannot go!" Cosminho pouted. "We have not had our fun yet."

"I am sorry, Cosminho. It is time."

"Oh," said the child. "At least when you leave, you will go away in your truck. He has a truck," he told the other children excitedly, "that goes va-room, va-room. We will all come to hear it."

The children rushed out and surrounded the pickup Jaime was driving tonight. I gave my arm to one spirit that had taken over the body of a woman who looked seventy. The child took my help gratefully enough going up the embankment but when we reached the road she shook free and ran ahead of me.

To ornament his dashboard, Jaime had bought a magnetized statue of Cosme and Damião, fully grown and clad as knights. He held their figures up to the cab's light.

"Ah!" the spirit children cried, bursting into applause.

"Vamos?" Jaime asked me.

I pulled the door shut. He started the engine.

"Va-room!" Cosminho shouted as we drove off. "Va-room! Va-room!"

BUT MARIA AND THE OTHERS didn't hold a Candomblé every night or even once a week. Most evenings meant an early supper, an hour of stale banter with my predictable callers, the lonely silence after the town had gone to sleep. I hadn't realized how badly this isolation, the tedium of small-town life, had been scraping my nerves until one morning at the hotel breakfast table when tears rolled down my cheeks.

Nothing like it had happened to me before. I was finishing a hard-boiled egg, feeling neither better nor worse than during eighty other breakfasts in Camamu. Then tears filled my eyes.

The coffee is too hot, I thought, and put down my cup. The tears didn't stop.

My eyes hadn't bunched up. I wasn't sobbing. The tears simply kept running down until my cheeks were wet. It was eight o'clock. Everyone else had eaten and left for work. I was alone on the porch at the back of the building, and for a moment I was too surprised to think of wiping my face.

It's a head cold. But my nostrils weren't plugged, my throat wasn't sore.

My instinct was to pack a bag and leave that day for Salvador. But I wondered whether the tears might not indicate progress of a sort. I had read—with aversion admittedly—about the brand of sensitivity therapy that aimed at stripping people of their bark. Perhaps for the spirits to reveal their truth to me, I had to be sanded the same way.

I would stay. Stay, and see whether this instability I was showing might be a credential for the occult.

"AND THE SHEEP," Nelson was saying, as though he could erase the week or two that had passed since our last meeting. "I must have two, and the goats—"

"Yes," I said. "Yes. Is this not the day the man from Nazaré is coming back to tell you the result of your work?"

"He could not come," Nelson said. "But he sent word with the bus conductor that the work was a complete success."

Suspicious. But Nazaré was a good distance away and messages in Bahia were often conveyed precariously. Two days ago, the fiancé of Sargento Jaime's oldest daughter had hailed me in the road to say that Valter in Ituberá was postponing his Umbanda ceremony one week and wanted to spare me a needless trip.

Nelson's wife was sitting beside him at the table, head resting in her hand. To what Nelson said, she was nodding, and by my reading she was so guileless a woman that if she had been instructed to lie, I'd have detected a telltale flush.

I said, "The man is going mad?"

"He has already begun to act strange. The man who was here will soon have his job. That will pay him much more money and make him happy. The night of my Candomblé approaches," Nelson said without a pause, "and I still have not bought—"

"I wanted to hear more about the work you can do to help me receive a spirit."

"It is very easy," Nelson said. "We can do it whenever you like."

"Perhaps the night of your Candomblé?"

"No! Earlier than that! Next week! Wednesday!"

"Does it matter that Wednesday is the town's festa?"

It was the day to honor Camamu's patron saint, Nossa Senhora da Assunção. For many weeks everyone had been reminding me of its approach. Dancing! they promised, holding a hand to their bellies and swaying to a samba step. Drinking! A parade! Dona Bela was even having the front of the hotel painted an optimistic lemon yellow that was soiling before the workmen had taken down their ladders.

"Yes, then Wednesday is bad," Nelson agreed. "Better earlier. This Friday."

"The day after tomorrow?" I had expected more time to decide how to think about it.

"Time enough!" he said. "Tomorrow for buying the provisions. Friday for the work."

My palms began to prickle as though they had been switched with a strap. Rubbing them together couldn't stop the hot itching. Through my mind the verse kept repeating, By the pricking of my thumbs, something wicked this way comes.

"What must I buy?"

"Seven bottles of cachaça. Seven metros of cloth—black, white, blue, red, purple—"

"Yellow," Nelson's wife prompted.

"Yellow. And lilac. Then seven rejientes."

"I do not know what they are."

"Rejientes," he repeated testily. "Then maize, red and white. Two white chickens. Three cartons of candles. A length of fuma da corda. Farofa, white and red. Seven boxes of matches."

"That is everything?"

He looked to his wife. She nodded deliberately.

"Friday?" I said. "It does not leave much time."

"It is an excellent day," Nelson insisted, "much favored by Oxalá." Unarguable; my notes said Friday was the time Oxalá dispensed his special gifts.

155

"I will ask my friends where to buy these things."

"I do not think it is a good idea for you to make the purchases yourself. The whole town will see." Nelson pulled down the lower lid of his good eye, the gesture for curiosity, gossip, unseemly talk. "They will all know that the foreigner is making a work."

"It is better if you buy them?"

"Less talk in the town if my wife buys everything. They expect us to make those purchases." At his side Nelson's wife went on nodding steadily.

"How much will it be?"

He garbled an amount that sounded like seventeen cruzeiros. I knew that could not be right. "I did not understand."

Again, something muffled with a seven in it. "Seventy?" I asked. Nelson bent to spit and his bowed head jerked impatiently.

"I have this much now." I laid three ten-cruzeiro notes on the table; five dollars. "I will bring the rest on Friday." My palms hadn't stopped stinging. "The afternoon?"

"The morning," Nelson said firmly. "Nine o'clock."

I left the house dazed. A gray sky was drizzling, and halfway up the mule trail I stopped and broke off a palm leaf to hold over my head the way the children did. I was five minutes late for my lesson with Marlene, and when she met me at the door she sent her maid at once for a bath towel.

"Where is your umbrella?" Marlene asked as I rubbed my arms and the back of my neck.

"I leave it on the bus for Ituberá."

"You left it," she said. "Deixei. The past tense."

"What is a rejiente?"

"Radiante?" Marlene repeated, correcting my pronunciation. "It is a happy man, one satisfied with his life and fortunes. Why do you ask?"

"Tomorrow I must buy seven of them for a sacrifice."

"Then it must be some other word," she said, a little crossly. "Rejientes," she tried several other stresses. "No, I do not know what they are. What sacrifice?"

"At nine o'clock Friday morning, Senhor Nelson in cidade baixa is doing a work for me. So that I will receive a spirit."

She shuddered and turned her head. "I do not want to hear about it."

"I am only telling you so that Friday night when I come for my lesson you will remember to ask who I am. Probably it will not be me at all but Xangô or the Old Black Man."

"Please!" she said. "Do not say more."

Rui, hearing of my plans, was even less enthused. He was one of the sharks from the snooker table, a young man with an oiled pompadour and a sulky mouth who might have stepped out of a 1956 time capsule.

On Thursday Rui would be celebrating his twenty-second birthday, and he had expected to spend an hour or two in my room drinking lemon batida with his pals, then capping the evening with a jaunt down the road for an eighty-cent whore. If I went to bed early to be ready for my spirit, his party could be severely truncated.

"Nelson is a damned fake," Rui said. He was missing his left upper incisor and the red gap made his grin decidedly devilish. "Last year when a robber stole money from my cousin, he went to Nelson to find out who did it. Nelson went through a whole work and did not come up with the name of the man. My cousin never did get his money back."

All the same, Thursday morning I went to Júlio's bank. Turning over my last exchange with Nelson, I had begun to think that it had been his temerity in asking for two hundred and seventy cruzeiros that had made him mumble and cough.

If I was right, he was asking nearly fifty dollars. I would pay it. I wrote out a check for three hundred cruzeiros and handed it across the counter to Júlio.

"You have already taken your money for this week," he said.

"I know."

Júlio already considered me a spendthrift. This money I was drawing represented sixty percent of his month's salary. "Nelson is going to do a work for me."

"You are going to give him three hundred—?"

"No," I said. "No. A part, only."

Júlio had a banker's conserving instinct. If I had told him how much I was prepared to pay, he would have harangued me for days after.

Back in my room I spent the rest of the day lying on my bed, staring at water stains on the ceiling. For the first time in the weeks in Camamu, my bowels had loosened. And since the bathroom had never been finished, I was forced up every twenty minutes to hurry along the street to a toilet in the empty house Zeca's family owned. It was a nuisance, this coincidence of contracting diarrhea one day before Nelson's work.

Did I believe I would be receiving a spirit the next day? Probably not. Yet when I awoke from a dream that night, I couldn't make sense of the few slivers of light the shutters were letting in. At the sight of those flickering white shapes I snapped on the overhead bulb. Before my head cleared I heard myself saying aloud, "What am I doing here?"

IT TOOK ME A LONG TIME to get back to sleep. I lay in the dark with my eyes open, ignoring the rats in the walls and recollecting the two other times I had brushed against the occult.

Twelve years before, driving with a friend down a rough Mexican road toward Guymas, I had pulled the car to the shoulder, shut off the ignition, and got out.

"What's the matter?"

"Later today we're going to hit a cow," I said. "You just bought this car and I'd rather you be driving when we hit it."

He laughed and slid behind the wheel. I walked around the back of the car to the passenger side. I hadn't felt a flash or seen an image of the accident. It was simply a certainty that spoke one time in my blood, a calm feeling because it was so sure. Nothing to shake or alarm me, either then or two hours later when we struck the poor beast taking its rest on the asphalt.

Since then I had felt several premonitions and I always yield to them and they never proved right again.

There was also the day that Betty, the rosy astrologer, charted my horoscope. Betty saw at a glance that I had none of those astral triangles that speak of passion or genius. Instead, she found several drab pairings that even her quick fancy couldn't make palatable.

"Unusually stable," Betty read from lines she had mapped. "Sensible. No strong urges."

Betty picked up my disappointment and as she traced out one line that didn't connect across her chart, she said encouragingly, "A little trouble there with your Mars. Maybe— No, it's nothing serious.

"Over all," Betty was forced to conclude, "it's a balanced chart that is very weak in spiritual force."

Just as one needn't love animals to be foolishly flattered when a cat comes to nestle, so my disbelief in the stars made it no less galling to find out how thoroughly they returned my low regard.

To make amends, Betty offered to lead me to my past incarnations. At her direction, I closed my eyes and hoped to convey a little spirituality in my descriptions of the scenes that materialized.

My ancestry being German and Swedish, the pictures owed a good deal to an illustrated edition of Grimm's Fairy Tales and to Ingmar Bergman movies. But my parade of woodcutters and gaunt Lutheran pastors gratified Betty, and she decided that together we could risk a passage up the astral planes.

"As you know," she began, "we are now on the third astral level—"

"What happened to the first two?"

"We are on the third astral level," Betty repeated. "There are twelve altogether. Close your eyes and advance to the fourth plane and tell me what you see."

I went obediently up a castle's circular staircase, reporting on the figures waiting at each landing. Mostly, the guides were nondescript, but on the eighth level I saw Billie Burke in her pink-spangled gown as the good witch of the south. On the tenth plane I came upon a rat as big as a whale.

"That happens sometimes," Betty said calmly. "Although usually it's a cat. Go on to the eleventh."

At the eleventh plane, a dim-featured, agreeable man took me readily the one last flight. We came out at the top of the tower.

"A man is sitting there," I told Betty, "wearing a suit of armor and a black hood."

"Ask his name."

"Richard Bruce, he says."

"Now ask Richard Bruce your true name, the one you've had through all your incarnations."

"He says," I repeated unwillingly, "it is Axel."

The only Axel I knew was in the title of Edmund Wilson's book, and it was possible that Sinclair Lewis had given the name to one of his small-town atheists, drunks, and janitors.

Betty was well pleased. "Come back for this time."

I opened my eyes and found Betty's radiant face floating above me. "How do you feel?" she asked.

"Rotten. And very tired."

When Nesio dropped by my apartment after dinner he found me still depressed. For a week he had been intrigued by stories of the traveling astrologer, more for her pink immensity than for any powers of divination. But after talking with me a few minutes, he decided against paying Betty a visit.

"This woman has only made you feel sad, Jack," he said. "Why should I go and let her sadden me?"

I WAS AWAKE AGAIN BEFORE SIX, aware of an early-morning racket from the road. The roosters were satisfied with their dawn and they kept quiet. But Zeca's Dalmatian was barking. The burros hitched next to the post office were guffawing among themselves. And those infants who were prodigies at screaming had been pushed outside early to get in an extra hour of practice.

Cramps were making my stomach feel kneaded. The fish and rice from last night's dinner had risen in my throat. I opened the shutters but the air in the room stayed damp and feverish.

At the hotel I risked a single biscuit, smeared with the fresh butter that tasted like custard. "No eggs today," I told Railda.

"Porquê?"

"I am going to cidade baixa in twenty minutes to have a work done for me by a pai do santo."

160

She raised a hand to shield herself and ran backward to the kitchen. Brincando, of course; Railda must be joking.

Down the road, I unlocked the empty building and went along the corridor to the bathroom. I wanted to get rid of the pressure on my chest but I couldn't bring myself to ram a finger down my throat. I did shower with special care, though, remembering that every spiritist but Nelson put a premium on cleanliness.

Except for my socks and trousers, I dressed in white. I shaved carefully and pared my fingernails. I brushed my tongue. By the time I was ready, I was a minute behind schedule and I trotted down the brick road for the trail to Nelson's door.

The running agitated my bowels and I soon stopped. Already I was wondering what to do if midway through the ritual I needed a sanitario. I hadn't seen evidence that Nelson's house had plumbing, though he may have had a toilet secreted at the back, something less grand and conspicuous than his house for Exú.

Nelson was awaiting me at his table. "My wife misunderstood," he said. "She thought it was nine hours tonight and she has not made all the purchases."

At her end of the table, Nelson's wife was looking blithe. More likely they had decided to wait until they had my cash in hand.

"Then we cannot go ahead now?"

They shook their heads in concert.

In Vietnam I once went along with a planeload of paratroopers in the Central Highlands while they made their monthly jump; the pilots and I were the only men aloft who were not jumping that afternoon.

The plane had almost reached the site when word came from the ground that it was too windy. The jump would be put off until further notice. The same mood that swept through the plane that day was passing over me now—annoyance and relief, in nothing like equal proportions.

"When should I come back?"

"Tonight at seven hours," Nelson said.

"I have not been quite sure how much the total ceremony would cost."

He began to list the ingredients once more. "Seven—"

"Yes. But how much?"

"Cheap!" Nelson assured me. "Only three hundred and fifty cruzeiros more."

It was within ten cruzeiros of the money I had brought along. Nelson, watching me folding that lone bill and putting it back in my pocket, thought fast. But I was quicker. Before he could speak, the money was buttoned away.

I said, "The senhor knows it does not matter to me which spirit I receive. For me, any spirit would be welcome. But do you have an idea which one we will be trying to summon?"

"Oxalá!" Nelson said it with his usual air of sweeping the chips to his side of the table.

"Oxalá?" I repeated, as I always did, to give him time to reconsider, to let any vestige of modesty or shame assert itself.

Nelson nodded contentedly. "Oxalá."

"Até logo," I said.

On the way back to my room, I stopped at the farmácia and bought two bottles of a pink liquid guaranteed to stop diarrhea.

THE NEXT TEN SOMNOLENT HOURS I passed dozing on my bed. My innards were apparently cleansed now and coated with the pink adhesive. But I didn't risk lunch, and I sent word to Marlene that I would be skipping our lesson.

At five o'clock, the sky itself went pink, first the clouds in misty patches, then the sunlight, until for a moment the world and I were a gauzy pink inside and out.

Ninety minutes more. At that thought, my heart and the sun sank together, and I went down the street to shower again, wash my hair, pass a razor over the upper lip where my beard first raised a shadow.

At Nelson's door it was his wife who greeted me and took me to the bedroom with the shrine. I went toward the bed but she indicated a stool covered with the feathery rag quilt. "You will be more comfortable there."

In front of me, my sacrifices were spread over the floor in much the arrangement of Nelson's work to unbalance the Nazaréan.

I considered marking one of the Jacaré bottles to see whether they were truly carted off to Ibirapitanga or stored away for the next client, and I had the chance when Nelson's wife stepped away for a moment.

But I thought: I am not here to expose Nelson or to exonerate him. I am here to receive a spirit. If he can conjure one with used cachaça bottles, I have no complaint. I might even be pleased to learn that the spirits weren't so fastidious as the Umbandists in Long Beach had made them out.

From the kitchen I could hear Nelson's budding daughter gossiping with the maid. Poor as his household was, Nelson employed an adolescent girl still poorer to ensure that his fourteen-year-old daughter grow up in the fashion of provincial Brazilian ladies. That is, that she might make her own clothes but never wash them, and bargain like a Teamster with her butcher but never cook the meat he sold her.

Over my head, cages of small drab birds were hitting their wings against the wooden bars. One cage hung so low the bird beat his feathers almost in my ear. I hunched my shoulders and pulled the stool away from the wall.

Nelson's wife returned. "We begin?"

Tonight I was going to question nothing, so I didn't ask where Nelson was or why we weren't waiting for him.

Only a single candle was burning amid the statues and paintings on the vanity table but Nelson's wife left on the single overhead bulb. She was wearing her usual white blouse and polka-dot skirt. Everything in the room was ordinary, commonplace. It reassured me that they hadn't contrived an extravaganza to dazzle the estrangeiro.

"What name do you want the spirits to know you by?" she asked.

"Jack." It was a boy's name but the alternative was Axel.

It didn't matter. Nelson's wife made a try or two during her prayer but the consonants in "Jack" were beyond her and I became "he."

Taking up two bottles of cachaça from the mat, she waved them over my head like Indian clubs. "In the name of Jesus, Mary and Joseph," she intoned, "cleanse this man and keep him free from pain and worry."

As she spoke, she passed the bottles over my shoulders and down along my thighs, crossing them a final time over my shoes.

"Thank you, Ogum," she said, putting the bottles back on the mat and picking up two more. She murmured, "Thank you, God," and repeated the gestures and the prayer.

She did it again with bottles that appeared to contain lemon soda. Perhaps what Nelson had been saying was "refrigerantes"—soda pop. For a moment she balanced a dish of farinha on my head. At all times, her voice was low and unhurried.

Whenever she passed a sacrifice over my face, my eyes instinctively closed but even then I was drifting into a pleasant reverie, thinking nothing, soothed by her voice and the gentle brushings of her hand.

"Now," she said, offering me a heaping bowl of popcorn. "All."

"All?" It looked like three pounds of popcorn.

"All."

I reached in a hand.

"No!" Nelson's wife pulled the bowl away. "This is the time for you to speak your every wish."

My voice sounded like an adolescent at his confirmation. "I would like," I began hesitantly, "to receive a spirit. It is not important to me the name of the spirit so long as I can do my share well."

"That is all?" she asked as I passed the bowl back to her. "You do not want to ask for money?"

I was there to receive a spirit. If Nelson defaulted on that, he couldn't redeem himself by foisting a million dollars on me. "No," I said, "that is all."

She took up a bowl of farinha. "Once more," she said.

The meal was spread across the bowl like a grainy mirror. I stared down into it and repeated my wish.

Now Nelson's wife took up the stack of cloths. The top one was black with a store's gummed label sticking to it. Tearing that away, she left a white blotch of paste. The cloths, at least, were new.

One by one she unfolded a cloth and dusted me with it while she said the prayer yet again. She rumpled my hair with the cloths and bore down very slightly on my shoulders and biceps.

At my groin, she whisked in rapidly, then gripped the cloth more securely to move down my legs and over the dusty tops of my shoes. Each cloth she used was tossed into a heap beside the bottles of cachaça.

I found a voluptuousness in giving myself to the light rubbing, the friction of the cloth over my knees. I thought, Being massaged by a nun would be like this.

When the cloths lay crumpled on the floor, she straightened up. "Now is the time you give the money to the gods."

"How much?" I asked warily.

She quoted an outrageous figure, enough to make me stiffen, ready to rise up from the stool and storm out the door. But I remembered that a few years ago the Brazilians had devalued their currency by a thousand percent and that the change hadn't worked its way into everyone's vocabulary. "I need a thousand cruzeiros," Ailton sometimes said, when what he meant was one cruzeiro—sixteen cents.

I pulled out my notebook and a ballpoint pen. "Would the senhora write the amount, please?"

She looked at the pen as though it were an invention from the next century. "Oh, senhor," she said, not embarrassed or ashamed but with a lifetime of regret, "I cannot."

I covered my hand over the book and stuffed it away. "I think I am to pay seventeen cruzeiros," I said. "And another one cruzeiro and seventy centavos?" It totaled three dollars.

"Sim, senhor," she nodded, grateful that the crisis was past.

I had the eighteen cruzeiros but not the coins. "Excuse me," I said. "I did not know what I was to bring."

"It is no problem." She left me and from the other bedroom I heard the daughter going through her purse. Alone in the room I shut my eyes against the cages strung over the walls like wicker prisons.

"Fifty, sixty, seventy," Nelson's wife was counting when she came back. "Here."

I took the coins, held them for a moment and passed them back to her. First with the bills, then the coins, she ruffled my hair and followed the outlines of my body with the money in her fist.

Finished, she threw the money down carelessly among the matchboxes and cigars. One final pass with a seventh bottle of cachaça and we were done. The ritual had taken forty minutes.

"Now go," Nelson's wife said. "At midnight, these sacrifices go by car to Ibirapitanga. The next thing is for you to talk with him. Tomorrow he will be selling firewood all day in Valença but he will return for supper. Can you come at five hours in the afternoon to talk with him about the second step?"

"I can."

"This ceremony went very nicely," Nelson's wife said. "It is much better when it is a prayer only for good things. It is more beautiful, the white line."

"It was beautiful," I said.

"Until tomorrow."

I was outside, walking along the lagoon and the rows of fishermen's shacks, when I met Júlio leaving the bank. "Are you feeling better?" He knew of my stomach trouble.

"I am feeling very good."

"FIRST THERE IS THE BASIN, like this—" Nelson was using his hands to describe a vat. "Of course it must be new. And white. That will be eighty cruzeiros right there."

We were grouped around his table again. The pile of wood in the hallway had shrunk substantially. From that, and from his grudging good humor, I surmised that Nelson had spent a profitable day in Valença. He was outlining now the equipment he would need for the next stage of my work: the ritual washing of my head.

Mildly I said, "I thought the last money covered everything."

"Everything!" Nelson agreed, positioning a wad in his mouth for the next spitting. "Everything. But now there are these small expenses for your cleansing next Monday morning."

"I bought a basin for my room above the post office," I said. "It is about this size." I made a slightly smaller circle than his. "And I paid four cruzeiros for it. The man asked five. But he took four."

"Plastic!" Nelson snorted.

"Metal," I said, reaching behind me to tap the door of his old refrigerator. "Four cruzeiros."

I looked to Nelson's wife for support and she nodded reluctantly.

"The herbs!" Nelson persisted. "You have seen our yard in the back. It is solid rock. We must buy everything: tapete de Oxalá, mange mecum, agua da levante, arruda, Guiné da caboclo, alecrim do campo, alfazima, amaci para lavar mutui."

"He does not know what mutui is," Nelson's wife chided him.

"I would guess that it is the Nagô word for head," I said.

"Head!" Nelson agreed. "You see those?" He extended his fingers. "You call them dedos," he said, using the Portuguese word. "But in Nagô, they are gadanu."

"Gadanu," I repeated. "Do you want me to buy the basin?"

"No, no," he said. "We will find one in a store here."

"So if I bring another—fifty cruzeiros, that should cover—"

"Everything!" Nelson said.

His wife had gone to answer a knock at the door and she came back now clasping a brown paper sack about eighteen inches high. The habitual resignation was gone from her face and she was beaming like a bride. "It came," she said.

Nelson took the bundle from her and ripped away the paper. Inside was a statue of a white man with receding brown hair. He was dressed in a robe of Chinese red and carried a book tucked under one arm. His expression was girlish and dim-witted.

"São Lorenzo," Nelson said.

He motioned toward his wife, who was regarding the figurine with a reverence and satisfaction that made us both smile.

"She has wanted him for a long time," Nelson said. "Of course he was expensive. And coming now, with the Candomblé, it is going to be hard to raise the money, but—" He nodded again to his enraptured wife.

"Do you know how much he cost?" Nelson paused to appraise either the statue or my gullibility. "Two hundred and forty cruzeiros!"

"For that? It is very nice, but—"

"Two hundred and forty! They do not have anything like him in Camamu or even Valença. He had to come all the way from Salvador."

"I have seen statues the same size in Rio de Janeiro," I said. "They cost thirty cruzeiros."

"Thirty!" Nelson marveled. "But you see, that is the way it is with everything here. Here, it is all exploitation!"

I WAS COMING TO THINK OF VALTER IN ITUBERÁ as the antidote to Nelson in cidade baixa, and by dawn on Sunday morning I was relieved to think that I'd soon be escaping to Valter's Umbanda.

When I got to the taxi stop, though, it looked as if I was going to miss the festa. Transportation between the towns was never certain, and for a norte-americano with a craving for precision, the system strained the nerves. Throughout the day, passengers for Ituberá sauntered down the hill and waited at the riverbank. If a jeep came, the trip was on. If not, not.

I drank a bottle of Guaraná, the sweet yellow cola, and ate hunks of grainy cheese the color of vinegar. On the corner, a long-haired man laid out cheaply made shirts and trousers along the curb. As he was finishing it rained. He covered his stock with tarpaulin. Two minutes later, the skies cleared and he pulled off the cover and straightened the pile, all without a customer or the prospect of one.

From time to time, the man selling cheese strolled down the street to inquire around the square for my ride. "They are going the other way," he reported as a truck roared past us. "Nobody seems to be going to Ituberá today."

I had been waiting nearly two hours when a wreck of a car clattered down the hill and stopped a half-block away. Once it had been as much a Land-Rover as other jeeps around town, but so many disparate parts had been welded and joined to its chassis that it no longer had a predominant feature. Where it wasn't rusted, the surface was gunmetal gray, with two assertive spots of the original blue finish on each front fender.

A head leaned out the open window, its features hidden by the kind of straw hat that horses wear. A scrawny black hand beckoned to me. "Where do you go?"

"Ituberá."

"Get in!" said Senhor Nelson.

He pulled from his pocket a bent door handle and worked it around in a hole until the door fell open. At the wheel sat a young man, not Nelson's son Francisco.

From the back seat I said, "It is the first time I have seen your car. Is it new?" The question would have sounded sarcastic in English, but by the placing of the adjective, Portuguese permits one to mean, Is it new to you?

Nelson snapped his fingers to show how long, long he had owned the jeep and patted the dash with the usual inscription in Bahian taxis: "Driven by me, guided by God."

En route to Ituberá, Nelson demonstrated that his taxi was no charitable venture. Brown men bearing machetes sat near the road and as we approached they jumped up to ask, "How much?"

Nelson hung out the window to collect fares. "Two cruzeiros."

"Other cars charge one cruzeiro, fifty centavos."

"Vamos!" Nelson told the driver. Without further haggling we were off, leaving the farmers staring sadly after.

Along the road, the distances were subject to negotiation but cab fare from Camamu to Ituberá was a fixed three cruzeiros. At the town square I pushed three bills into Nelson's hand. "You do not want to go further?" he asked.

"From here I can walk." If Nelson and Valter had never met, I didn't want to be the one to introduce them.

I climbed the path to Valter's terreiro a step ahead of a rain storm. The hall was already packed with people, but it was during a lull and Valter could come over.

"Have I missed much?"

"Not too much. The opening ceremony you already know. Now we are having the ancient feast of the spirits."

The center of the hall was studded with palm trees in green pots. A white cloth had been spread as though the floor were a banquet table and then laid with candlesticks, vases of flowers, bottles of beer and soda. In one corner a vast black woman, encircled by steaming tin serving pots, was ladling out rice and beans, pork and chicken, with a generous hand.

I asked Valter what god was being honored today.

"This is our yearly feast for prosperity," he said. "We ask that all the spirits grant a good living to the people of the town."

At a motion from Valter, his shy eldest son spread a fresh white cloth over a school desk. "You can write more easily here," Valter said.

A girl delivered to me a mountain of beans and rice shored up with walls of pork. A minute later she was back with so many bottles of beer and lemon soda that the desk looked like a chessboard.

When Valter was sure I was properly welcomed he withdrew into his shrine. The dancers took their places, the drums gave a roll, and the chanting began for the King of the Little Forest. Rei da Matinha, the chorus sang. With the breathy r it sounded like "Hey, da Matinha!"

I held out my notebook and pencil to Valter's son. "Write your name for me, por favor. All of it." I had been forgetting to ask Valter's last name and this seemed the easiest way to find out.

"Ersival Gomes da Silva," the boy printed.

"And the full name of this school." He went to ask his mother and came back to print another two lines.

"So when I leave Bahia, I could always contact your father by writing to Senhor Valter da Silva," I said, reading, "Escola Municipal Senhor do Bonfim, Ituberá, Bahia, Brasil?"

"Sim, senhor. If you want his other name it is Petronilho. Valter Petronilho da Silva."

"Where is Deoclides tonight?"

"His little girl broke her arm and he took her to the hospital in Valença. José—do you remember? From the Firestone fazenda?—he went with him."

"The last time I was here, you had a bad stomachache. And your father's brother was in the hospital with a hernia."

"The doctors gave me medicine and I am better. My uncle, too."

It reminded me of a debate I had overheard in the Long Beach terreiro. The congregation was not disposed to reveal its dissensions to a stranger. But when I asked what the dispute was about, they wouldn't lie either.

"We are having a testing of our faith," a Brazilian man admitted. "In the last few weeks a number of us have had either illnesses or bad accidents. Some of the members wonder why the spirits are not taking better care of us."

"That must be why Tony called me this morning," I said. "He warned me to drive with particular care on the way home tonight. He said that sometimes after spending a day with the gods, your members are in such a state of euphoria that they don't take the proper precautions when they leave."

"That is one explanation," the Brazilian said.

At Valter's terreiro the singers were still entreating Rei da Matinha to appear when with a flourish the spirit burst from the shrine. He was dressed in a costume made from gold material shot with a lighter figure, something like the upholstery for an occasional chair.

Below his bare arms the tunic cleaved to display Valter's neat brown ribcage. From the way his shorts ballooned, they might have been bloomers. Over all this hung a pale green cape ending at the knees.

Valter's face was transfigured with the sweet piety I had seen whenever Iemanjá used his body. He passed among the congregation offering blessings, then sat in the middle of the banquet cloth and buried his nose in the white blossoms.

"That is the King of the Matinha?" I asked Ersival.

"It is the king as a small boy." He snickered at the sight of the child king sniffing the Angélica petals with gaudy delight.

"When you were a little boy yourself," I asked him, "did it frighten you to see your father receiving a spirit?"

Obedient and industrious, Ersival was seventeen. He worked days as a mechanic and went to high school at night. I could imagine him living much the same life in East Los Angeles. Except for the father in a gold playsuit.

"Then it frightened me," the boy said. "Not now."

From our talks on other days, I knew that two of his sisters received spirits but that he, his mother, and the other children never had. "After so many years," I asked, "do you still like Umbanda?"

Ersival hesitated, treading a line between truth and disloyalty. "Yes. More or less."

I rested my recorder near the dancers to capture the ecstatic shrieking when the spirits descended and the changing timbre to the voices as the gods began to speak.

Since the dancing went on eight hours, I could catch that eerie moment many times, and although there were several arid stretches there were also fragments of great beauty. Valter's heavy daughter staggered into a trance and when she recovered she was dancing like a thistle. Her body whirled past the open window. Moonlight glistened on the folds of her white satin gown, and her solid flesh looked ready to dissolve.

When the child king released Valter, Ogum took his place with a hearty "E-yuh" and knelt to pray in a voice that clipped and isolated each syllable. As the singing resumed, a wide-eyed child sheltered under Ogum's arm and sang along with the spirit, her voice a little late and sharp. That, I realized, was what Bahian women sounded like at their prayers. Forcing up their voices to sing piercingly through the nose, they were just that—strident little girls.

Even before midnight the dancers were flagging, but Ogum rallied them as though they were contestants in a marathon. A cousin of Deoclides had arrived to report that the child's broken arm had been set, and Ogum pulled the man to me and watched benevolently as we shook hands. The man introduced himself as Dadão José.

"And he," Ogum added, pointing at me, "is an ameriqueiro." In Portuguese, that godly garbling elevated my nationality to a profession.

Each dancer who was mounted by a spirit came by my table to pronounce a blessing. In Valter's Umbanda there was no kissing, only fervent handshakes and a loose embrace. Even the most placid mediums needed a guiding touch to maneuver around the room, but Valter's two daughters were especially violent this night, and they clasped my hand feverishly.

Ediva, who had whirled past the window, now fell twice. After her spirit had finally released her, she showed the other women ruefully a spreading dark bruise on one knee. Her sister Elza was even larger, and when she collapsed she fell into unconsciousness.

"Hoy!" she moaned as they brought her around. "Hoy!"

She patted her bosom in distress, and then she screamed, "I have arrived! I have arrived from the house of the dead!"

When I spoke with Elza later, she sounded abashed about the force of her visitation. "It was Xangô," she said. "He is much harder on me than Sereia the mermaid."

Dadão José was standing a few feet away from my table. I was getting up to ask that he remember me to his cousin when the drums started a new song and Dadão flew across the room in one long spin that dashed him into the far corner. He stayed there vibrating until Ogum approached and touched him at four points across his shoulders.

But it appeared that Dadão's spirit had a low threshold; a moment later his body had sunk on its knees to the floor and this time it took three men to raise him. They moved him slowly around the circle as though he were walking off an overdose of drugs. His hands were stretched straight ahead, and every few minutes his body convulsed and he screamed, "Eeee!"

When I looked at my watch again, it was past one o'clock in the morning. Ogum had gone, so had most of the spectators. Valter himself was leading the dances in a plain white shirt and gray slacks.

Another hour went by.

Dadão's spirit was inexhaustible, bouncing his body on its own inner spring. But the girls had wilted, and the oldest drummer kept calling, "I am tired!" His two colleagues were slumped down, asleep with their heads on the drumskins.

Valter tried to enliven the circle. He pranced like a pony. He strutted with his thumbs up in the style that used to be called Truckin'. Finally he broke away and came to me. "Normally, we would go on to dawn but they seem to be tired."

"I understand why."

"Do you think your tape came out all right?" It was the broadest hint Valter could permit himself.

I punched the replay button and Ogum's hollow prayer echoed around the hall. The few women who had stayed looked up and smiled. Even the drummers revived.

We listened for about five minutes. Then, in the midst of a chorus

173

for Xangô, an elderly woman jumped from the bench and flew at the machine like a white moth.

She stood in front of me, shaking and cawing, until Valter rose and went to her side. With a very small touch of asperity he explained to her spirit that it had been duped by a machine. The Umbanda was over for the night. The spirit should go home.

"MY SISTER WILL NOT BE ABLE TO DO YOUR LAUNDRY," Ailton informed me one day. "She has gone to stay with relatives in Valença."

"When will she come back?"

He shrugged. "My father has a new woman who does not like us either. I do not know when my sister can return."

From the first stack of clean linen, I had pictured Ailton's sister as a long-limbed mulatta with wicked eyes. Until one noontime, on her way home from the ginásio, the girl came upstairs, and with proper ceremony Ailton presented me to a timid round bundle in a blue and white school uniform.

A few nights after his sister left, Ailton came pounding on the door at ten o'clock. It was a chilly night but he was wearing a short-sleeved shirt, frayed cotton slacks, and open sandals.

He wriggled past me and went to the corner where I stacked the newspapers from Salvador. He peeled off a few sheets, spread them over the floor, kicked off his sandals, and lay across the papers. He curled up and closed his eyes. All of this without a word to me.

"Ailton."

He pretended to be asleep.

"Ailton!" I prodded his ribs with the tip of my sandal. "You cannot sleep here."

"I am asleep."

"Listen: it is cold and you have already got the grippe. Go home where you have a mattress and blanket."

"I do not have a mattress at home. I sleep on the floor at home too."

"Go home."

"My father does not want me anymore. His new woman does not like me. If I cannot stay here, I have to go and live with my mother on the farm."

"Your mother is alive? But that is better still. Go and live with her since you do not get along with your father."

"If I go to the farm, I must work in the fields for six cruzeiros a day. There is no school on the farm." He opened his eyes long enough to give me a stricken look. "My education would come to an end."

"Ailton, you cannot live here."

"I will make no problems."

"You cannot."

He was squeezing himself tighter as though he could disappear from under my eyes. "Ailton, you are an intelligent boy."

"Graças a Deus," he mumbled into his chest.

"You may be too sensitive. But that will pass. Do you know what I mean?"

"No."

"Sensitivo," I repeated. "Have you never heard the word?"

"No," he said. "What does it mean?"

"It is not important. What I am saying is, you have not used your intelligence very well."

That opened his eyes and brought him upright on the papers. "Why? Why do you say that?"

"When you told me that you were starting night school and that your books would cost thirty cruzeiros, what did you do with the money I gave you?"

"First I bought the briefcase for my schoolwork—"

"For your lottery tickets."

"Then I bought books. Four of them. If you do not believe me, I will go to get them right now. Though my father will be very angry to have to get up and open the door and he will beat me."

"I know you have arranged to borrow the books of Jaiminho's sister. I know that you have not gone to class at all and that you hide down in cidade baixa at night so that I will not see you when you are supposed to be in school."

"Who told you that? Duba?"

"A friend of yours."

"Duba is a friend of the devil!"

"I was sorry because I think it would be good for you to go to school. I am not angry. I am only telling you now so that you will understand that you cannot stay here with the excuse that you want an education."

"Let me stay just for tonight. Tomorrow I will go to the farm and live with my mother."

"Get up."

"If you do not let me stay," he said, wiping his nose on the hem of his sleeve, "I will sleep in the street."

"Go home for one last night. Leave for the farm in the morning."

"If I go now, I will sleep in the street and you will never see me again."

"Go home," I said, pulling him up by the elbow. He got to his feet stiffly and went with dignity to the door. Going down the stairs, his round black head did not turn back.

"Até logo," I said. He didn't answer.

As he threatened, I never saw Ailton again. Jaiminho, the sergeant's son, told me that he had left for the farm where his mother picked fruit.

About three days after he had gone, one of Ailton's smallest acolytes stopped me in the street.

"Has Ailton gone to Estados Unidos?"

"I do not think so."

"He said you promised to take him there," the child said reproachfully. "To drive your car for you."

ZULMIRA, THAT FRAIL, SAINTLY WOMAN whose family seemed to constitute the bulk of Nelson's terreiro, was leaving his door in a fluster when I arrived for my ceremonial head washing.

"Tudo bem," she replied politely to my greeting, although everything clearly was not well.

When I reached Nelson at his table, he was still grumbling to himself. "She promised me a goat for my Candomblé and she has brought me a duck."

176

"Ah," I said.

"When I first met her in Salvador many years ago she was flat on her back," he said bitterly. "She could not move! She had not been out of bed in a week. Do you think she remembers that now?"

"Now, thanks to God, she has twelve children," Nelson's wife said with a sigh.

"A duck is not a goat," Nelson said.

"No," I agreed.

"A duck," he repeated, as though I still harbored doubts, "is not a goat.

"Ah," he spat, "they are all like that."

His wife hoisted up from her stool and went out to the rocky slope in the back, where garlands of green herbs were drying in the sun. Dressed entirely in white today, complete with a white turban, she looked like an authentic priestess as she crumpled a leaf and held it under my nose.

"Guiné," she said. It smelled like sour clover.

I asked Nelson whether I might watch the animal sacrifice for his Candomblé later in the month.

"The sacrifice itself is not important. I will show you something much better."

He sprang from the table with an agility remarkable for a man who usually scuffed along the floor and came back holding his wife's card of needles and a glass brimming with water.

"Watch," he said. "Very few people can do this."

Nelson balanced a needle on the lip of the glass. Using the edge of a match, he pushed the needle out to the surface of the water where it floated near the center.

He looked to me for applause, and I congratulated him, though it looked like a high school science class trick.

When Nelson tried again, the second needle sank. But he launched a third and a fourth, and they each floated into the orbit of the first needle, swinging around and attaching themselves to it.

"I can do ten," Nelson said.

As he spoke, the three needles also sank.

"I do not know how it is done," I said.

"You do not! Very few people know! It involves the Sign of Solomon."

Before I could question him further, Nelson's wife beckoned us into the bedroom. In front of two lighted candles, a white enameled basin awaited me. It was filled with a brown fluid that looked like the result of a backed-up sewer.

Taking a place at his drum, Nelson sang, "Oxumare, o li, li." His wife tucked a bath towel under my collar.

"O la bomba," Nelson sang. "O la la bomba."

She prodded gently at the back of my head and I lowered my hair into the brown water.

And found that it smelled wonderful, like pastureland on a spring afternoon. Nelson's wife was praying under her breath as she soaked my back hairs with her cupped palm. When she finished, my hair smelled like a hayrack. She rubbed it dry and handed me a comb.

"That is all?"

"For now," Nelson said. "Come back on Wednesday afternoon for another ritual."

I handed over fifty cruzeiros. "Will that be the last?" I had a vision of Nelson and me growing old together, me endorsing over my Social Security checks.

"The last," Nelson said.

"I will receive a spirit on Wednesday?"

"Not then," he said. "But soon."

"Maybe the following week. At your Candomblé."

"Before!" Nelson insisted. "Before that!"

"Até logo," I said.

"Até logo," Nelson replied. "Remember on Wednesday to bring your present."

"My present?"

"Yes," he said. "It will be time for your present."

MEANWHILE, Camamu's annual festa was upon us. When I went for yet another complaint to Zeca about the staircase, he spread his hands as though before a holocaust.

"The festa! It is impossible to get workers now."

"I see that you have found several men to paint your house."

As we spoke, the façade of the rambling house Zeca shared with his widowed mother and his brothers and sisters was being smeared with a watery pink paint not too different from my diarrhea medicine.

"They are not carpenters," Zeca said.

In fact, every unemployed man, which in Camamu meant a good percentage of the population, had been enlisted by the mayor to join in the cleanup. For a few cruzeiros, men with scythes were hacking away on the hillsides at a year's accumulated weeds. Others strung a line of colored lights and small pennants along the block between the church and the snooker parlor. Three houses of every four had been slapped with fresh paint, until the only eyesores were the post office and the church.

"Since this is a festa for the patron saint of the city, Nossa Senhora da Assunçao," I remarked to the man who managed the municipal waterworks, "would it not be an agreeable gesture to paint the church?"

He made the thumbs-down gesture that meant Camamu was without money, poverty-stricken, irredeemably and forever busted.

"Will there at least be a priest?"

"Yes, he comes from Salvador and spends the night."

At dusk on the evening of August 14, the colored lights came on and along the street the children yelped and clapped their hands. Those few dozen bulbs lifted a lid off the town and made the night almost cheerful. At the hotel I said, "Camamu should leave up its lights all year round."

"But then what would we do for the festa?"

And the truth seemed to be that the lights were the festa. After dinner Júlio and I were leaning out my window, and I said:

"Perhaps I am wrong, but it begins to appear that this festa I have been hearing about since May, with people saying, Yes, it is boring tonight but wait for our festa, that this long-awaited celebration consists of people putting on new clothes and walking back and forth between the church and the corner. Can that be correct?"

179

"Yes, it is idiotic." But Júlio's scorn may have been due to disappointment: his own new pair of bib overalls hadn't arrived at the post office in time for the promenade.

Whatever I might think of the festa, it was attracting crowds from the countryside. The first day, in the hall of the hotel, I tripped over a fat woman setting up a portable piano. She plunked an experimental chord and handed me a peeled orange.

At the bar a shabby impresario from Valença dragged in an accordion player and before the first chorus was over had collected a crowd of fifty people. The boy played well, did not play "Lady of Spain," and his histrionic flourishes, his flashing up and down the keyboard, were forgiven him because he was blind.

On the festa's second day a loud and unresonant bell at the church rang its lead clapper at five A.M. and every half-hour afterward. Dona Bela, who usually had to count her beads to a radio mass, was pleased to tell me that the visiting priest had held a morning service.

At the social club, which was also a gymnasium when itinerant wrestlers came to town, folding chairs and tables had been set up and a band imported from Valença.

"We are called the MACH 5," its leader explained to me at dinner, "because when we started there were five of us. Now there are eight. But I do not think we can be the MACH 8, can we? It would not be scientific."

The club's officers, responsible householders such as Zeca's older brother, had voted to let all women into the dance free. The men, however, would have to pay twenty cruzeiros each to enter the club, then another thirty for a bottle of cheap native whiskey.

Steep rates, in a town where a laborer earned six cruzeiros a day. After five hours of drinking beer and sulking, Rui led an expedition of young men to the club steps. There he pounded on the door, made threats, and at last vomited across the doorsill.

Brazilians were not overly endowed with a capacity for liquor and most of the year they were nearly abstemious. But the festa justified—demanded—public drunkenness, and grandfathers and fifteen-year-old boys staggered together along the street, full to the ears with fermented sugarcane.

With everyone out strolling, complex relationships unknotted, and I discovered that, except that families in Camamu were rarely separated, this festa might be their annual reunion.

I learned that Sargento Jaime's prospective son-in-law, a robust brown man, was the brother by a different mother of the china-white president of the high school futebol team.

Dona Elza, the mãe do santo, was apparently aunt to half the town.

Bela at the hotel was revealed to have seven brothers, one currently serving as mayor, all fanned out around Camamu in strategic shops and businesses.

And Marlene, though she showed no inclination to do so, could boast of being a distant cousin to Zeca and Joaquim.

Late in the afternoon, I locked my room, inched down the disintegrating stairs, and headed for the baixa. Glum in a chair, Nelson hardly looked up when I came in. "It is time for the last part of my work," I said.

"Yes it is," he said, without stirring.

"Have you been uptown for the festa?"

He looked as though I were making sport of him. "The festa!" he snapped. "Many people doing nothing."

Giving me her hand, Nelson's wife was subdued, too. "Yes, thanks to God, I am tudo bem," she said.

They left me at the table among birdcages and a dusty framed still life of a watermelon. On a cupboard I saw a tinted photograph taken about the time they were married. Twenty years had smoothed most of the anxiety off the bride's face but time had dealt harshly with Nelson. It was hard to reconcile that bland unwrinkled face with the rutted features of the man who returned now carrying a brown pill bottle.

"Shake this," he said.

A silvery globule rested along the bottom of the bottle. I shook the bottle hard and watched the droplet break up and repair itself.

"Ten, twenty pieces, and then it is one again," Nelson said. "It comes from Africa."

"In English we call it mercury."

"No!" he said, as though I were trying to fox him. "No! It is azougue!"

According to the dictionary I consulted that night, azougue was the

Portuguese term, masculine gender, for the element mercury.

Nelson unstopped the bottle and let the ball graze my palm. "What do you feel?"

"A slight warmth."

"Ha! That will lengthen your lifeline." He showed me again the black gutter that ambled down his own palm.

"The twenty-fourth of August is my Candomblé," he said. "Today a man who promised me an ox—the same man who once came here groaning with pain"—Nelson clasped his head and rolled his eye—"and left totally cured, he wanted to give me a goat. A man should not promise a house and give a bedroom."

"No."

"The people of Camamu," Nelson went on, "think of nothing but eating and drinking and buying beautiful cars. I do not ask anything for myself, only for the saints. I am not like the padre who comes down from Salvador for one day every three months. I live here, not in Salvador. I do not have a fine church that is locked every day or a beautiful car to drive in. I do not want those things. I want only to serve the saints."

He rose from the table and retreated to the bedroom. His wife came to keep me company. "Have you been dreaming since we washed your head?" she asked.

"Yes, I dreamed that my cheeks were on fire, red and burning. When I woke up they were hot."

Nelson's wife listened with a wise smile, nodding her approval. I asked whether other people had told her their dreams.

"They usually dream of whiteness and the sea," she said. "But your dream was good, too, thanks to God. There has been nothing about the ritual so far, thanks to God, that has not gone well."

I brought out an envelope with fifty cruzeiros and a silver key ring I had brought from Rio. Its medallion showed in bas-relief the statue of Christ atop Corcavado mountain. "I brought this present," I said.

Still nodding, she caused the envelope to disappear into her pocket. At the front door we heard voices. Then four prosperous-looking black people negotiated the piles of wood in the hall and fell on Nelson's wife with cries of delight. "Minha comadre!" the matron said, embracing her startled hostess.

The husband looked about Nelson's age but fleshed out and fit. A young son in a well-tailored suit took my hand. "A pleasure." His sister, immaculate in beige linen, flung me a nod while she went on glaring at her parents for inflicting Nelson on her.

Nelson's daughter had hurried in with a clean cloth to spread over the table, and I drew Nelson's wife aside. "It is an inconvenient time for my work," I said. "I will come back."

"Oh, yes, senhor, please." Her eyes were darting with the dozen things she must do. "Come back another time."

THE NEXT MORNING I was shaking off a different dream when from the street arose a burst of sour loud noise. Instead of opening the shutters, I pulled on my pants and headed for what remained of the staircase. Midway down, the last fragments collapsed and I fell eight or ten feet into the stairwell.

I lay there on top of the splinters giving a perfunctory moan and inspecting my bruises. Nothing seemed broken. But my shoulder ached. The tip of my spine was sore. My left forearm was raked and bleeding.

Outside the door the music had got louder and I heard the stamp of dancing feet. I pulled myself out of the dusty hole and brushed at my pants. Then, feeling rather too much like Ailton, I went brandishing my wound to find Zeca.

An enormous white truck was parked at the curb directly in front of the post office. Three columns as thick as smokestacks supported a platform high in the air, and up there a dozen men in red band uniforms were playing an old carnival song by Caetano Veloso.

Around the tires, two hundred children were doing a wild samba. Ten or twelve of the older boys had stripped to the waist and they waved their shirts like anarchist flags.

Zeca was watching the commotion from his porch.

"Three weeks!" I held up my arm, sorry to see that the blood had already coagulated. "For three weeks I have asked you to find a carpenter to repair those stairs."

He studied my arm and shook his head, as though he had warned me a hundred times. "You must get that treated," he said.

Three months before, I might have cursed him lightly in English and gone my way. Now, after the nights with Rui and his friends, I could string together all of the country's unforgivable insults. Zeca heard me out with the same sad expression.

"I want a carpenter today!" I concluded. "Today, understand? Son of a whore!"

This last was spoken to our shoes and could describe either my vexation or himself, as Zeca chose.

He reached forward to touch the arm that hadn't been scraped; Brazilians believed that anger must evaporate at the touch of a hand. In the event they were right, I pulled my arm away from his conciliatory fingers.

"Today!" I repeated, lumbering off.

But where to go and nurse my grievance? With the stairs collapsed, my room was probably inaccessible. I decided the hotel was the best place to display my stigmata.

Arousing resentment against Zeca's family proved easy enough. On paper, the family's estate was impressive and included many houses and a fazenda that produced dendê oil. But its obligations were always greater than its income. Workmen would not refuse outright to serve these white-skinned Protestants with an honored Portuguese name, but, as with my bathroom, they'd contrive delays and excuses, hoping the project, for which they knew they would never be paid, might be abandoned.

All the same, Zeca and his relatives lived in Camamu as natural superiors. There were several things I already regretted saying—that Joaquim was a lout, that a younger brother was half-witted. But the harshest thrust had been that if they were truly short of money, their twenty-two-year-old sister might get a job.

This was the girl who had been Júlio's sweetheart for a week. Until Rui's gang made such cruel fun of her buckteeth that his infatuation cooled. She hung about in the street all day, patronizing the cooks and servants as they ventured out to take the air. Once in a while she pulled hair with girls she had hated since high school, but mostly she simply

184

waited for another young professional man less sensitive to public opinion.

By propping up a few timbers, I found I could hoist myself back to my room, and I retreated there while the dancing went on beneath the window. No carpenter appeared. Occasionally the white leviathan outside would head down the hill, fifty children in its wake, to assault the cidade baixa. Whenever the racket returned, I knew the truck was camping again in front of my door.

By evening I hadn't decided whether I would try to get to Ituberá for Valter's night of obligation for São Roque. "It is particularly pleasing," he had told me, "because of the parade of the little ones."

I needed either Valter's presence or Maria's green tea. But during the lesser celebrations in Camamu, I had found the taxi drivers drunk in the back seats of their jeeps. And my shoulders and shins were still aching from the fall. And although the town seemed to see the justice in my denunciation of Zeca, I was feeling more than merely ashamed.

First I had caught myself weeping for no reason. Now I was shouting at a hapless young man over a trivial accident. Worse, I had been ready to punch him. Why?

I wanted to believe that the spirits were the cause, that they were bringing my submerged dread to the surface. Or, that being too far-fetched, that I had been away from the writing of fiction for six months or more, damming an outlet for emotions I should be purging on paper. True, I had been writing an account of my experiences in Bahia, but telling the truth was not enough. I was learning that the worst work of fiction did more for its writer than any book of fact.

Far more important than the release it gives him, fiction permits a writer to shed for weeks and months the self that has ideas and preferences. Writing a novel, I could ignore the personality that chose blue shirts, drank cognac, laughed out loud at "Tender Buttons."

It was this reward of fiction writing that I was missing now. An only child, I had grown up with a room of my own, and yet even there I would make caves at the back of my closet, crouching there, hiding when no one pursued. Other boys might want to be Captain Marvel; I longed for the secret of the Invisible Man. As a novelist, I had found it.

185

But in Camamu I was always there, through the days and nights, a physical presence in view of the entire town. Every hour I was exposing my inconsequential tastes—hard-boiled eggs, fresh butter—and aversions: tripe, cacau, the incumbent American President.

It wasn't only their scrutiny I found wearing, it was the awareness of myself they were forcing on me. Instead of spending my days transparent, I had to see myself as they did. Even when the sight was not entirely comical, this being called upon to observe me, after years in which I had lost interest, was an intrusion.

And that being so, it was intolerable that I should be offering to us for examination a fraction of myself that spoke Portuguese like a vaudeville comedian or grinned, blushed and shrugged like a fourteen-year-old.

Locked away as they were, any new thoughts were languishing. I had started to think in Portuguese only enough to be clumsy on both ends of my tongue. Surrounded by a people who lived off their feelings, who joked incessantly and relegated philosophy to their priests and generals, I felt doubly disarmed, reduced to trying to charm a population I wasn't fluent enough to impress.

That they forgave my defects, that they even behaved as though they could see past my lumpish disguise was no consolation. I was unable to forgive as well as they did, and in only the weeks from May to August, I was beginning to doubt that there was a self worth knowing.

This self-pity was interrupted by a clatter and a yell. A friend of mine was leaping up the debris in the hall, followed by two boys from the high school football team.

"Hoy!" he called. "The stairs finally went?"

I waved my insufficient wound at him. The few light scratches elicited more tongue-clucking than they deserved.

"You told Zeca his sister does nothing all day?" my friend asked neutrally.

"Does she?"

"Nada," he agreed. "All the same, she is very angry. But that is not why I have come. Tomorrow, I must have a serious talk with you."

"Have it now."

"Not in front of them." The athletes were hanging out the window, shouting to dancers in the street. "Later."

"I have the curiosity that kills cats," I said. "I will give them batida and we can walk to the back."

With a glass in their hands, the long-haired boys were content to loll at the window. My friend and I went to a dark corner where cement had been poured for a shower.

"Did you see the man I was talking with earlier today?" he asked. "When the truck had gone and the street was empty?"

"A fat man with a mustache?"

"He is one of the state prosecutors. He believes that you are an agent."

"Two months ago, Júlio told me something like that. I thought he was joking. An agent of what?"

"He is not sure. Perhaps for your government. Perhaps for a terrorist group. But he says that you being interested in Candomblé must be false since there are no Candomblés in Camamu."

"Police are the same everywhere."

"He asked me why the children come here, and the boys and girls from the high school. I said to use your tape recorder. He had heard that you were teaching the young ones to make fun of the national anthem."

"I know where that idea came from."

"People here are often false," my friend said, "smiling to your face but—are your documents in order?"

"My visa runs another couple of months. I planned to have it renewed again."

"They may search your room."

"Tonight would be a good time," I said. "I have decided I will go to Ituberá. Where there is no Umbanda, either."

We walked back to my table. "Here." I picked up a sheaf of notes. "Look."

"You know that I believe you." Nonetheless he looked and murmured approvingly when he saw the name of Iemanjá.

"Have I ever said anything against your government?" I asked him.

"You said you hoped your own President would be removed from office. You told us that you were waiting in Camamu in exile, like Perón, and that when he was gone, you would return to the United States and be President in his place."

"What did the prosecutor say to that?"

"I told the prosecutor nothing, except that you were doing what you said you were doing. But it will be better if right now you do not criticize any government."

The futebolers had finished their grape batida. "Ready to go?"

"Ready," I said.

"You are going to see Nelson?" one boy asked.

"Not tonight. But Nelson has been doing a work for me."

"Nelson has a good heart."

It was an astonishing accusation. I looked sharply at the boy, who was touching his heart piously. But with the other hand he was making the Brazilian turn of the wrist toward his pocket that indicated a ladrão, a thief.

"You are saying that Nelson likes money?"

"I said Nelson has a good heart," the boy said a second time, also repeating his gesture. "I would never say anything bad about Senhor Nelson. I would be afraid."

I locked the door and we jumped down the few remaining struts to the street.

"No brincando," the boy insisted. "I am not joking. I would be afraid."

A CHILD IN A WHITE SHEET was carrying a statue of Saint Roque as gingerly as though it were the old saint himself. On either side, two smaller children marched ahead with candles to light the way. The tallest boy came next with a Brazilian flag.

Leaving Valter's terreiro there had been six of us. As we passed the open windows of the shacks, children ran out to claim a candle and their mothers followed behind in white skirts. It was a tranquil walk through the blackness. I was glad I had come.

Valter walked at the rear, singing from a hymnal and looking up when we crossed the footbridge across the rushing white river to keep an eye out for the toddlers. Not far past the bridge, we turned slowly and retraced our path. I wanted to concentrate on the children's voices echoing to the edge of the forest but I couldn't put aside the picture of a fat prosecutor going through my bags. I told Valter I was going to hire a jeep and go back to Camamu.

"We will be starting the Umbanda soon," he said. "It is our night of obligation. I had hoped you could see it."

"I am sorry," I said. "I think I may have an appointment in Camamu. But I thank you for letting me walk with the children."

On the ride back to Camamu, all sorts of calamities occurred to me, the worst being that since no one in the town read English, my papers might be confiscated and taken to an official in Salvador to pronounce on them.

At the post office I scrambled back to the second floor. The lock had not been forced. If a policeman had searched my room he was expert at his trade.

All the same, I resolved not to leave overnight without storing my notes with Júlio at the hotel. He was a banker. Better still, he was a careerist who habitually referred to the military president of Brazil, with no snide or negating hand gestures, as "boa gente," good folk.

WHATEVER HIS OTHER POWERS, Nelson had the magician's instinct for surprise. Two days, three days, I went for my final work and each time I was put off with an excuse. The river was too low, Nelson's wife said one day. Or, he has been called away on urgent business.

I had puzzled over Nelson's never wavering in his assurances that I would receive a spirit when the ritual was concluded. Self-protection should have led him to say that of course it would depend on my spiritual force, that there was only so much that even a pai do santo skilled in Nagô could do for a man if the spirits did not choose to mount him.

But Nelson had never faltered, and now I wondered whether he might not have hit on the more subtle scheme of not concluding the rites at all. I would be stalled, worn down by delays, until at last I would lose interest and stop coming. Nelson could tell the town, The gringo got impatient.

So I went back yet again on Saturday night, eight days after the work had begun, expecting to hear another reason why the time was not auspicious.

Instead, Nelson met me at the door and ushered me at once into the bedroom with the shrine. On the stool stood an imposing urn wrapped in tinfoil, tied with ribbons and festooned with flowers. The purple tulips were made of wax, the roses were cloth. But sprigs of wildflowers and Angélica were twined among the artificial blossoms and gave off a scent as corrupt as gardenias.

With its rim of flowers, the pot stood two feet high and nearly as round, but it looked oddly seaworthy, unsinkable; a get-well gift for an admiral.

"Look!" Nelson rummaged around inside the urn until he pulled out a package wrapped in druggist's paper. "Perfume! Soap!" He fingered the royal blue tape wound around the mouth of the urn. "Ribbon! I am not a man who promises an arm and gives a hand. No! I am not one of those."

The center of the great vase was filled with thin white crescents. "Coconut?" I asked.

Nelson nodded with satisfaction. "This is the best work a man can do," he said. "It is the same work I did for Zulmira when she was near to death."

"How many do you do in a year?"

"Like this?"

"No, of all kinds. Twenty?"

"More! Fifty!"

"One a week."

"Some weeks, three! Four!"

"When we finish, this sacrifice will also go to Ibirapitanga?"

"This will go into the sea," Nelson said. "That is why the tide and the level of the river have been important. A fisherman will take your sacrifice by canoe to a spot near the island called Pedra Furada."

Manuel had told me about the island, "the rock with a hole." It was said to be a sacred place for many spiritists along the coast. "Do I go with him?"

"He goes alone. Early on Friday morning he returns once more and offers a second prayer at the place on the water where he left the offering."

"After that I am ready to receive a spirit?"

"Certo!" Nelson was in fine humor, rubbing his hands, hardly spitting at all.

"You have an animal sacrifice at midnight Thursday for your Can-domblé," I said. "I would like to see it."

"Claro, claro." He offered a rapid prayer to Iemanjá and then began the chants. Nelson sang as though he were planing wood, moving his rough voice over the surface of the music and eventually leaving it smooth.

In Portuguese, he sang, "I remember that you created me from the red mud."

And, "O father, O my good father. O mother, O my mother."

In Nagô he chanted, "Capungaru ku ku ru ku." And: "Ai, obaluaé."

Nelson's wife slipped in and sang the chants an octave higher. "O my small craft, forgive it, Mother mine." And, "To my seven men, I am singing. O I will name them. O I will call their names."

We sat together for an hour. Nelson was not a man to promise a recital and give a medley. Every chant and gnomic Portuguese chorus was repeated at least twice, and Nelson sang them with absolute—the word kept insisting itself—sincerity.

THE STATE PROSECUTOR DISAPPEARED for a few days and I could forget him. Then one morning he was back, hanging over the low yellow wall in front of the hotel. "Bom dia," I said, on my way to breakfast. He scarcely nodded.

While I was buttering crackers in the dining room the prosecutor peered around the corner at me, and when I had finished he was seated in the red plastic chair in the lobby, looking intently at a month-old newspaper. But since he was a guest at the hotel, none of this behavior in itself was aberrant.

For a week Professora Marlene had been in bed with the grippe, and after breakfast I walked the few doors to her house to ask when we might take up our lessons again. At my knock, she shuffled out looking black under the eyes and green everywhere else.

"You are still sick," I said. "Let us wait another few days."

"Sit down a moment," Marlene said wanly.

"Go back to bed. We can talk when you are better."

"No, sit."

There were two straight wood chairs along the corridor and we sat side by side, as on a trolley.

"I have a new schedule at the school," Marlene said. "It is very heavy. I do not think I can go on teaching you."

She looked miserable from her flu. I said, "I am sorry."

"I can try to find someone else for you," she said. "A boy from the high school—"

"No," I said. "I think not."

"I am sorry, too," she said. "But it is just too much."

"I understand." I was sure I did.

"If you change your mind about a boy—"

"I will tell you. Now go back to bed. I hope you are better soon."

"Thank you," Marlene said.

I climbed the beams to my room and went to the window. The prosecutor was resting on his arms against the wall. We both watched the ten-year-olds kicking a black and white futebol in the street. The man glanced up to my window but when I stared down from the greater height, he withdrew into the hotel.

I wanted to get away if only for a night. From a heap of notebooks I dug out a schedule of Candomblés in Valença that Dona Mira had given me. As I remembered, she would be having one tonight, a simple ceremony according to her apology, a routine night of obrigação to the spirits.

I packed my papers in a flight bag and took them across the street to Júlio's room at the hotel. The prosecutor was nowhere in sight. I walked to the bottom of the hill just as a bus was pulling out for Valença.

The bus ride gave me two and a half hours to think, and the farther we got from Camamu the sillier my suspicions looked. Marlene had told the plain truth: she had too much work. It might require an inflated civic pride for a Bahian official to believe that Camamu deserved its own American spy. But it was even more deluded to imagine that my harmless activities were worth a full-time government prosecutor.

Not that I doubted that, once aroused, the Brazilian authorities could be disagreeable. I had seen and believed Haskell Wexler's film about the torture of Brazilian political prisoners. And at the moment Brazilian reporters were in jail on the charge of "offending the dignity of public officials."

But apart from a few trysts my own activities in the claustrophobic town were known to tudo mondo, as they said in Portuguese; to the whole world. After all, half the time it had been a police sergeant who drove me to the Candomblés.

That thought, supposed to be reassuring, set off a new line of speculation: what if Sargento Jaime's off-duty taxi service wasn't motivated by an eagerness to lay by a few extra cruzeiros but by his official diligence?

And if Jaime was suspect, what about the afternoon last month when Zeca brought to my room a stranger, a mulatto with gray, ungiving eyes? I would like you to meet my friend, Zeca said. Without emphasis he added that this friend also happened to be a lieutenant in the police.

The officer refused batida, whiskey, coffee from my thermos, water. During the twenty minutes that we made laborious chat, the gray eyes never left my face. I suppose you have a passport, he said once, but did not ask to see it. On leaving he pleaded a friendly interest and carried away paperback copies of my novels.

Approaching Valença, I put aside those thoughts and looked forward to my next few hours. Except for Mira I knew no one in the entire town, and it would be a respite, this return to the impersonality of city life. Alone I would eat a sandwich. Alone I could drink a cold beer. I would speak to no one. In twenty-four hours I wouldn't grin once.

The bus stopped at a park by the river. As I got off, five pretty girls in school uniforms darted around the bus. In the mild press of people, they didn't turn to stare after me.

I walked to the first corner without a single eye catching mine.

"Jack!"

The call came from the farmácia across the street. I walked over and looked past the door. Behind a counter the chunky lead singer from MACH 5 was looming genially. "You have come to see Mira?"

"Yes."

"I knew it was you, even across the street. Some of the band will also be going to Mira's Candomblé. We will look for you there."

I bowed out, grinning as though my mouth were pulled by rubber bands.

"Mister!"

At my elbow it was Adimir, a book salesman who had stayed overnight at the hotel in Camamu in May.

"Come for Mira? I am going too. Where are you staying? I suggest the Hotel Universal. I will come by for you at eight o'clock. We can have dinner and get to Mira's before her Candomblé begins."

"I thought tonight I would just watch from the back of the hall."

"Yes, of course."

Adimir was punctual to the minute, and when he arrived I really wasn't sorry to see him. In Camamu he had done magic tricks—stunts with empty beer bottles, making coins disappear—small arts that might win a salesman a few friends in a strange village.

The first time he had palmed a twenty-centavo piece, I had grabbed at his closed hand. "You are holding it there."

He held out a withered claw and said so naturally that I wasn't embarrassed, "No, that is just the way my hand grew."

Now he knew the several shortcuts to reach Mira's hall. Once we arrived, he marched me directly to her inner room. "You remember the American?"

The blouse of a slave, ten skirts of a washerwoman, it didn't matter; Mira looked more desirable than I remembered.

She grasped my hand. "Oh, not tonight! This is going to be nothing! Next Sunday in Ibirapitanga we will have costumes, flowers. The mayor has invited our whole troupe. Look!" She waved a script and I could read stage directions: Enter Xangô. "We will have a true pageant. This, tonight—"

"I have been looking forward to it."

She sighed and gave a command. Men pulled out overstuffed throne chairs from a closet and dusted them off for Adimir and me. Along the sidelines, black men and women were watching from the benches but I hadn't seen a sign at these ceremonies that any favors to me were resented. Rather, the regulars seemed pleased that their terreiro knew the proper way to receive guests.

The ritual was short, barely three hours. It was also cleanly, temperate. The music was never melancholy, and Mira's dancers were disciplined and graceful. Perhaps it was their absence of any excess that made the night seem mechanical. One man who fell into an unbecoming shiver was hurried instantly out of sight.

Mira was assisted by a female martinet who sat on the throne next to mine and received the obeisances of the dancers as though her blessing were an act of charity.

"I would like you to meet my mother," Mira said.

I took the firm hand that was offered me. "Your real mother or your first mãe do santo?" I asked Mira.

"My real mother. But she is also a mãe, Dona Bela da Conceição."

"The senhora must be the mãe do santo of Dona Maria in Camamu."

"I am," the woman allowed. "You know Maria, then?"

"I saw her only last week." Before the festa, I had called on Maria and found her with head in hands, complaining that none of her remedies were bringing relief from a severe pain.

"She has been sick," I said.

"Yes," said Bela, in a tone that suggested she already knew or that she had anticipated shortcomings in Maria that would cause her to ail.

At the center of the room, Mira was delivering up her body to a spirit with the least possible ado. She had said that she received Ogum and I listened for traces of the same god that used both Maria and Valter.

But the spirit's voice was coarse. Its body paced restlessly, hands clasped behind its back, offering brusque prayers for the congregation.

I had seen this gruff figure before but I couldn't think where. I was only sure that it wasn't Ogum.

Then I remembered Long Beach, our hostess under the control of Pai Ubiraja. Tonight Mira's leg didn't drag nor was her mouth smoking cigars. Otherwise, the resemblance was marked enough for me to intrude upon Bela's regal silence.

"Your daughter is receiving Ogum?"

"Now? No, now she receives an Indian called Ubiraja."

I admit to being surprised, at least until I reassured myself this way: the songs and prayers had survived through centuries, as had certain performances. In their childhood, both Mira in Bahia and Vonda in Rio had seen other horses mounted by Ubiraja. Perhaps not realizing it, they had been absorbing his ungainly stride, the rough cob to his voice.

American theater producers often sent out road companies with leading ladies who modeled their performance on the Broadway original. If I hadn't been astonished to see Mary Martin being impersonated in Chicago or Ethel Merman in London, I need not be overwhelmed that a touring Ubiraja had made it the six thousand miles to California.

"YOU CANNOT GO ALONE AT MIDNIGHT TO CIDADE BAIXA," Júlio said firmly. "It is far too dangerous. Rui and I will come with you."

His sense of style didn't permit Rui to open his eyes entirely, but the slits seemed attentive and agreeable to the idea.

"Have you ever been to a blood sacrifice?" I asked Júlio, sure that he hadn't.

"Claro," he said. "Of course. My older brother receives a spirit and I have gone with him. Chicken blood is quite tasty."

"Tonight Nelson is killing a pig."

"I do not know about the blood of pig. It is probably not the same."

Down the cobblestones to the river, the only sounds were our heels echoing ahead of us and the crickets in the grass. In the course of the ten-minute walk, we passed a single black youth, and it was he who seemed skittish at the sight of us, particularly Rui.

Nor, it seemed to me, was Nelson wholly at ease with these two young strangers. Covering his nervousness, he took up a story as though our arrival had interrupted it, and he spit after every sentence, sometimes after each phrase.

"—it was a woman from the first floor," he said. I deduced that the incident had taken place in Salvador. "I did the work she requested and then she came to me with three bananas! Three! Two for me and one for the spirit!"

I glanced to Júlio, who was listening with strained politesse.

"I told her that since the god she had offended was Omulu, she could expect to have the inside of her mouth infested with every kind of horrible wound. What else could she expect when she came with an offering so skimpy?

"I saw her eight days later," Nelson went on happily. "Her lips were swollen, she was spitting out terrible pus. She went to the doctor.

"He told her it was cancer!"

Nelson looked for the effect on Júlio as the more responsive half of his new audience. Rui had tilted his chair against the wall; if he wasn't asleep, his eyes were closed and his mouth gaping.

Nelson said, "She came begging back to me, but I just looked at her. I was not willing to help. No! Why?

"But the woman had a little girl and I felt sorry for the child. I ordered the woman to come to me, and when she kneeled, I touched her forehead. I told her, Take this water and sip it three times. Then wash your mouth with the rest.

"She did as I told her and her wounds were immediately healed. She went away and I never saw her again.

"There was the man who was supposed to repair some furniture," Nelson continued, sure that without such rhetorical tricks as a dramatic pause, his story had made its impact. "He took thirty cruzeiros from a man and his wife and then never showed up again. They came to me in a terrible state.

"I said, I will get the money back. But tell me, do you want to see this man again?

"No, said the man.

"Yes, said the wife.

"So at two o'clock the next afternoon, at just the hour the husband was away, the carpenter stopped by the house to pick up a coat he had left behind, and he felt bad and paid back the thirty cruzeiros and they never saw him again."

The Rabelaisian interpretation to those events hadn't seemed to occur to Nelson. Now he was saying, "There was a woman who was getting very fat from stealing chickens at night and eating them—"

It was half past midnight and I had to cut in, "Senhor, what time were you expecting to start your sacrifice?"

"I await the man to do the killing."

"What time will you finish?" Júlio asked anxiously. Rui's days were as unencumbered as his nights, but Júlio had to be shaved and in a shirt and tie by seven A.M.

"Four o'clock." Nelson went to rouse his son, Francisco, and Júlio and Rui jumped up together.

"We go." Rui screwed up his face and gave dry imitations of Nelson's spitting. "Bad!" he said feelingly. "Very bad!"

"And he makes many mistakes in grammar," Júlio whispered. "We go."

"What about all the danger for me alone on the street?"

"By four o'clock," Júlio said, "the bandits will all be in bed."

They were out the door before Francisco came from the bedroom rubbing his eyes. I went with him past the kitchen to the rock pile at the back. While Francisco gathered sticks for a fire, his father took a candle and led me up the slope to an indentation in the rock that made a natural pen.

"There he is," Nelson said, pointing to a black hog asleep in the crevice. "And here are the ducks." He shook his leg and four white wings kicked back at him.

Inside, the house was filling with neighbors. Among the women was Zulmira, looking ethereal despite a pair of blazing red slacks. There were also sleepy children wrapped in pastel cotton blankets, and a sinewy brown fisherman with the first inch of an accumulating belly. His helper was a teen-age boy with pert, wicked features.

"SeSe," Nelson said, introducing the fisherman. "He took your offering out to sea last week. When we have finished here, he will go again for the final prayer."

SeSe pulled off his clothes until he got down to a striped bikini that rested low on the oaken crests of his buttocks. Then he clamped a straw hat far back on his head. Meeting SeSe was establishing that the errand to Pedra Furada had not required a virgin.

When the fisherman left to inspect the hog, Nelson retired to the bedroom and sang one chant to his own lagging accompaniment on the drums.

Climbing back up the rock, I found Francisco, SeSe, and his young hoodlum helper huddled around the sleeping pig. Our only light came through the open kitchen window. Francisco went to fetch a smoking oil lamp, which he held toward us as we slid and grappled to keep our footing on the rock.

SeSe had located the long-handled ax and was hefting it in one palm. Then, with a grunt, he and the boy approached the hog. I was standing two feet behind them. Though he was holding the lamp, Francisco trailed behind me.

Nelson's son had the resentful and immobile face of a star of black mobster movies, and tonight I expected to see him at the forefront, very likely wielding the ax himself with a lusty "Ha."

But as time for the killing approached, the boy had turned his head away and was extending his arm full-length to bring the lamp in the vague direction of the pig without having to look. At first I thought he was joking, but he kept his eyes resolutely on the kitchen window.

Standing so far away, and with his arm shaking, Francisco was bringing the lamplight nowhere near the hog. With no resistance from him, I lifted the lamp out of his hand and he ran down the rock pile and into the house.

I moved forward another two feet with the flame. SeSe already had the ax poised above his head. His helper was standing back with his arms stretched wide, ready to grab for the pig if it bolted.

The sound of the ax was muffled by the animal's hide and the pig itself gave no yelp. It was quiet in the yard. At that first blow, the animal hunched together and seemed to wait for SeSe to finish the job.

He brought down the ax once more and this second swing left the pig dead or dazed. The boy grabbed the head and SeSe the hindquarters, and they half lifted, half rolled the body onto wooden planks near a kettle of steaming water.

Then, using a machete, SeSe sawed across the hog's throat. The boy stood by and held out a tin basin to catch the blood. The pig's neck was thick. Under the blade, the black body kept twitching until a meager trickle of blood leaked from the throat and the hog lay still.

With a dipper, SeSe scooped up scalding water out of the kettle. Carefully he wetted the pig's shoulders. Handling his machete like a razor, he shaved off the black bristles in long easy strokes.

He worked steadily, pausing only to soak another stretch of flank. The skin emerging under his hand looked white and fragile, like a peeled orange.

He left the legs and the snout unshaved but otherwise he caught every thick black hair. His knife he wiped periodically on the pig's ribs and he washed away the loose hairs with more hot water. Women came to the doorway to watch but the wood smoke from the fire drove them back inside.

I liked Francisco for his squeamishness and I thought I knew the cause. When he returned, the butchering was nearly over and I asked him, "Did your father buy this pig for the Candomblé? Or had you raised it yourself?"

I hadn't seen the hog in the backyard but it could have been fattening out of sight in its rock crib.

"We had him eight months." He understood the point of my question. "But I have never liked the killing."

With the hog shaved, SeSe was sawing at its head. The surface of the rock was slippery with blood, and he kept shifting position to get a purchase that would let him cut deeper. The helper had hunched down to hold the hog by the ears while SeSe hacked past the cords of the throat.

From the kitchen the women handed out a wicker basket as big as a laundry hamper along with another tin basin. SeSe severed the head, yanked it free from the body, and tossed it four feet into the basket. The rest of us jumped out of the way of splattering blood.

The pig's feet came away with less effort. Still using his knife as a saw, SeSe rent the shining white body from shoulder to groin. Pulling the pan of blood closer, he brought out five scoops in his cupped hands from within the hog's ruptured belly. By moonlight the blood looked as clotted and dark as borsch.

Pulling herself up the rocks, Nelson's wife stood in front of the house for Exú. She uncorked a bottle of cachaça and sloughed clear cane whiskey over the statue and over the skull near the back.

"Go away now," she said to Exú softly, a lover's adieu. "Go now. It is time to go. You must go."

She left the bottle half full beside a burning candle and went back to the kitchen.

SeSe had finished gutting the hog. The second basin was heaped with heart, liver, intestines. Deliberately, he flayed and quartered the carcass, cracking its ribs and hip bones with blunt strokes of his knife.

He had been tossing the meat into the wicker basket on top of the pig's head but now he dug down and handed the head to Nelson. "It is for Exú," Nelson told me. "Later."

The pig had vanished from the wooden boards and SeSe was scrubbing them down with boiling water. Through the kitchen window I saw Nelson's daughter discover the pig's heart among the piles of meat and snatch it up as though it were a ruby.

"What next?" SeSe asked Nelson's wife. "The ducks?"

I held the lamp again while he laid hands on an angry duck. Its squawking alerted a big black rooster, which gave a few clucks of protest but didn't leave his straw nest.

SeSe's helper held out another basin, and SeSe planted one bare foot on each of the duck's agitated wings. He pulled up the neck and stropped off feathers along the arch from the breast to the duck's bill. With his knife he made a new mouth low on the neck.

Once more blood drained out slowly. When the duck did not die fast enough to suit him, SeSe clamped back its wings and dipped its limp head into his kettle of boiling water.

I had been kneeling to keep the candle close to SeSe's knife. Now when I stood up, I felt faint. In front of my eyes I saw a thin screen made of straw, and past this screen, SeSe's brown arms, the last furious beating of duck wings, the firelight, the kitchen door. But everything overlaid with a straw scrim. Trying to clear my head, I only brought the weave of the screen into focus, a pattern of interlocking chevrons.

I looked around to see whether there wasn't a mat or toweling hung somewhere in the yard that my eyes had seen and registered. But there was nothing that resembled this dun-colored pattern. I blinked my eyes again. The shade persisted. It was only when I crouched down again, still dizzy, that it lifted.

My balance had come back and I stood up again. But for the killing of the second duck, I held out the lamp at waist level. Crouching had caused the faintness, or possibly the wood fumes had. Now, on my feet, I was appreciating the unflustered way SeSe let the duck's blood before he dipped its twisting head into the kettle.

Beyond those few early pats on the drum, Nelson had made no attempt at providing a ritual, wandering instead along the dark corridor to the kitchen and giving orders to the women by the stove.

His killing accomplished, SeSe came inside for further instructions. I followed behind. Blood had dried like chains around his wrists and ankles, but the exertion had left him exhilarated.

"First he will wash," Nelson said to me. "Then he will go in his canoe to the place where he left your sacrifice."

"The Candomblé starts tomorrow night at nine o'clock?" I asked.

"Tonight," Francisco corrected me, pointing to his Japanese wristwatch with its window for the day of the month. "It is nearly dawn."

MOST BRAZILIAN SPIRITISTS do not believe that animals have souls or that they return reincarnated to earth. Should they be wrong, however, and Nelson's hog looked down the next night from his sty in the sky to observe the Candomblé, he must surely have felt that he had died in vain.

I was, as ever, prompt. A dozen people had already gathered around Nelson's table, most of them kin to Zulmira. It struck me as odd that Nelson's wife was wearing a shamrock green dress instead of her white satin robes, but I sat down at the place they cleared for me and waited for the rites to begin.

From deep in the house, I couldn't see the front yard. The next day Júlio told me that he and Rui had led a platoon to Nelson's from the snooker parlor. They milled about on the riverbank for an hour, waiting for the show to start. Finally Nelson's wife sent out plates of pork, which they had eaten with their fingers, and grumbled and climbed the hill for home.

While I waited inside, Zulmira's snubbed-nosed teen-age twins induced me to play a game. We would each conceal one, two, or three unpopped kernels of corn in a fist and then guess what the total from our three hands would be. We played for an hour and I was winning with no difficulty when I overheard Nelson say to a black man crowding into the room, "No, no drums tonight."

"No drums?" I asked one twin, Cosme.

"Later," he said conspiratorially.

Perhaps, although it was contrary to Dimitri's notion of etiquette, Nelson was thinning out the crowd before he began his Candomblé.

Cosme was a cheat. He hid extra husks between his fingers to make his bets come true. But he was also clumsy and they usually fell out on the floor. His brother Damião was honest but he took so long deciding how many kernels to keep in his fist that the game lacked any sustained excitement and even the smallest children drifted away from our table.

At midnight I said, "I do not think there is going to be a ritual."

"No," Damião agreed readily. "Nelson has been trying all week, but he could not find a house big enough. So he has just had the feast."

"Why did your brother tell me 'Later'?"

"He wanted to keep our game going."

The fishermen had been pushing for hours along the corridor to the beer in Nelson's refrigerator. But when I went to take my leave, Nelson was alone, gaunt and lifeless on his stool. I shook his hand and said good night.

"Até logo," he answered listlessly.

It was the first time he didn't think to ask when I would be coming back. I wondered whether, given tonight's setback, Nelson had decided he should stick to peddling firewood.

SUNDAY MORNING AND I WAS EATING a piece of dry yellow cake with sugar frosting when a policeman came into the hotel and out to my table on the porch. I had seen him many times standing watch at the bank door, so timid and kindly looking that one sharp word would have disarmed him. Today he approached in full regalia, his tan shirt encrusted with emblems, a visored cap, even a pistol.

I said, "Bom dia, senhor."

He blushed and walked to the railing to spit. He stayed there leaning on his elbows and gathering strength.

When he came to my side, he dropped his voice although we were alone on the porch. "Senhor, the lieutenant of police would like to see you in his office."

"Certainly."

"There is no hurry. Ten o'clock?" It was already after nine. "And please you will bring your documents."

"I do not know where the lieutenant's office is."

"Oh," he waved his hand westerly, "it is only up the street. You will see it."

The office proved to be a rose-colored bungalow two blocks from the hotel. Its interior was a dark green except for posters of an electric yellow lettered in red: WANTED TERRORISTS. NOTIFY THE POLICE.

Beneath the heading were photographs I had described to Ed Houser —two dozen young faces, mostly white and male. One girl pretty as an ingenue smiled out from the bottom row. Usually the men wore white shirts and ties. I supposed the police had gone back to their high schools for the pictures.

A young clerk was typing at a small table. Behind the single desk, a bald man with moist lips looked up from behind dark glasses. It occurred to me what an injustice it must seem to be an ugly Brazilian.

I announced my name. He regarded me with aversion.

"Sit," he said at last. "I just wanted to have a chat with you. Entirely informal."

"Fine."

He took up the list of formal questions he had prepared: name, age, occupation. When he asked on what date I had arrived in Brazil, I opened my passport and pushed it across the desk. He fell on it avidly, turning to the address for notification in event of death. "You are a son of California?"

It was by adoption but I said, "Sim."

"He is here on a tourist visa," the lieutenant said significantly to his clerk.

"That was for the first ninety days," I said. "In Rio I received this extension until October." I reached across the desk and pointed to the official stamp of the state of Guanabara.

"I have never seen this stamp."

"It is from your own government. If you wish to see two others, turn the page. Three years ago, I had my visa extended and again last year."

"There is nothing here that says what your profession is. You claim to be a writer. Where is your card of identity?"

"I do not understand."

"This!" He pulled from his pocket a laminated green card issued by the state government of Bahia. "To prove what you are."

"In my country," I said, "we do not have such documents. In the United States," I went on, neglecting to add that I spoke only for the white middle class, "the police do not stop people walking on the street and demand to see their papers."

His expression said that when he got around to America do Norte, he would attend to the oversight. "You have nothing to prove that you are a writer?"

"I have copies of books I have written."

"No," the lieutenant said, "that would not do. I mean a certificate, an authorization."

"I do not understand what the problem might be," I said. "I have a valid extension for my visa."

"Senhor," he said, his voice rising, "we do not have folklore here. You say you are interested in Candomblé but if a man wanted folklore of that type he would be in Salvador where they have great pageants."

"Last week in Valença, I told Dona Mira that I was not interested in pageants. You have heard of Mira?"

"I do not know Valença," he said primly, as though I had mentioned Sodom or New York.

"The whole world knows her folklore. But she also conducts a small Candomblé, and that to me is more interesting."

"You are not living in Valença."

"Here there are more fathers and mothers of the saint. Dona Maria, Dona Luzia, Dona Elza. In cidade baixa, Senhor Nelson—"

The lieutenant turned on his clerk. "Old Nelson does Candomblé?" The boy shrugged and went on typing.

"In Ituberá," I said, "there is Senhor Valter."

"I do not know Ituberá," the lieutenant said, defiant now. "But if I were interested in folklore, I would not come to Camamu."

I was not going to lecture a Brazilian on the difference between folklore and magic. We sat silent for a few moments.

He took up my passport again.

"I do not like this," he said. "I do not like it. Look!" he demanded of the clerk, who raised his eyes briefly to my visa. "This official in Guanabara. I do not know him. Have you ever heard of him?"

The clerk ignored the question. I said, "He is the chief of the office of foreign visas. If there is a doubt about his signature," I went on blandly, "you might call him on your telephone."

The guard from the bank crept in humble as a truant and took a bench by the wall. The lieutenant made a show of writing down my name and the number of my passport on the back of a lottery ticket. When he pushed the passport back, I rose to go.

"I do not like it," he said again.

I reached over the desk to shake his hand. Against his will, he touched my fingers as though they might explode.

AT THE HOTEL THAT AFTERNOON, the women were talking about me in the kitchen. As I came down the passageway, Dona Bela's meek husband warned them, "O americano," and the girls hushed and ran water in the sink.

Ah, I thought, now it will be like that.

But then at night Railda and Alda came knocking at the door, ready to drink batida and record a new love song by Roberto Carlos. A dozen children drifted up the stairs to listen, followed by a delegation from the high school, including perky Julia, tall and solid Rita, solemn Margarita. When they were gone, the young men from the bar arrived full of beery condolences.

"He is very ignorant, that lieutenant," one fellow assured me. "The whole world knows that for years he could not get a job until his friend, the prosecutor, got him hired by the police."

Their consolation held me overnight. Then, the next afternoon, the toothless mailman downstairs put three letters in my hand, snatched them back again, and went to a ledger to make a notation. "New regulations," he said.

"A nuisance for you," I said.

He sighed and shrugged. He didn't seem resentful about bearing his share of the nation's security.

DURING THE FESTA, I had felt a delicate pluck on my elbow and turned to find Dona Luzia promenading in a new brown dotted swiss. Huddling on the sidewalk, we had set a date for the work that was to bring me love. Over the next ten days, I settled on a victim.

I ruled out the local beauties as not comprising a fair test. I'd never know afterward how much of any success was due to the spirits and how much to my own enterprise. But there was one beleza who had passed through Camamu briefly on the way home to the town of Ipiaú.

We had talked only a few moments and although I saw to it that we traded addresses, unless the spirits intervened, there was little chance of our ever meeting again. I did not have a photograph but as I set off for Luzia's I had in my pocket a scrap of paper with the address in Ipiaú.

My route took me past the snooker parlor, where a schoolboy named Urbano spotted me carrying my flight bag with the tape recorder inside. "Jack!" he shouted. "You are not going back to America?"

"Partway. I am going as far as Luzia's."

Rui said, "We go too." Eight young men put down their cues and bottles and fell out on the street to march behind me.

"I am not going for a Candomblé." Surely they knew that at eight in the morning there wouldn't be drums or cachaça.

"Luzia is going to do a work for you?" Urbano guessed.

I nodded but said nothing about its nature. At the path to her house, I turned to them. "I will see you all tonight."

"Tonight?" the boys protested. "We will stay now. We will go in with you." But Rui was a good sergeant; he looked at my expression and prodded them back toward town.

When I stepped inside Luzia's house, a husky farmhand was buttoning up his yellow rayon shirt. Luzia had been massaging and praying over a strained muscle, and the man said his shoulder already felt better. He left; she nodded for me to follow her into the chamber with her shrine.

Everything I had read about love potions in Brazil came from times past, and usually the charms had been sought by women. Sometimes slave girls strained coffee through the crotch of a nightgown in which they had slept two nights and then served a man a cup at breakfast and again at dinner.

Gilberto Freyre had listed several ingredients for magical charms in previous centuries: hair from the armpit or genitals, sweat, nail parings, tears, saliva, sperm. Or sorceresses might make a doll of wax or cloth and, as they prayed, spread its legs.

For café mandingueiro—witches' coffee—the mãe do santo mixed a potion of sugar with clots of her own menstrual blood.

Without being ungallant, I could assume that Luzia's change of life was behind her and could hope that she'd have other recipes to prescribe.

Her small roncó was spotless, the doorway hung with fresh strips of green and red oilcloth. On the altar, the handkerchief covering a glass of water was as white as befit the King of Snows.

Two grandchildren, Sebastião and Manuel, seven and eight, had crowded inside with us and they sat giggling on a stool. Luzia's slender sister also slipped in, taking no room at all.

Luzia fitted herself into a corner so her profile faced me. She lighted a stick of hand-rolled incense and held it under my nose—faint, sweet, hardly pungent. Inhaling the fumes, Luzia propped the thin stick in a candleholder, where it burned to ash as we spoke.

Breathing deeply, Luzia closed her eyes. The boys watched her face solemnly. Somewhere else in the house the baby Raimundo was crying.

Luzia's bosom rose and fell until her pulse seemed to race and she gave the gasping dry sound I had heard from Valter—"hup, hup," like stifled coughing.

"May God grant you peace," a husky voice said from Luzia's lips.

Her sister knelt and kissed the spirit's pale brown hand. She was raised up and had her own hand kissed in turn. I did the same. The children squirmed and pinched each other to be next, accepting their blessings with contented smiles.

"Who is Dona Luzia receiving?" I whispered while Sebastião was being lifted from his knees.

"Ogum Beira Mar," Luzia's sister answered. Ogum of the Seashore.

"What do you want of me?" Ogum asked.

"I have come to ask for love."

"I will bring you happiness." It wasn't until later, hearing the tape, that the ambiguity struck me. "And I will safeguard your health. What hour do you prefer?"

"What hour?" I turned to the sister. "I am supposed to say what hour?"

She nodded decisively. "What hour?"

I had been inclined to leave the date and hour for my assignation to the spirits. But clearly I was expected to say something, and since I knew how early the people of Bahia retired, I said, "Eight o'clock?"

"Eight o'clock tonight?"

Too precipitous; the trip from Ipiaú alone would take two hours. But I said, "Yes, tonight."

"You must be bathed with green leaves," Ogum explained. "From head to toe. Then you will have a powder rubbed into your wrists. And before you go to bed, you must say a prayer to your protecting spirit. This guardian angel will receive your prayer and grant the happiness you seek."

"At eight hours tonight I am only to be cleansed with leaves?" I asked, relieved not to be causing havoc in Ipiaú.

"Eight hours here," Ogum agreed. "Now I will leave you."

The four of us went forward again to bow and kiss the hand.

Luzia slid easily back into herself and asked her sister what Ogum had recommended. "The bathing," her sister said, "and the powder and the prayer."

From a shelf, Luzia pulled down a pamphlet so engrimed with dust and oil its pages looked like parchment. It was a book of prayers published in São Paulo. From the introduction, I saw that it was the work of Kardecists.

"You may like to copy this," Luzia said, finding a prayer to the protecting spirits, "so that you can repeat it tonight as you go to sleep."

"Wise and benevolent spirits," the prayer began in Portuguese, "messengers of God that perform the sublime mission of aiding the living and teaching us the paths of progress and truth—"

Luzia escorted me back to her dining room table while I copied out the three paragraphs. Her son, Antonio, had come in from the yard, and he smiled to see his mother and me bent over the prayer book. His children were hanging on her chair. Angélica, who could barely crawl, was trying to pull herself into Luzia's lap.

"I am asking for different works at different terreiros," I said. "I am glad this is where I came to ask for love."

Back in my room I read through the prayer aloud, stumbling over words like "permanecem" and "interessais." It was already noon when I looked at my watch and saw that the date was wrong. It showed 30 in the small window and I was sure it was only August 29.

I couldn't understand how the mechanism had gained a day. My night hadn't been more restless than usual, and even if I had changed the date in my sleep, it would have taken two full revolutions of the hour hand. And then I doubted I could have set the time correctly.

It might be that the stem had come loose while I wound it. But, again, why was the time accurate and only the date one day ahead?

I made a note of this inexplicable event but I was annoyed. If this was Ogum of the Seashore manifesting himself, he had chosen particularly trivial means.

Then I recalled that while I showered that morning I had dropped my watch. Picking it up, I'd looked to see that it was still running but had not checked the date. Now I banged the edge hard on the heel of my hand.

Once, twice, three times. I couldn't make the date jump forward another notch. But I was sure that with enough physical force it would.

THAT EVENING LUZIA HAD MORE VISITORS. As I entered, a brown-skinned man was describing the symptoms of a serious ailment. Next to him, pulling at his trimmed goatee, sat a younger white man out of the pages of a Russian novel. When he could leave his beard alone, he was clasping his hands and biting his lip.

"Has she had anything strange to eat?" Luzia asked the darker man. "Or only the usual beans and rice?"

"It has nothing to do with what she has eaten!" the anguished man burst out. "Come!" He addressed the other. "We have wasted enough time. We must find a car and get going."

He rose without saying good night and rushed out the door. Grimacing his apologies, the other man hurried after.

"Brothers," Luzia explained to me. "The moreno brought the young one here because his wife is very ill." She held out her arm rigidly, stiff as death. "They have been married only four months and she is expecting a baby as well, so the young one is very worried. The moreno thinks the girl has been taken by a bad spirit. It sounded like that to me, too."

"If you want to go to her—"

"No," said Luzia, excusing herself, "the husband wants to take her instead to the hospital at the Firestone fazenda."

At the back of the house, six women were working around the stove. After I had spent ten minutes alone, Luzia's son led me to the terreiro, where Ogum Beira Mar and the women were already waiting.

Ogum showed me to a small room I had seen before only from its threshold. Once inside, he faced me on a stool toward a door that opened onto the meadow behind Luzia's house. In the perfect darkness outside, a single candle burned like a polestar. Ogum lighted three more candles at my feet and picked up an array of green branches heavy with diamond-shaped leaves.

Touching the ground, Luzia's sister said, "Da licença, Ogum," and retired to stand at my shoulder. She held a small basin of clouded water. Ogum took each of seven switches in turn, dipped it into the basin until the leaves glistened, and moved it down from the crown of my head, across my body, as Nelson's wife had done with colored cloths.

With each pass, Ogum chanted and the women behind me joined the song:

"The Son of Our Lady,

"Jesus, commands that he be clean,

"The Son of the orixás."

Again my hair was tousled. But the branches itched and tickled as the cloths had not, and I shifted my arms to protect the tender places.

When all the branches had been used, Ogum scooped them up, careful to retrieve every leaf, and carried them out with the little water that was left in the basin. In a moment, he came back inside and handed the empty basin to Luzia's sister.

Taking my hand in his, Ogum pulled at each finger, a gentle downward pressure not hard enough to pop them from their sockets. Then his own hand continued to move in a flowing motion toward the door, as though he were ushering out the psychic wastes from my body.

He went around to each side of my head and blew once, vigorously, in my ears.

Then, bidding me to stand, he pulled downward on my arms, repeating, "Give me strength, God. Make me strong, Goddess."

212

Still standing, I was led by the spirit back to the shrine room and the stool before its altar. Luzia's sister held out a vial of green powder and Ogum took a small heap in his palm.

The spirit made the sign of the cross on each of my wrists, daubed a bit of green into the crook of each elbow, made crosses on my biceps, forehead, thorax, the nape of my neck. Hoisting my pants legs, he traced a pale green cross on each calf.

"I am going to prescribe for you now," the spirit said, taking his seat in the corner. "When we finish, I would ask that you stay seated before this altar for half an hour. Please look at the time."

"Dez para nove," I said. Eight-fifty P.M.

The women had clustered behind me, straining to hear the spirit's every word. Luzia's two sons entered the shrine room and crouched against the wall.

"First, bathe five times with this liquid." As Ogum pronounced the words, Luzia's sister handed me a brown bottle of the size for cough syrup. At the bottom were a few spoonfuls of a solution that foamed as the bottle changed hands.

"Add a few drops to a liter of water," Ogum said, "and bathe thoroughly with it.

"When you have finished, light one of these." The sister now held up a blue stick of incense. "This is enough for five treatments. Make certain the smoke reaches everywhere." To demonstrate, Ogum lifted a sandal and wafted the smoke under the sole of his foot. "Let it permeate your clothes."

Next, Luzia's sister gave me a small capsule, almost empty. "Drink three glasses of water, lukewarm, not cold, mixed with this powder," Ogum said.

The label read, FORMULA: PENICILINA G BENZATINHA. But in Brazil all bottles were reused many times, and I was sure I wasn't being given a penicillin compound. The teaspoon of powder inside looked caked and gray.

Ogum of the Seashore asked me, "Do you understand these instructions?"

"Yes, senhor."

"On sexta-feira"—Friday—"it will be better if you eat no meat. Do you have the prayer now for your protecting spirit? Remember to repeat that."

The sister leaned across me to address Ogum directly. "Before you leave us, we would like to ask you about the moreno who came here with his brother. We think the wife of the brother is possessed by a bad spirit and that you could help her."

"That is true." Ogum spoke with detachment. "But if the husband refuses my help, I can do nothing."

"We do not understand him," said one of the younger women. "If he loves his wife so much, why will he not let you cure her?"

It was obvious the episode with the distraught husband had upset them. They drew closer to hear what Ogum would answer.

"Some people remain ignorant," Ogum said. "It is not that they are bad people or wish for bad things to happen to their families. But since they are ignorant, we can only pity them and pray for their enlightenment."

The family listened, agreed, and started to talk among themselves. "I heard him say he was going to ask for transfusions," Luzia's son said pityingly. "He will end up spending all his savings on blood and she still will not be better."

In the corner, Ogum was taking his leave less smoothly than before. Luzia choked several times as though she might vomit. Then her eyes snapped wide and she folded her hands in her lap.

"You go?" she asked me.

"Ogum suggested that I stay seated here thirty minutes. Ten minutes more."

"Of course," Luzia said.

The voices behind me were so loud that one might think the family was arguing but they were in accord: the husband was ignorant, exactly as Ogum had said.

"I think that he—" Luzia began. But no one was paying attention to her now.

At nine-twenty P.M. I rose to leave. "Make this sign," Luzia said and coached me to cross myself in front of the altar.

214

With the vial in one pocket, the brown bottle and the blue incense in the other, I left the terreiro amid a chorus of "Até logo." It was early enough for the first bath, and back in my room I hunted about for a liter bottle. The one I found reeked of batida but I washed it out and poured in a little of the soap.

The empty house where I showered was dark, the water was icy coming out of the shower. Usually I tried to wash at noon when any sun had warmed the pipes. Now I backed under a rush of cold water and poured the contents from the batida bottle over me from the top of my head to my heels.

In my room it took three matches before I got the incense smoldering and could fumigate myself and my clothes with the curls of smoke. Next I drank the powder in a glass of warm water. It tasted like perfumed eraser dust.

Girls from the high school had seen my light behind the shutters and they ran upstairs to conduct a few interviews with my machine. It was their latest fancy:

"Tell the audience here at the Clube Jacques, Maria," the compère would say into the microphone, "what color eyes you like best in a man." The answer was always blue.

The girls left. I thought my day was over. But just before eleven there was another hesitant knock at the door.

Thirty minutes later I was finally alone. I recited Luzia's prayer and shut off the light. To the spirits, I added a last companionable word:

Tonight was very satisfactory, I told them. I am grateful for that surprise you arranged. I've been waiting a month or more for that particular beauty. But remember our contract: a visit from Ipiaú.

I did admit, however, that while Nelson's three-week advocacy with the spirits had produced a bad fall, a stupid quarrel, and an interrogation by the police, this single day with Luzia, if not yet answering my prayer, had already fulfilled one of my pleasantest daydreams.

CONVERSATION WAS FLAGGING, which was unusual with Valter, Deoclides, and me. Drinking our coffee, we were a little constrained, repeating the jokes about how much sugar Valter took in his cup. There were minor signs left to learn, lesser chants—all minutiae for which I didn't have the heart this Sunday morning.

To make conversation I asked Valter, "You have been a caboclo in Umbanda all your life?"

"Yes," he answered. "I have never done anything else."

"If you had not received the spirits, what do you think you might have done?"

"Farm work." Behind his bifocals Valter's worn face became reflective. "Or perhaps I would have worked as a builder."

"You surprise me. Your work in Umbanda requires so much teaching, I thought you would say that you would have been a teacher."

"I like the classes of Umbanda." He hesitated to say it. A teacher was a grand figure, beyond a man's aspiration. "But I do not—"

At that moment, two black men pushed open the door of the terreiro. One hung back while the other walked to our table and presented himself to Valter.

His radio had been stolen at the Firestone fazenda, he said, and he wanted the spirits to name the thief.

"The saints do not like to do works on Sunday," Valter told him. "But if you work at Firestone, then this is your only day to come here."

The man nodded.

Valter handed a one-cruzeiro note to his ten-year-old son. "Buy candles. Or," he added to me, "muilas. Muila is another name for candle in the language of Umbanda."

The boy went lagging off. By the time he was back with a package of eight thick white candles, we had finished our coffee and Valter went directly to his abasé.

I asked Deoclides, "Can the gods always name the thief?"

"Not always. But many times."

The harsh, labored speech from the inner room told me that Valter had not received Iemanjá or Rei da Matinha. It must be either Ogum or Tupinamba. I guessed the latter, and when Deoclides listened, he agreed it was the Indian.

The plaintiff disappeared inside. His friend and I sat on a bench outside the door. It was open a crack, and I hoped to overhear Tupinamba's advice.

But I missed everything because one of Valter's three-year-old twins came running into the terreiro. Giggling, Crispim climbed onto my knees and put his bare feet in my pockets. His cousin, the same age, snuck up from behind and tweaked my ears. The more I shushed the children, the louder they squealed. With twenty agile fingers, Crispim wrested off my watch and the other boy unbuttoned my shirt.

It wasn't until Crispim rushed away to nibble on the blackboard eraser and his cousin to lick the slate that I could ask the other man what Tupinamba was advising his friend.

"The saint has described the thief," the fellow reported. "His height, the color of his eyes, the color of his skin. It was the man my friend suspected. The spirit says to stay calm and keep an eye out. Next week the thief will try to sell the radio. That is when my friend can get it back."

The victim emerged looking grim, and Deoclides motioned me inside. Tupinamba was offering a loud, disjointed prayer. When the spirit had finished, Deoclides explained to him that I would be returning Tuesday night for instructions about my work.

"That is good," Tupinamba said. "Sunday is the wrong day for this. Monday, Tuesday, Wednesday, Thursday, Friday, Saturday I am here to help you, but Sunday should be set aside for prayer, not for works."

Deoclides and I left, but Tupinamba stayed in the abasé another twenty minutes. As we talked softly, I could hear his stentorian praying punctuated by the ringing of the silver bell.

At last Valter came out from the abasé. He was veering so badly I jumped up and half carried him to a chair. He shook his head to clear it and smiled apologetically.

At that moment, Valter's wife peeped in at us. When Valter was only her husband of twenty-three years, the woman went about her chores not paying him much attention. At two o'clock in the morning, I had seen her with a sheet folded across the dining room table, pressing one of Valter's red satin outfits with a wedge of metal that had a chink for hot coals from the stove. Between strokes, she would blow on the coals, taking care not to sear her eyebrows.

But the instant Valter gave himself over to a spirit, his wife tried to become invisible. Now, satisfied that she was not intruding, she passed Valter a canister of ground herbs.

"We make our own incense," he explained, "a compound of several plants: cravo, carringa aruanda, erva doce, and alecrim de tendal—all mixed with white sugar. It is a blend that invites only good spirits. Bad ones smelling it know that they are not welcome and they pass us by."

He carried the incense to his altar. "Are you ready for lunch?"

"Senhor, this must stop. You should not have to feed me every time I come."

"It is our pleasure."

At the door to his house, I still intended to disengage myself but his daughter Elza had already set a place for me. Valter held up my plate as proof that I was ordained to stay.

That table setting proved to be a ruse. The meal was far from ready to serve and as we waited I made the mistake of telling them about my works with Luzia and Nelson.

I was describing the ritual at Luzia's when the first of the food was passed to me. It was a platter of bones and greasy tidbits, and the sight of the wads of gray fat prompted me to lie:

"No, I cannot today," I said. "The mãe do santo told me not to eat meat for five days."

"Five days?" Deoclides looked with wonderment at Valter. "I have never heard of such a thing."

The exaggeration made me uncomfortable but not as queasy as the plate I could now hand untouched to Valter's son. I said, "The abstinence is supposed to increase my spiritual force."

"Eating meat does not affect that," Valter said. "At least not as we understand the wishes of the spirits."

But that temperate reaction faded when I got to telling about my initiation at Nelson's hands. I had barely started when I thought Valter would slide off his chair laughing.

"Oxalá!" he cried to Deoclides. "The pai do santo was going to bring him Oxalá!"

218

It was such heartfelt laughter that I laughed at their laughing. Sitting along the wall, even Valter's wife gave little chirps of happiness.

"Who do you think he *would* receive?" Deoclides asked Valter, jerking his head in my direction. "I imagine Ogum."

Valter appraised me levelly. "Yes, Ogum."

Emboldened by the merriment, Valter's wife said, "I think, Oxóssi."

Jorge Amado had described Oxóssi as a finicky eater. I attacked the cold macaroni with more brio.

"Perhaps," Valter allowed, looking at something beyond my forehead, "perhaps Oxóssi."

"I would have been more than satisfied with an old man." I said velho, not preto velho. "Old black man" might sound patronizing.

"Oxalá!" Valter repeated and they laughed again. "How much did he charge you for this work?"

"I did not add it up. Each time I went, there were new expenses."

To put an end to the subject, I turned to Deoclides. "When a man comes as the one came today to locate his radio, how much does he pay?"

"What he wishes."

"There is never a fixed charge in Umbanda," Valter said. "If they pay nothing, the work will be done all the same."

"Do you remember, months ago, you told me about a man who practiced Quimbanda?"

"André. Yes, he did Quimbanda. But he has gone away. The police did not like what he did." From the satisfaction in Valter's tone, he would not be crusading for André's religious liberties.

"It is time for the bus," I said. "I will come back Tuesday night to talk with Tupinamba."

"You will stay here overnight," Valter said.

"No, at the hotel in town."

We wrangled agreeably for a few minutes. Valter always claimed my staying would displace no one, but the times I had spent the night there his three youngest children had been routed out to empty a double bed for me. I argued that any family with thirteen people under its roof didn't need a boarder.

The truth was less self-sacrificing. On my way to Valter's terreiro that morning, the cashier in the café near the bus stop had greeted me with an unprecedented exuberance. When would I be returning? she asked. And where would I be staying?

"The hotel is very noisy," she volunteered. "I live alone. It is more tranquil."

The girl herself was sallow and small-eyed, with a span best measured in ax handles. But I had been going to her café many times without getting so much as a good day. I reckoned that if Luzia's soaps and powders were producing this powerful effect, I could not afford to waste a single night under Valter's chaste roof.

TWO WEEKS HAD PASSED since the conclusion of my work with Nelson, and as yet I hadn't felt the stirrings of a spirit. I was debating whether to go down to the baixa and tax him with the failure when SeSe knocked at my door.

He had put on a clean white shirt and he twisted the brim of a plastic hat with a crown as high as a helmet's. "I was passing by," he said guiltily, "and I thought, Why not go and have a bate-papo with the American senhor."

"Seat yourself. Would you like batida?"

In one quick move, he nodded and shook his head. I poured out two stubby fingers and handed the glass to him where he had settled on the edge of the bed. He drank the liquor down in the style of Cosminho. "More?" I asked.

SeSe smiled bashfully and made the same contradictory head gesture. I poured more.

He drank and handed back the glass.

I drew up a chair and waited. We smiled at each other. Thirty cruzeiros, I was thinking. Maximum.

SeSe, as I was to learn, was thinking sixty.

"Senhor," he said at last, "you are not angry with me?"

"Angry? Why should I be?"

"You remember, senhor, the night of your sacrifice to Iemanjá? It was I who took it to sea and I who returned the next week to the same spot."

"I remember."

"You did not wish to pay me a little something? To pay me what Senhor Nelson promised you would pay?"

"I gave the money to Nelson," I said. "Did he not pay you?"

It may have been his mustache, which had grown an odd sandy color on his swarthy skin until it looked like an exterior row of yellow teeth, smirking when his mouth was closed. Or it may have been his excessive servility. Whatever the cause, I trusted SeSe no further than Nelson. But on the off chance that his story was true, I gave over the money he asked.

"There is no reason to tell Nelson of our talk?" SeSe said imploringly. "He has a bad temper. If he knew that I had come here—"

I nodded and shook my head, and saw him out the door.

The next day he was back, more abashed than before, to plead for medicine for his sick daughter. "There must be an epidemic in Camamu," I said.

"Senhor?"

I reached in my pocket. "I hope your daughter is better soon."

On Sunday he came while a quartet of girls from the high school was recording, between helpless giggles, the song "Ironia" by Paulinho da Viola.

"This is not a convenient time," I said.

"I have nothing else to do," SeSe assured me, slipping in and casting admiring looks at the brown calves beneath the short blue skirts. He stood in the corner, his eyes never rising more than three feet off the floor.

The girls left, SeSe stayed. "I need boards for my house," he said. "The rain—"

"How is your daughter?"

"My daughter?" He hesitated, regretful I was sure, that he hadn't tapped that sure vein a little deeper before seeking out this new lode. Too late—he had mentioned the timber. "She is better, thanks to God."

"How much money do you need?"

"One hundred." He gave me a peculiarly seductive smile, as though we weren't talking about a few strips of board but the women he would buy for me.

"Nothing," I said with a sigh.

"Fifty." SeSe winked rapidly, as though he understood my straits and didn't want to shame me any further.

"Nothing." I surprised myself with the aching regret in my voice.

"Nothing?" he said in disbelief.

"Nada." A lovely word, with slumberous despair in each of its syllables.

"Nada?"

When he left, we were both shaking our heads and only mouthing the word. An hour later, Duba ran up the stairs. "Jacks!"

Duba was sure I would be astounded to see him. Evidently I had conveyed my second thoughts about failing Ailton for every Monday morning, looking distraught, Duba told me that he was off to a farm and wouldn't be back to Camamu for at least a year. The first few times the story had been good for a modest going-away present. But every weekend since then he had been bounding to my door, expecting a welcome worthy of a year away.

"I have just seen Senhor Nelson in the baixa and he told me to tell the gringo—to tell Jacks—to come to his house right away. It is urgent!"

Four months in Camamu had redefined that word for me, and I got to Nelson's the next afternoon at three o'clock. His wife received me in the tender manner she usually reserved for her plaster saints. "Come in! Come in! He will be so glad you are here."

Nelson leapt from his bedroom and pumped my hand. "That fisherman," he said immediately. "He has been bothering you?"

"He came by a couple of times."

"And told lies about me?"

I gave Nelson an edited account of our transactions.

"Liar!" Nelson said. "Thief and liar! I will fix him! He will not get away with this!" He ground his thumb into the palm of his other hand as though he were tightening a screw. "He will be sorry! Oh, yes! He will regret the day!"

I felt a nasty thrill at the prospect of Exú's revenge. "What will you do?"

"He will never come to another Candomblé of mine," Nelson announced awesomely. "He will never be permitted in this house. And you must have nothing more to do with him. Remember that!"

"I will remember. While I am here, senhor, I wondered whether you would repeat into my recorder one song from that last part of my work. It is the one that ends with the line about the evil hen. I am afraid I may be mistranslating it. Do you know the one?"

Nelson looked blank. I spoke the phrase as I had understood it. " 'Evil hen—ma galinha—roosting on the holy cross.' Do you recognize it?"

Nelson's wrath against SeSe had worked up his bile and left his voice rasping and black. "You sing it," he said, pointing at his wife.

My microphone also pointing in her direction, she dropped her eyes and rubbed her hands. After a few false starts, she sang:

"Green plague, O my Jesus,

"Green plague, O my Jesus!

"Magdalena seated at the bottom of the Cross."

"Oh," I said, "Magdalena. Thank you."

"Claro!" Nelson answered grandly.

"One thing more: I was wondering when I might expect to receive a spirit."

Nelson looked to his wife; it was the question they had anticipated. "Monday," he said. "Come back Monday at three o'clock."

"I will be here."

"Senhor," Nelson's wife said at the door, "he was glad to see you today. It has been a long time and we did not know what lies the fisherman might have spoken about us."

FOR THE FIRST TIME SINCE I ARRIVED IN BAHIA, Valter invited me to enter the abasé and watch as he received his spirit. Kneeling before the altar, he rattled off a lengthy ritual prayer as fast as a child reciting in class. When he had finished, he picked up a string of chalky white beads and held them so that the candlelight hit their surface and made the facets glitter.

He clasped his hands and stared at the beads. Slowly he set them swinging. I looked at my watch.

Two minutes and forty seconds later, with a terrible wrenching cry, Valter's body fell forward in a spasm across the altar. Deoclides stepped up, removed Valter's bifocals, and lifted the beads out of his hand.

A voice from Valter's crumpled body laughed gravely, "E-yuh, e-yuh, e-yuh." The spirit rose and put out its hand. "How are you, my son?" We gave the three-part clasp.

Deoclides fell face down on the floor. He moved his body first to one side, then the other, until the spirit lifted him up and embraced him. I started my tape recorder and sat forward on the low stool.

Before he had spoken a few sentences, I recognized Tupinamba. He and Rei da Matinha, the Indians, pronounced each syllable with an elaborate distinctness. Despite his hollow rhetorical tones, Ogum spoke more naturally.

"I have come to ask for a work, senhor," I said. "I also have questions I would like to ask."

"We expected you tonight," Tupinamba said. "Several of the orixás are gathered here with me while I speak with you. Oxóssi is here—he is the master of your head, although as yet he is not reaching you. Besides, Oxóssi is not the kind who helps men to get on well in life. Mostly, Oxóssi likes to drink.

"But Iemanjá has come, along with some caboclos you do not know."

"Graças a Deus," I said, to all.

"Before we get to your questions, my son, there are matters the orixás desired that I explain to you.

"First, you make a mistake going to see a man who promises that you will receive the spirit of Oxalá. Such a man must be motivated only by money. The spirits remember that it was for thirty pieces of silver that Oxalá was delivered over to his enemies. They detest money and never ask for it. If a man demands payment for his works, from that alone you may be sure that he does not have genuine contact with the spirits.

"There is something more: you are going from Candomblé to Umbanda seeking works—for health, for assistance, for love. It is only confusing to the spirits, my son, these requests from so many different sources.

"I do not know which caboclo informed you that you must not eat meat for a period of time after a work. But that is a fallacy. The eating of meat has nothing to do with whether or not a body is closed to evil influence and open to receive spiritual benefit."

Tupinamba paused for a shallow gulp of breath. For a moment he sat recovering with his eyes closed.

"We would recommend this: do one complete work to bring yourself all the blessings of the spirits. Content yourself with that work alone. If properly offered, the one work will do more for you than all these fragments."

"Sim, senhor."

"We can return to that subject," Tupinamba said. "I am ready to answer your questions."

The machine squealed as the tape ended. Tupinamba fell back against his chair and waited while I snapped open the compartment and reversed the reel.

When I was ready, Deoclides touched his wrist and Tupinamba opened his eyes. It had been less like sleep than as though the spirit's consciousness had sunk below the surface of Valter's mobile brown face.

I had written out my questions in Portuguese, looking up any unfamiliar words, correcting the grammar. But the first one seemed frivolous, given the aura of pomp that surrounded Tupinamba. I skipped down my list.

"What must a man do, how should he conduct his life, to be pleasing to the spirits?"

"To the spirits," Tupinamba replied in measured tones, "the most important quality is sincerity. Sincerity and faith. The spirits love a man who is honest, who keeps on with honest work, who holds his mind in a kind of prayer to the Almighty. For such a man, the spirits respond by giving him the strength to accomplish good work.

"If it is your aim to progress in the spiritual life, you must tell only the truth. But I tell you this, my son, today one should not live with both eyes open. Open the one to goodness, but close the other. For besides the astral spirits, there are evil spirits who live only in the material world, attracting only evilness. Close one eye to such spirits.

"I am quite aware that this is being recorded and that later you may

225

listen to my words elsewhere, either alone in quiet or with one or two other men. But even if you were to let two thousand people hear what I say, I would speak the same and always repeat the same true words: sincerity and faith."

The Indian chieftain paused. "That was your first question," he said with a mirthless "E-yuh." "I am ready for your second."

"I would like a description of the universe that the spirits inhabit."

"The spirits who live in this universe, to help people down here, are spirits who have not yet gathered unto themselves sufficient light to move beyond. They are not yet completely purified.

"Through the pai do santo, they come to do good, acquiring more light and eventually reaching the stage that will allow them to pass to another realm.

"That was number two," said Tupinamba, apparently pleased with his answer. "Three."

"Perhaps your last answer fits this, too." This had been my first question, the one that made Deoclides uneasy. "But I will ask anyway: Why do the spirits help men? Why do they bother?"

"What motive?" the spirit asked. "Is that your question?"

"Yes, why?"

"God understands that some men are good, that they are worthwhile. He cannot enter into their bodies himself but he sends his spirits to help them. The first spirit who comes into a man and encounters there both sincerity and honesty will bring the others.

"There are men who do bad things, spiritually as well as physically. They do not act from the heart but because an evil spirit has taken hold of them. These men, when they are inhabited by bad spirits, must fight them. Some of these spirits come directly from the devil.

"But those who receive good spirits may suffer as well. Everything that Jesus suffered on earth, the beatings and the crucifixion, everything that was imposed on him simply because he was a gifted man trying to bring goodness to everyone, all of those trials and sufferings may be visited on those who receive good spirits. Because they are following the same path through the same world.

"Question four," the spirit demanded, as though he were shooting clay pigeons.

226

"If the United States accepted the spirits, what difference would Umbanda make in American life?"

"Men who live a materialistic life can never be happy," Tupinamba said. "But to live a life of the spirit, it is necessary to have help, the help of our celestial Father, to purify the mind and the body.

"Later, man will be only spirit, as Ogum is, as I am. We are not afraid to go anywhere, to work wherever we are needed. Here or with the African tribes—wherever Umbanda is practiced.

"I have reached a level where I do not need clothes. I do not eat. I do not drink. I can now devote myself to the spirituality of others.

"All nations need to ask the spirits to bring them a better life, to make contact again with their guardians and their protecting spirits. On this planet of earth, all men must learn to live with the spirits. Question five!"

"Those were questions enough for the patience of the senhor," I said. "Perhaps we could talk about my work."

"I know the work you want, my son. It presents no problem. You can start when you wish and be confirmed on the first day of the new year."

That morning in my room I had discovered teeth marks on my bar of soap. By January, I would be as desperate as the rats for a change from rice and beans.

"I doubt I can remain that long, senhor. I have already been in this forest a long time."

"Look, my son, we know that you have parents but that you do not have a wife. It is true that you have had a lady friend for some years and that she has had no news and she is worried about you. The date when you were supposed to return has passed and you did not come back. So naturally she is troubled."

I was sorry to hear Tupinamba sounding like the Norwegian woman with loop earrings who used to read the future for my mother at "The Leaves" on Nicollet Avenue. What he said was true enough, and all known to Valter from our Sunday morning talks. But to pass the evenings in Camamu, I wrote often and no one at home gave signs of worrying.

"I had in mind a shorter work," I said, "only the one to open roads. The work for well-being and happiness."

"Such a work exists," Tupinamba allowed. "It is not a simple one. This man"—he inclined his head toward Deoclides—"can supply you with a list of the materials you will require. The work you request is in three parts."

"Three?" Nelson had left me wary of tripartite works.

"The first whenever you wish," Tupinamba said. "Nine days later, the second. Five days after that, the third."

"Fourteen days?" I thought of Luzia condensing her work to a single day, and I was sure that, had I asked, Nelson would have performed three impossible works before breakfast.

But counting out the days, Deoclides made a few economies. "If you start next Friday," he said, "then nine days later is the following Saturday, and five days after that would be Wednesday, the nineteenth of September."

As we were calculating on our fingers, Tupinamba had receded. Deoclides saw the signs of his fading, and he sprang up and poured a glass of water from an earthenware jug.

The body in the chair was rocking and trembling. After the first convulsions, the voice had become feminine and cajoling, and I thought it was addressing Deoclides. But he ignored it and stood with the water ready in his hand. At the next jolt, the soft voice halted. The body gave itself to a prolonged shaking.

Gasping, Valter opened his eyes and swallowed the water to stifle his moans. "Oh, God," he whispered, like a man who had been kicked in the belly.

"It is terrible," I said.

Deoclides laughed and poured out more water. "We are used to it."

When Valter recovered, Deoclides left the abasé to compile the list of supplies for my first work. While we waited, I played Valter a section of Tupinamba's advice to me.

"You remember none of that?"

"Nothing," he said ruefully, as though his lapse of memory were a shortcoming.

We listened to Tupinamba describing the way the spirits gathered more light unto themselves. "You are taking that tape back to your country?" Valter asked.

When I said I was, he started to say something, then stopped and shook his head. Since he couldn't explain what we were hearing, he seemed to wonder what the materialists of Estados Unidos would be likely to think.

Deoclides returned with the list and I glanced through it. Most items —the candles, the metros of cloth—would be easy to find. Then there was the chicken. "I suppose I can buy a chicken in town," I said doubtfully. "Live, I suppose?. It must be alive?"

"Vivo," they agreed together.

THE STATE PROSECUTOR WAS STILL INTERESTING HIMSELF in my activities but since he was often called away from Camamu, the surveillance had become sporadic. One night I saw him posted in front of the hotel, keeping track of who went in my door. A week later, he followed me into the post office and watched as the postman counted out letters into my hand.

The prosecutor was turning his head almost upside down to read a return address, and I grinned and held the envelope out to him. He may have blushed but he looked.

That night, a friend who had witnessed this performance assured me that I had improved myself in the opinion of the law. "You did not clutch the letters to your body," he said. "You held them out for anyone to see."

"If I were a secret agent, my letters would be in code."

"Just the same, I talked with the prosecutor afterward. For the first time since he came here, he did not ask more questions about you."

"He is sure I am not a spy?"

"He is less sure that you are one."

"If he is not suspicious anymore, then I can finally say to you what I have been waiting to ask: how much money do you want in return for selling me all of the secrets of Camamu?"

"Oh, do not say that," my friend whispered. "Please do not."

I HOPED TO USE THE PAYING of another month's rent as the occasion to set things right with Zeca. I found him in the light company's office, seated behind a pile of bills.

"Sit, sit," he said uncertainly. "I thought you were angry with me."

"Did I not wave the other day when I saw you driving a car?"

"Yes, I was driving." He puffed out his chest and smiled at the memory. "But that was not my car. I was only driving it for a friend."

"It is time," I said, "to pay the rent again."

His eyes darted around the room. "There is one thing," he said unwillingly. "My family does not like the boy Duba. They do not like having him visit you."

"Duba has gone to a farm." Or, at least, one Sunday had passed without our usual reunion.

"But while he was here, he said many bad and false things about my delay in having your stairs repaired. They are good now?"

"They are good. Now."

The previous week, a downcast white boy, coerced somehow into the job, had arrived and fashioned within an hour a set of steps strong enough for tap dancing.

"Duba spoke very badly against my family. He is not a boy you should associate with."

As Zeca knew very well, Duba had only sided with me, repeating what he had heard me saying. But the town's tradition demanded there be a sacrifice. "He has gone to work on a farm," I said again.

"But if he should return—" Zeca paused.

I gave in and laid the memory of the loyal boy across the altar of reconstructed steps. "I do not expect to be seeing Duba anymore," I said.

I HANDED BACK TO DONA LUZIA her brown bottle and empty vial. "I have done everything Ogum Beira Mar told me," I said. "But I would like to know about the ingredients."

"The soap was of Ogum," Luzia said. Disappearing behind her oil-cloth curtain, she came back with a commercially bottled pink soap with OGUM in block letters on the label.

She said, "There are other soaps for mães do santo who receive Iemanjá, Oxóssi, Cosme, and Damião."

"And the gray powder?"

"That was a powdered chalk, to close the body to evil." She ran her hands down her thighs as though she were sealing the pores.

"What became of the young woman who was so sick? Do you remember? Her husband was very worried. You thought she had been taken by a bad spirit."

"She is better," Luzia said. "He took her to the infirmary at Firestone and she has improved very much."

"You never did see her?"

"No," said Luzia, without rancor. "Her husband did not understand about the spirits."

STANEILL PULLED HIS CAR IN FRONT of the café in Ituberá where I had been waiting. "You have the frango?" I asked.

He answered by dragging up from the floorboard a fat red rooster. It gave a desultory flap and nestled in his arms.

"I will be right back. I have the rest of the sacrifice in my room."

The Hotel Santo André did not light its stairs. I felt my way to the room, where the purchases were laid out on the floor next to a chamber-pot.

Nearly everything on Deoclides's list had been cheap and simple to find. From the clerks in Camamu I had gotten none of the sidelong looks Nelson predicted if I did my own shopping. Showing the list, I folded over the heading Deoclides had written—"For the First Work." But when a man in Brazil bought white candles, seven cigars, and five scraps of colored cloth, his intention stood revealed.

Since stores sold dendê oil only by the liter, I had cadged a small bottle from Dona Bela at the hotel, and I stored the packet of corn in my typewriter case to keep the rats from getting it before the spirits did. For those first items I had spent less than two dollars—the cigars were a penny and a half each, the remnants of cloth six cents apiece.

But four metros of white bramante, a white fabric as heavy as linen, came to eight dollars plus another three dollars for the rooster Staneill got.

A young mulatto with dashing sideburns and square white teeth, Staneill had attended high school in Camamu before migrating the eighteen miles north to Ituberá. As we drove up the hill to Valter's, he said, "I have found another pai do santo for you. José Napolean is his name. He is not so famous as Valter but people say his works are very strong. Also, if you want to go to Itabuna, there are three pais do santo there."

"What about in Ipiaú?"

"I do not know. I could ask for you."

"We will see."

We drove past the cemetery, down among the wild thicket, across the narrow bridge that led to the terreiro. I was braced against the right-hand door as far as I could get from the trussed-up bird nesting at the base of the gearshift. Even so, he stretched his neck and slipped his head trustingly under my pants cuff.

In front of Valter's house, a few women in long white skirts were enjoying the night air. "You did not see Deoclides on the road?" Valter asked us. "No? We will wait a little longer for him."

"I found everything on the list," I said. "But this: 'one bottle of malaso.' "

"No," Valter corrected me, "that word is malafo. It is the same as cachaça." He sent one of his sons running down the hill with one cruzeiro, sixteen cents for a bottle of liquor.

"Deoclides should have written cachaça," Valter said. "It is enough that you must learn one new word for each thing in Umbanda without having to learn two or three."

Inside, Valter's son, Ersival, was waiting for me eagerly. Two weeks before, he had asked me to find him a job in Rio and I had sent letters to my friends there, asking about his prospects.

"Only one answer today," I said, "and that one not very encouraging."

I had brought the letter, though it was written in English, and I showed him the paragraph that said the Burroughs Corporation was hiring only young men who had completed high school and then only after a special test that eighty percent of the applicants failed.

"Burroughs," Ersival said, pronouncing the name as though it meant mules.

"They manufacture and install computers." At his blank expression, I reached for my dictionary and found the Portuguese word. "You know, computadors. Computadors. You know."

"No, senhor."

"They are machines for storing facts. You are a mechanic. It would be a good field to learn. But I am still waiting to hear from my other friends."

The boy looked as doubtful as I felt. And Elza, his twenty-year-old sister, wanted to go to Rio, too, though she refused to consider work as a maid and as the eldest girl in the house had never done anything else.

By nine o'clock Valter gave up on Deoclides and, Ersival leading the way with the kerosene lamp, we crossed the road to the terreiro. The women came after, gathering up their full skirts for the climb to the door.

In the shrine room, Valter put on a priestly green outfit over his white shirt and brown trousers. With Deoclides absent, Valter was left a man shy and he pressed Ersival to serve in his aide's place. Because he wasn't a filho do santo, the boy had to be coached often, and throughout the ceremony I caught him smiling apologetically at one or the other of his sisters.

At a signal from Valter, we slipped off our shoes or sandals and passed through the men's roncó into a hidden court. At last, O Templo.

It turned out to be a very ordinary-looking patio, an enclosure surrounded by high fencing and studded with palms and fronds. Rough flagstone had been embedded in the earth, except at the center where a thick tree arose, its trunk dividing the oblong space into two separate bowers.

Valter led me to the one at the rear. There a white paper had been spread across the stones. Without speaking, he showed me how to stand at an angle to the paper and squat without letting my stocking feet touch it.

Hunched over, legs extending onto the stone, hands on my knees, I waited while Ersival and the women each lighted white candles and placed them around the outline of my body. When the last was in place, Valter spoke directly to the tree trunk:

"Let us elevate our thoughts to our celestial Father and make this sacrifice for Jack, a man of progress. A man of peace. A spiritualist. A human being.

"For you to permit him to come to you, I ask permission to make this work with your assistance."

Valter stared hard at the flickering candle until he stumbled backward. Ogum of the Seven Swords caught the body with a loud "E-yuh!" He straightened up inside the human frame and returned to the tree.

"Huh! huh! huh! Praise be our Savior Jesus Christ," Ogum said.

In an African dialect, Ogum sang chants to Xangô, to Oxalá, and to a spirit called Sindo. Each taking a cigar, he and the six children of the saint passed them three times over the length of my body and shook loose the accumulated bad currents into the glass of water at my feet.

Ogum draped black, purple, and red cloths over my head and shoulders. He unwound a spool of thick white thread across my forehead so that loops hung over my eyes like bars of a cage. The yellow band of material he laid across my feet, the white one across my knees in a way that covered my hands as well.

A few days before, I had visited Maria for my work to have the spirits assist me with my book. Her ritual also involved cloths, grain, candles, and as I waited it out patiently, I felt Tupinamba had been right: I was overdoing my demands on the spirits.

From the waist down, my body had gone numb, but whenever I shifted on my haunches, the edges of flagstone cut my legs. Behind me, Ogum had started on the bowls of meal, passing them down my spine.

The cigars and the maize went into a large brown sack placed just behind the glass where my bad energies had been grounded. Ogum removed the scarves from my head, feet, and hands. Holding each in front of my eyes, he tore it in half and dropped those pieces into the sack.

Ogum of the Seven Swords now pulled on the joints of my fingers as Ogum Beira Mar had done at Luzia's. He also pulled on each toe, repeating, "Success, happiness, riches, health."

Ogum measured out a cup of cachaça into a white bowl and, scooping it up with his hands, laid his dripping fingers liberally over my hair and again down the length of my body. When he was done, I was both damper and more fragrant than after the moist leaves at Luzia's.

Ogum gestured for me to rise. The women had opened out the four metros of white linen to serve as a canopy over my head. They were all standing on their toes and stretching their arms high. Even so, my head poked into the cloth.

I was glad to be on my feet and off the rough stones. Ogum approached with my red rooster in his hands, the bird bucking and screeching as though it had a presentiment.

Standing at my side, Ogum raised the cock to the top of my head and then, clamping the wings firmly to its body, he rubbed it down my face, along my shoulders, over my chest, waist, crotch, thighs. Three times the angry red feathers batted at me.

Like a parachute collapsing, the canopy was dropped. I was enshrouded from head to foot in white cloth and tugged and prodded back over the stones and up the stairs to the abasé. A stool was nudged against the backs of my legs. Still enmired in the bunting, I sat.

Through the cloth I saw only the diffused glow of a single candle. From instinct rather than any breathing or scuffling, I gathered that someone had been delegated to watch over me.

From the secret garden came singing. I heard the phrase "in the crossroads." The chorus gradually grew louder as Ogum and his children came back inside.

Reaching under the white coverlet, the spirit unbuttoned my shirt and drew with chalk crosses on my breastbone and the nape of my neck. Meticulously his fingers worked the shirt buttons back through their holes. He poked through his hand again and made the sign of the cross

235

with a liquid that smelled like bay rum.

At a tap on my back, I stood again. The linen was drawn off me. Ogum handed it to the women and waved them away. The two of us were left alone before the shrine.

"You have completed the first of the three nights of your work," Ogum said. "For five days I would ask that you drink no cachaça. Can you comply with that request?"

I took cachaça to mean all liquor, wine, and beer. "I can."

Valter's wife tapped at the door and crept inside. Ogum gave a short "E-yuh" in greeting and waited for her to speak. "There is a man here who wants to see you."

"Let him enter," Ogum said.

Staneill came in, subdued and respectful, and kept his back to me. "I have a problem with my job. I would like to consult with the senhor about it," he said nervously.

"Tonight I am engaged on this one work only," Ogum replied. "We also have nights of obligation that are open to all."

Staneill backed out of the abasé. To me, Ogum said, "After the bathing, you will be informed about the conditions of the second part of your work."

I retired. It was a few minutes before Valter tottered from the abasé. Even in the shadowy light, he looked flayed from fatigue.

"Senhor," I said, "receiving is too hard on you."

"It leaves me very nervous," Valter said, smiling to show that he wasn't complaining. "Sometimes, after a work I cannot get to sleep at all."

I recognized that sort of fretful exhilaration. Finishing a novel, I often lay awake until dawn, too tired to work, too aroused to sleep. It felt as though more nervous current was flooding my system than I could absorb, and the only answer I'd found was to let the energy exhaust me until by seven or eight in the morning I would sleep for an hour.

I said, "What will happen to the sack that Ogum filled with cloth and cigars and meal?"

"It has already been thrown into the street."

"At a special place?"

236

"No, it may be left anywhere."

"And the cock? Was his gullet slit?"

"The ceremonies vary," Valter explained. "This first night has been a cleansing to propitiate Exú. Sometimes the cock is then killed and its body is thrown into the street with the sack. But this was also the beginning of a more significant work. In such cases, it is better that the cock go free."

"What happens to it?"

Valter shrugged. "It is free."

"Is it not likely that one of your neighbors will capture it and have it for dinner?"

Valter laughed his own easy way, not in the challenging "E-yuh" of Ogum.

He said, "They know that if they should eat the frango, all of the accumulated bad feeling that had been removed from your body would pass into their own. Up here, when people see a strange bird, they know it is from a sacrifice and they leave it entirely alone."

"And the long white linen cloth? It is always four metros?"

"It varies with the size of the person. With our people, three metros are usually enough."

"It went into the sack with the rest?"

"No," Valter said, "not the bramante. That is put aside and saved for confirmation."

"Each prospective filho do santo goes through this same ceremony?" Valter gave me a look I didn't understand. I went on, "That means that if I were to become a filho, on the first of January the terreiro would use this same linen for my confirmation?"

"Certo," Valter said. "These cleansings and prayers you have begun are the highest works of Umbanda."

"But it is not my choice. The spirits must decide whether I will receive or not."

"It is their decision," Valter agreed.

Staneill was waiting for me in the jeep. He seemed apprehensive about whether I resented his infringing on my time with the spirit. As we rattled across the planks of the footbridge, he said tentatively, "Senhor Valter is a very fine person, is he not?"

"I think he is."

Reassured I wasn't angry, he relaxed. "I came back while they were wrapping you in the sheet. There is a crack in the shutter. I could see you. You looked—" The rumbling laugh shook his whole body.

"Did you watch Ogum release the chicken?"

He nodded. "After they wiped you all over with him"—Staneill's laughter was getting dangerous, the headlights of the jeep were darting around the narrow road—"and they let him loose over the wall of that garden.

"But the best was you with that white cloth hanging down, and them leading you like—" He dropped the wheel to stick out his hands and jerk his head like a doddering old man. Our right-hand tires bumped along in a low ditch.

"I am sure it was all very comical. Yet you are going back?"

"Yes," said Staneill. "Yes!"

SACKS OF MAIL ARRIVED IN CAMAMU EACH NOON but they often lay unopened for two or three days while the postman struggled with registering outgoing letters or traded gossip in the street.

That explained why the letter he handed to me on Monday afternoon, although it came only a distance of ninety miles, had been postmarked a full week earlier.

The envelope was edged with yellow and green stripes, but the letter inside had been written on vivid pink paper. It contained a warm invitation from the object of my work with Luzia for me to come calling in the town of Ipiaú. As it happened, the letter had been mailed on the same day that I completed my baths with Ogum's magic soap.

SO IT WAS IN A MOOD SOFTENED AND CREDULOUS that I strolled down the path later that afternoon to my appointment with Nelson and

238

whatever spirit he might induce to join us.

Midway down the hill, four or five urubus were contending on a garbage heap with a couple of tame turkeys. The birds picked the green rims of cacau and clawed over crumpled cigarette packs for a taste of rotted banana.

I said, "Urubus!"

At the sound of their name, the big birds jumped apart guiltily and spread their wings for the nearest tree.

Farther down the path, I heard a rustling in the grass which sounded like wind or children playing. But a small boy who had been lagging behind on the path suddenly rushed forward and gave me a push on the legs.

"Cobra!" he whispered.

Side by side we ran at least ten yards before we looked back. There was nothing on the trail. Still, I chose to take the boy's warning as one more good omen. By the time I slipped into the chair next to Nelson at his table, his task for the day was already half done.

Then, within no more than a minute, he undid the advantages I had handed him. "You have been to Valença?" he demanded accusingly.

"Not since Dona Mira's Candomblé."

"Mira! I know about Mira!"

He barked out a story about Mira being so negligent that she once let the sacrificial meat stand for three days and then served it cold to her followers.

"Do you like cold pork?" he asked suspiciously, as though I hied to Valença in pursuit of it.

"No."

"No one does," Nelson said. "No one likes cold pork."

That story put him in mind of another. I heard for ten minutes how a man in Salvador once played Nelson false and the price he had paid.

"Three days later, he lost his job at Petrobras," Nelson concluded grimly.

"That reminds me," I said. "Do you remember the man from Nazaré who wanted a work done against his supervisor?"

"I remember."

"Did you hear more from him?"

"He was here today!" To his wife in the kitchen, Nelson called, "What day is today?"

"Segunda-feira."

"Monday! Today! He said that my work had succeeded completely. The other man is finished."

"Not dead?"

"Not dead. But—" Nelson tapped his own black temple.

"Crazy?"

He nodded. "Doido."

"What was the supervisor's name? João, I remember. But his second name?" I tried to sound as though I were making conversation but Nelson screwed up his eye at me.

"It was not important that I know. The spirits knew him."

"Since my own work," I said, "I have waited several weeks to receive a spirit, but so far—"

Nelson cut me off with a discourse on faith, spiritual force, how important they were to the receiving of spirits.

"But as I remember," I interrupted him, "the work you did for me was aimed at increasing my spiritual force to the point that I would be able to receive."

"Certo! But what about the drums and music? There must be drums and music!"

"I did not know."

"Sim." A prolonged sighing "yes" that said the whole world knew that much.

"Could we have the drums—?"

"Today? Claro!"

We rose together for the bedroom. At the dressing table I pulled a stool close to the flame of a candle. Nelson rolled out his largest drum from a corner and tapped the skin indifferently.

As I have said, Nelson's voice had its own raw power, but his rapping on the drumhead was ignominious; the high school boys had wrung more music out of my straw mattress. Nelson's wife sat beside him on the bed adding her faint amens.

240

I stared at the flame but my eyes strayed to the gawky figure of São Lorenzo. He held two books to his breast in the way twenty-three years ago girls had carried algebras and histories through the halls of Washburn High School. Beside me, Nelson was knocking out a mélange of chants from earlier Candomblés.

Whenever I left off staring at Lorenzo, the corner of my eye fastened on Nelson's hands, the aimless way they dropped, picked themselves up, fell again on the drumskin and never made more than a toneless thud.

All at once, a light bulb overhead burst on the room like an early sun. It grew brighter and brighter until I could see the layer of dust over the statues on the shrine. Its power went on growing, so bright after a minute that I was squinting in the windowless room.

But I knew the reason for this light, and it was neither a revelation nor a trick by Nelson and his wife. The same sudden illumination sometimes hit my own room after the power had failed throughout the city for an hour or two. Electricians found the problem eventually, and as they repaired the wiring, the level of current fluctuated, greater for a few moments. Up and back, the filament went from a dying ember to a light as white as a plutonium explosion. Now at Nelson's shrine the light diminished and finally went off altogether. I went back to watching the candle.

We had been working there for twenty minutes when Nelson's hands bounced off the drum a final time. Ritually he said, "Thanks to God."

"I did not receive," I said, nothing accusatory in the way I said it.

"Today, no!" Nelson said. "Not today! You must come back in one week."

I laid three bills beside the candle. "Segunda-feira, three o'clock again?"

"Certo!"

"And I will—?"

"You will receive a spirit!"

At the bottom of my suitcase, along with a bathing suit gray with mold, I found the book on self-hypnosis I had brought from Los Angeles but never read.

Before the next session, I would study the book. Meantime, on my table the pink letter was waiting for an answer.

I wouldn't send one, at least not now. Possibly later from Rio or Los Angeles. The charm of the affair had rested entirely in the logistical challenge it posed to the spirits. The bedding itself was not worth four hours of rough roads.

Yet I was grateful. If ever again I had dealings with Ogum of the Seashore, I'd make the next wish less contentious.

AT THE HOTEL, the girls in their morning caucus decided that I was working too hard. Alda was delegated to speak to me. "You go out to these Candomblés and you come back and shut yourself in your room," she said, placing a bowl of beans by my plate. "You are eating less and less. You have even stopped asking people to your room to use your tape recorder."

I had no rebuttal. She went on gently, "My cousin in Salvador was a law student. He studied all the time. Day, night. He never went out or enjoyed himself. It was always work and more work.

"One day he went insane. Just like that. There was no warning. He was living in a beautiful apartment with paintings and expensive furniture. One day he took a knife and destroyed everything, cut up the paintings, ripped the stuffing from the chairs. It was a terrible thing."

I said, "You have seen my room. If I go crazy, there is not much damage I can do."

"At least stay and have dessert with your coffee," Alda entreated me. "We have marmory tonight."

WE WERE LOITERING DELIBERATELY AT VALTER'S TABLE, none of us impatient to get on with my ritual bathing. My own reason was practical: There was a ripping cold wind outside, and from a word dropped last time I deduced that tonight's washing would be no symbolic ritual but a real scrub, with me naked in the water. For his part, Deoclides had been working in the fields since daybreak and he looked grafted to his chair.

Valter, too, had cause to linger. Once we began, he would have to submit to still another mounting by Ogum. Thinking over the reluctance of the mães and pais do santo to receive their spirits, the way they postponed ceremonies or begged off doing works because of a cold or stomachache, I was struck again by how much they behaved like novelists, concocting similar excuses for the same reason: to avoid throwing themselves into the trance that would let them see their characters and hear them speak. Wasn't it possible that in another place and time, Valter might have done his creating on paper rather than out of his own flesh?

As we sat together, I extended the kinship of Umbandist and writer to the subject of money. In the world's view, any contempt that a poor, scrupulous poet shows for the rich hack must spring from envy, and the world is seldom entirely wrong.

But when an Umbanda chief says, "My gift comes from God, and I have no right to seek money from it," even the rationalist writer would agree that what he has been given to write was equally a gift, that his vision was never earned or deserved but was a little less compromised the nearer he could present it to the pure state in which it first appeared to him.

When I listened again, I heard Valter detaining us now with the sort of gossip that probably brightens any minister's household. He was telling of a neighbor—a woman his entire family knew—who had come to him lately with an ailment. When Valter recommended that she see a medical specialist in Salvador, the woman had protested: "O senhor, I am so tired. So tired. Cure me here! Cure me here!"

To convey the woman's complacent feline sighs, Valter's voice shot up a register, to those upper reaches just short of falsetto that Iemanjá used whenever she visited him. Doing their homework around the rim of the table, Valter's children cheered loudly and he repeated, "O senhor, cure me here!"

The talk turned to reports out of Salvador that a man aged one hundred and twenty had taken a young bride. Valter's wife was treading her sewing machine in the corner but the news caused her to turn on her stool. "My grandmother lived to be a hundred and thirty-six," she said.

"Yes," Valter sneered. "But she had to go around like this."

He put his fist to his forehead, giving us a bent-over woman who moved like a tripod on her two legs and the cane that grew out of her nose. Again the children cackled with delight.

It was after nine o'clock when Valter rose and stretched. "Vamos."

He carried a white tablecloth and a basin. Deoclides brought candles. We crossed the path and unlocked the terreiro.

"You can take off your shoes and stockings here," Deoclides said. "Then put your feet up on a bench until we go. The floor is very cold."

"The washing is held in O Templo?" I asked. He had hurried away to help Valter and didn't hear me.

When I joined them in my bare feet, they were pouring liquid into a tin can from an old yellow bottle. "Remember," Valter was saying, "three times with this." From a second bottle he spilled only a few dark drops into the mixture.

Valter held up the white cloth and pointed out the symbols embroidered in red at the four corners. All were five-pointed stars, two with an arrow depending from the bottom, two others with a triangle.

"This is a cloak of purity," Valter said. "I am now entrusting it to the filho do santo."

Deoclides folded the cloth over his arm and took up the basin and tin can. Together we went jogging out of the hall, down the uneven steps and back across the path in the direction of Valter's house. The river wasn't far away, but like any constant noise it had been easy to forget. I hadn't considered that my bathing might take place there. We ran to the bank. Between my toes, the mud was slimy and cold, and every twig and stone nicked my citified soles.

When I stopped to roll up my pants, I reminded myself that as a child I had considered going barefoot a treat. Why this squeamishness now? After all, it was only—I was almost sure—mud.

Deoclides was waiting for me by the bank where a ridge of rock was breaking the current and causing the river to snarl with white foam. The rock he was standing on overhung the water like a pulpit.

Over the rushing noise he shouted, "You can put your clothes there." It was a high black rock where they would be safe from spray.

I shucked off my corduroy pants and unbuttoned the black shirt with four pockets. Reluctantly I pulled a white T-shirt from over my head. At that moment, clouds that had been shrouding the sky parted. Along the dark riverbank there were only the flashing white waves and my body, shining like an icicle.

I stepped off the rock into the turbulent water. "All!" Deoclides shouted, meaning my shorts.

To get them off, I lifted each leg high and tried to pass a wet foot through without soaking the cloth or losing my balance and falling into the current.

When I succeeded I threw them on top of the heap of other clothes. The noise of the water sounded louder when I was naked. I barely heard Deoclides telling me to turn around.

My back to him, I faced the white river and the moon. From over my shoulder he handed me the can. It was full of a liquid that smelled like Nelson's herbal shampoo. "Drink three swallows," he said. I made the gulps rapid and minuscule.

When I finished, Deoclides took the can out of my fingers. The remaining contents he poured over my head.

For months I had been taking cold showers and this should have been just one more. But there may be shocks, as well as pleasures, against which the body never builds an immunity. At the first touch of icy water down my spine, I shuddered, shook. And heard him dipping the can into the river for another load.

At that moment, it crossed my mind that the entire ordeal was a hoax, that no Brazilian or African had ever been forced to stand naked in a rushing stream by moonlight and suffer cold water poured down his back.

Valter had a sardonic humor. I had seen proof of it this very night. Tomorrow around the table, he would be saying, "And then he trembled like this—" and his children would scream until he did the impersonation over again.

The second canful, because I had time to dread it, was larger and colder than the first. It felt like a beer vat being emptied on me. The third was worse yet but bearable because surely it would be the last.

I listened for Deoclides to call me out of the river. What I heard was him drawing another can of water.

Some years before, I had ridden in a jet fighter-bomber in South Vietnam. After the pilot showed me how to strap myself in the navigator's seat, we had taken off, out to ravage a jungle glossier and more appetizing than this forest in Bahia.

We cruised aloft, and then suddenly the pilot put the plane into a dive. I was excited, afraid; but, mostly, stimulated.

He dropped a load of 500-pound bombs from the plane's belly. I was glad: the worst was over. Then he yanked on controls that took us straight up again. Pulling "G"'s they called it, and my eyes rolled to the back of my head. I could taste the blankness and felt as though I were drowning in pure air.

I was going under for the last time when the pilot leveled off and my senses came back in layers. First I could breathe. Then I could hear, and from the front seat I heard the pilot chuckle. I experimented with unloosening my knuckles and tried to smile. I started to take a tentative interest in life around me. It was then that he began the second dive.

Five times that day the jet plunged toward earth. Five times it braked in mid-air to soar aloft. Five strangulations, each one taking me past the wish to die. That instrument of misery had been a B–57 that had been built, as I recalled, at a cost of four million dollars. How astounding to me, shivering in a river at Ituberá, that Deoclides could produce the same effect with a rusty tin can.

Six times he scooped and emptied. I was dead and buried by the time I listened for the sound of the can filling again.

Nothing.

I rubbed my eyes and swiveled my neck. Deoclides was beckoning at me to step up on a narrow ridge of rock below his own platform. When I had scrambled there, he threw the white cloth over my head.

Six cans of water had cleared my head but not dispelled my suspicions. I hiked up the cloth enough to be sure my clothes were still spread out five feet away. The joke would be even better if I were left naked on the bank with my clothes tied in wet knots. Or if they were whisked away entirely, to be cut down later into rompers for the twins.

I did indeed see Deoclides's hand stretch out to the rock and grab my shorts. But he handed them over, then held my elbow while I got them on. Even with the cuffs rolled, the legs to my pants seemed three yards long, and I was lurching and slipping on the rock trying to work my way into them.

Deoclides ran me back to the terreiro as fast as I could manage still veiled. Once up the stairs, I heard, "E-yuh, e-yuh" and knew that Valter had ceded his consciousness to Ogum. Walking backward, the spirit pulled me over the doorsill of the abasé, lifted the cloth off my head, and blew a handful of green powder in my face.

I was trying to clear my throat and brush the green stain from my shirt when Ogum waved me to a chair. "What you have just completed," he said, "is the Banho de Amací. If you have your notebook, I will tell you what went into the three separate bathings you have had.

"First—this is the one you sipped three times—came the herbs: sepo de alho"—garlic—"folias de fuma a costa, dandá de caboclo, Espada de Ogum, and the espadas of four other saints: Oxalá, Santa Barbara, São Jorge, and Cosme and Damião.

"The second bath was with Sangue de Oiá, sometimes called sal grosso. The third was with Sangue de Pagé, or blood of the chief of the tribe. Those ingredients came from the bottles you saw."

Ogum was speaking quickly with no catches of breath. "The cleansing is always done in a river," he continued, "never a lake or an ocean. A filho do santo bathes the men, a filha do santo the women.

"To the spirits, this separation is not important. The saints do not concern themselves with matters of that sort. But the caboclos seem to believe that it will cause disagreeable talk among the townspeople if a man is allowed to wash the women. So that rule is observed. It has no religious significance.

"The powder I blew at you is called Pemba de Oxalá and it helps your protecting spirit to respond to you. This ceremony always precedes the second work and, like it, is dedicated to Iemanjá. Do you have questions?"

"The senhor is sure that every candidate to be filho or filha must go through this bathing?"

"E-yuh, e-yuh. You found the water cold?"

"Except that I have every confidence in Deoclides, I might have thought it was a joke on me."

"E-yuh, e-yuh," Ogum laughed mirthlessly.

STANEILL HAD UNDERTAKEN TO FIND THE ROOSTER and the dove for the second of Valter's works. I had barely booked my small dirty cell at the hotel in Ituberá when he was at my door, a bird under each arm.

He flung them down on the cement floor, where they huddled forlorn. One bird was white, one was brown. Neither was a dove.

"Staneill, where is the pomba?"

"There," he said, pointing to the darker bird.

"Staneill," I said, "a chicken is not a dove."

"É pomba!" he cried with conviction. "It is a dove!"

We were staring at the sheaf of soiled feathers when a fellow boarder passed in the hallway. I beckoned him over. "Would you call that a pomba?"

"No," the man said, "it is a chicken."

Staneill looked around as though he had landed on a foreign shore. "Not a pomba?" he demanded of the other man.

"A pomba is smaller," the man said. "A different bird altogether."

"Oh!" Staneill exclaimed. "A pomba!" He turned to me. "You did not want two chickens! You wanted a chicken and a pomba!"

"It is all right," I said. "Now I have the white rooster for the final work next Wednesday. All we must do now is find a dove for tonight."

But there were no doves to be found. A woman who bred them said that hers had retired for the night and they nested out of reach. We drove to other suppliers; they were temporarily out of stock.

The whole shopping trip this time had been tedious and unsatisfactory, though the list was half the length of the first. A bottle of white Martini wine was no problem, nor were the white maize or the single glass cup. But none of the three shops in Camamu carried bees' honey and I had no luck in Ituberá, either. Finally, a child who was tending the bar across from the hotel offered me fifteen small plastic packets of mel and I took them.

The instructions had specified a bottle, but I was trusting that the spirits now accepted modern packaging. In the event they proved inflexible, however, I kept asking at every store I passed and on the edge of town a shopgirl produced a squat bottle of a brand of honey called "Yuky."

By the time the jeep pulled up to Valter's house, the chickens had got to the corn and out of a half-kilo sack there was only a handful left.

None of this amused Valter. He regarded both the depleted sack and the unappetizing honey with misgivings. But he could provide a dove, and the ceremony would go ahead as scheduled.

Tonight I was not the only celebrant. A taciturn black man, his skinny wife, and their plain-faced teen-age daughter would undergo the second work as a family. They waited around the table while my sacrifices were being inspected, and under the girl's chair I saw a creditable gray cock.

At eight o'clock, Deoclides left with a filha do santo to administer the ritual bathing to the family. Valter and his children led me to O Templo.

"I am very glad I do not have to go through the bathing again," I told Valter as he set candles around the center tree.

"Before you are confirmed, you must be bathed again," he said, smiling to himself.

Certain of his silences and the looks he shared with Deoclides had been disturbing me. Since we were alone for a moment, it seemed a good time to disabuse him. "Senhor, I am not going to become a filho do santo. By the time of the confirmation ceremony I expect to be gone from Bahia."

He went on pressing the soft bottoms of the candles into the flagstone. "If you miss the confirmation at the end of December you must wait a full year," he said. "There is no other ceremony."

"Yes, I understand. But I will be gone."

Crispiano ignored his mother's objections and came toddling into the templo. He spied his sister and snuggled in her lap while the rest of us sat or squatted in a circle. Valter pulled the silver bell from his pocket, gave two clear peals and launched a syncopated clapping that opened the ritual.

The first prayer was brief and bidenominational, invoking as it did both the orixás and the Virgin Mary. The singers were just completing the first song when out of the cloudless black sky, a light rain fell across the court. Valter picked up his paraphernalia and directed us to walk into the terreiro backward.

We were inside and shaking ourselves dry by the time the bathers came running up the stairs. The women were dressed again in bandanas and full skirts; only the husband had the embroidered cloth draped over his head, but since Valter was not yet receiving Ogum he didn't get green powder blown in his face.

Deoclides came to where I was sitting. "The water was even colder tonight than when you went in."

"Impossible. It would have frozen."

"Do you remember," Deoclides called to Valter, "that he thought it might be a joke?"

Deoclides's smile was usually melancholy but now he laughed, truly laughed—the same wholehearted laughter of Staneill. Whether or not these works were affecting my spiritual development, they were surely improving the digestion of my hosts.

Nor was that the end to the hilarity. When the rain passed, Deoclides went to O Templo to prepare the altar again. He had barely stepped outside when I heard him laughing even more uproariously, laughing and choking so that Valter hurried out looking worried.

Soon they were back, Valter decidedly unhappy. "It was not a cock that you brought," he said to me. "It was a hen."

"Not a frango?"

"A galinha."

When he recovered, Deoclides announced that my bird had seduced the gray rooster, and he had caught them at it in a dark corner of O Templo. Was it too late to get a rooster? I asked, chastened. Valter spoke with his daughter and Elza was gone and back in minutes with a brown fowl whose sex and genus she vouched for.

At last we four petitioners were taken outside to the trunk of the tree, where Deoclides had laid out two saucers of meal and two mixing bowls. After the first song, Ogum took command of Valter's body, announcing himself with the guttural laugh.

Ogum took me first, then the family as a unit, passing us over with maize, depositing most of it in the two empty bowls but throwing the last handful in the air so kernels fell like hail against the leaves of the tree.

He poured honey and Martini wine into the bowls and into the glass I had brought. In woods around Ituberá the family had collected a liter of wild honey. Its amber purity clearly pleased Ogum more than my offering, which seeped from its jar in orange chunks, like marmalade.

At a nod from the spirit, Deoclides located my latest brown bird behind a palm and brought him forward. Ogum demonstrated how to hold him, its wings pulled back and its legs together. He himself gripped the head. Accepting a long silver knife from Valter's wife, the spirit cut the cock's throat.

The bird hardly stirred in my hands. Its blood ran first into the glass of honey and wine, then into the bowls, and last onto a saucer of honey. Only near the end, when it had leaked out almost three cups of blood, did the bird kick and flutter. At another nod from Ogum, Deoclides felt its plump breast for a heartbeat.

He found a low pulse and passed the body back to Ogum. The spirit hacked at the wound, now coating over with red mucus, to make it larger.

The bird was dead. Deoclides took it from me and tucked the dangling head under a wing, folding, shaping, straightening, until the cock looked like an oval feathered ball.

The blood transfixed me. Despite the sweetening and diluting, it shone dark red in the glass. I was sure we would have to drink it. My consolation was that there would be four of us to share the single cup.

When its time came, the family's gray cock died harder. Even as Deoclides was molding its feathers, it pulled out its head and went dragging a few last inches over the stones.

The songs had stopped. We were finished and being moved backward into the hall. The family was taken straight to the shrine but Deoclides detained me in the roncó with a pull on my sleeve.

He lighted a candle, took a scrap of paper, and carefully wrote a word on it. Passing the paper over, he gave me a look full of meaning.

"Mulheres?" I said. "Women?"

He took the paper back and wrote, "Not for seven days."

I was still slow. He was telling me something, I thought, about the ritual for the mother and daughter in the other room.

He pointed to the "not" and to "women."

"I see," I said. "Like no cachaça for five days."

"Sim!" he nodded vigorously. "But this is the only restriction this time. For seven days."

We came out of the roncó to find Ogum gone and Valter sitting at the desk. The family was arranged along the wall. In two hours I hadn't heard them speak to each other or even show much interest in this ritual that next January first would make them son and daughters of the saint.

Deoclides showed Valter the slip he had written for me.

"I explained the restriction," he said. "Do you want me to speak to the other man?"

Valter looked across the room to where the man sat hunched next to his wife of twenty years. "It is not necessary," he said.

RETURNING TO NELSON'S HOUSE ON MONDAY, I found Zulmira, summoned to lend her unearthly soprano, and Nelson's robust daughter also waiting at the shrine. Nelson's wife had bought the gray powder that went "whoosh!" when it was ignited; from a brazier behind me there were frequent loud reports.

Those accouterments were to no avail. Nelson exhausted his repertoire. Remembering the book on self-hypnosis, my eyes never left the flame. While Nelson sang, I labored to clear my mind and leave it spacious and hospitable.

But the more I concentrated on going blank, the more one idea persisted. It grew stronger—an idea that had been tantalizing me for the past week but it never looked more beguiling than at this moment. When Nelson left off drumming, I would share it with him.

Staring at the candle tired my eyes, but just as I was letting the lids close I caught a glimpse of Nelson throwing a triumphant glance to the women behind me, and he beat louder on the drum, as though it took a rush like a sexual frenzy to make the spirit come.

Half an hour. Forty minutes. The women's voices dropped. We were all uncomfortable and tired of the stuffy room. Tired of me, for not summoning a spirit with more dispatch.

"Enough," Nelson said with a last, sorry beat. "Next week. The third time it never fails."

"And if it does not happen the third time?"

"Always!" he said. Nelson's wife nodded, a ponderous dipping of the head. "Three times, always!"

"Because, senhor, after the third time I think I shall leave Camamu."

Saying it was like awaking from a dream. I looked around the filthy room, smelled the incense and the dendê oil, and I wanted to escape that house to a place where the light and the emotions were thinner, the colors pallid but clean. A place where people worshiped no god more accessible than the sun.

I said, "I will be leaving soon for Los Angeles."

FOUR HOURS LATER, Alda asked at dinner, "When are you going back to Los Angeles?"

"I only decided today," I said. "I think I am nearly finished here."

She went to her tiny room under the stairs and came back with the unflattering photograph that had been taken for her police documents. "As a remembrance," she said.

Railda brought her photograph, equally bad, and both girls prevailed on Dona Bela's daughter, who could write, to put loving inscriptions on the backs.

Bela herself came to the table to cluck. "You will be leaving a real falta"—a lack, a shortage. As though I were absconding; and thinking about breaking the news to Valter, I felt as guilty as an embezzler.

"When do you leave?" The boys from the high school had come by for help with their English lesson.

"Not before my birthday?" José protested.

"Or mine?" the others shouted.

André Carlos went to my typewriter and pecked out in Portuguese, "Jack, you are part of our hearts and so you cannot go away." The others thought that, even as brincando, his language was excessive and they refused to sign their names.

"You are right to get out," Júlio said. "This town has nothing. Do you know that today the bank director's wife took me aside and warned me that I was drinking too much?"

"That joke is five months old."

"She was not born in Camamu. She does not hear everything right away. Tomorrow I am going to tell the director that if his wife wants to run the bank, he should go and supervise the kitchen."

He was smiling regretfully and it took me a moment to understand that he was outraged. "She said, It will look bad in your efficiency report to Salvador if my husband must say you are drunk every night."

"Put it out of your mind," I said.

"My mother is dead—that is what I should have told her. My mother is dead and I do not need a new one."

"Forget it."

"I will return to school," Júlio said. "I will not be a banker at all. I will be an orthodontist."

"Then having the sister of Zeca for your sweetheart has produced one good result."

"You laugh," Júlio said, "but have you ever seen me drunk?"

"Never. That is why I laugh."

At about that time the lights dimmed and then went out all over town. Past the starlight at the window, my room was dark. "Look at that! No lights!" Júlio said scornfully. "You are smart to be leaving."

"It happens to other great cities. Once it happened in New York."

The boys struck candles and we went on drilling for their test. But the lights were still off at ten P.M. when I went downstairs to let them out and lock the front door for the night. They disappeared up the street shouting, "So longie!" and "What time is?"

Out of the shadows, someone lurched against the door. "Let me in," he whispered.

I had met the fellow once or twice, the first time at Luzia's Candomblé but I had never seen him sober. A lost-looking delinquent of twenty or so, his face was white as mashed potatoes and his eyes were pink and prematurely rheumy.

"I am sorry. It is late. I am going to bed."

"Let me in," he repeated. As he spoke, he stretched a hand toward my frango.

"No!" I said. "No, no. Thank you. No. Good night. I am sorry. Good night."

I swung the big door shut and locked it. He was still tapping as I went up the stairs.

I thought how tolerant and generous, albeit legalistic, Luzia's Ogum of the Seashore had shown himself to be. Confront him with a seven-day ban on women, and out of nowhere he produced a willing young man.

MY LAST DAY IN CAMAMU was the first day of spring and the morning dawned contemptuously beautiful, as though to show that Bahia was equally pleased to be quits with me. Throughout the day I divested myself of rubbish. The desk went to Urbano, who had been the first to ask for it; the straw mattress and bedding to Dona Bela; the pick of books to Staneill, who, not reading English, made his choice by the cheerfulness of the covers and carted off *Cymbeline* and an Ivy Compton-Burnett but left behind *Dead Souls*.

Júlio got the shaving mirror and a swatch of flowered cloth to cover his night table. "Now," I told him, "everything is gone and I can be off to see Nelson."

"Still?" he said disapprovingly. "Even on your last day?"

"He guarantees that this time—"

Why was I really going? Partly so that forever after I couldn't think that perhaps the third time actually would have been the charm.

Today Nelson had drawn on his full reserves. Passing the bedroom I saw Francisco rolling out a second drum, and Zulmira had showed up with a friend, a fine-looking girl from Salvador. From my experience with his monologue, the newcomer had been exposed to thirty-five minutes of Nelson's past, safely done with the woman of the cancerous mouth.

"—and he felt bad and paid back the thirty cruzeiros and they never saw him again." Nelson stopped to spit and point me into a chair.

To my pleasure, Nelson continued, "There was a woman who was getting very fat from stealing chickens at night." I had often wondered about the fate of that fat rustler.

"Nothing could be done to stop her. There is a woman right here" —Nelson paused portentously—"in this very room, whose chickens were among those being stolen."

Zulmira, the only other female present, blushed and looked to the window.

"That woman will confirm that I am telling the truth," Nelson said. "I spoke with the spirits and told them that whenever the fat woman stole a chicken, she must come to me and tell me.

"The very next morning, she came. The woman who knows this story, the woman who is in this room today, was also with me when the fat woman arrived.

"To her, the fat woman said, 'I think that by mistake I ate one of your hens.' You had to feel sorry for the fat woman. She could not help admitting what she had done. The spirits had taken away her power to lie. She paid for two chickens at ten cruzeiros apiece and she went away and the stealing of chickens stopped.

"There is a woman in this room who can tell you that everything I have said is true."

Zulmira had regained her poise and stared now at Nelson as though she too were hearing the story for the first time. Her passivity seemed to goad him, and he said harshly, "A woman who receives the spirits must be ready at all times to do so. If I ask her to receive and she says no, that is her right. But if she says no to me and then I learn that she has been receiving spirits for another pai do santo, then I have the right to punish her."

I wondered whether Nelson had caught Zulmira's Iemanjá in the terreiro of another man. Whatever the circumstance, clearly enough it was a warning, though Zulmira had assumed her most seraphic countenance and looked impervious to all earthly messages.

When Nelson's wife called to us, we trooped to the bedroom and got to work. I stared at the black center of the flame. I stared at the sight of the flame pulling away from the wick and dancing to a downdraft, as though the flame itself were a yellow moth.

I stared until my vision folded down on either side like curtains that had been drawn to make a smaller screen, and I saw nothing from the corners of my eyes. I could feel the muscles of my eyes as they became fatigued. Behind me the sound blurred; I had stopped hearing separate voices.

Progress at last? I might have thought so except for the taunting voice that floated up from some interior dimness: your eyes are tired. That's all. If this is spiritism, then every motorist who drives on a rainy night is a medium.

Zulmira had caught the beat and received Iemanjá. She was whirling behind my back like a mad thing. Nelson's drum went on and on, so long that finally my eyes grew accustomed to the flickering flame.

Gradually the muscles relaxed and the lids lifted again. My spine was sore from slouching to get the flame in my line of vision.

Nelson saw me stretching and sneaking a look at my wristwatch, but he kept on repeating the familiar chants and introducing new songs so involved and tuneless that even Iemanjá, goddess of waters, could only hum along helplessly.

We gave the spirit a full hour that day and another ten minutes grace period. Then Nelson hit the climactic beat and the room was quiet. Iemanjá came to my side and washed my hands in a basin.

"I feel that your spirit will soon visit you," the spirit said, her eyes skimmed back.

To Nelson I said, "I may be one of those people who will never receive a spirit."

"No!" he said, as though I had slandered myself. "You will receive! Do you see those?"

On the altar a string of green and white glass beads were wrapped around a rock the size of a fist. Nelson said, "When you put those beads around your neck, you will receive a spirit."

"Good, good. I will remember to buy some in Rio."

"In Rio!" Nelson's wife exclaimed in alarm. "He is going to buy them in Rio!"

"No!" Nelson said. "Here! Buy them here! They are not expensive! They are cheap!"

"When I come back to Camamu—"

"When you come back," Nelson repeated disconsolately.

"JACK!" Urbano's ten-year-old brother shouted from down the street. "When do you leave?"

"If it does not rain tonight and I can have my last work with Valter in Ituberá, I will leave tomorrow morning on the five A.M. bus."

"Grief!"

Sargento Jaime couldn't make this final run to Ituberá, but he promised to send his driver. I paced the street waiting until Geraldo arrived, an hour late. There was no gasoline to be had in Camamu, he said. But we might be able to make it with what he had.

It was a night with stars low enough to scrape the treetops and I wondered whether I would be sorry tomorrow when I had left these dirt roads and seas of green grasses.

After my apologies to Valter for our lateness, I held out for Deoclides's inspection the small bottle of perfume I had bought for the last work. "It may be too little."

"No, it is enough."

"I have also brought the white ribbon and the candle. The white cock is already here in Valter's yard. And at the farmácia I found vinho recorislituinte Silva Araujo. But I do not know what it is."

"A tonic," Deoclides said. "It is important in the ritual." He yawned and smiled. "You will see why. You will be glad you found it."

Valter said, "You will be leaving soon after this final work?"

"Tomorrow morning."

"And you will come back when?"

"I do not know."

He had asked that I send to an Umbanda shop in Rio for three books he needed. They came earlier that day and now I handed them over: *Baths and Defumations, Food for the Spirits, The Cross of Caravaca.*

That last volume included a two-inch tin cross in a plastic envelope stapled to the cover. According to the instructions, any disease could be cured by holding the cross while the appropriate prayer was recited.

When the books arrived, I had looked up the cure for cancer. Over the past thirteen years, a combination of surgery and cobalt radiation had kept my mother alive, and I wanted to see what her treatment might have been in a Bahian village.

"This prayer must be delivered on five consecutive days and nights," the book said, "being careful that the afflicted person hold the cross. After each prayer, the person must say three Padre Nosso and three credos."

The prayer:

"In the name of the Father, the Son and the Holy Ghost, I order that these malignant tumors disappear from the body of (insert name), in the same way that the devil disappears when he sees the sacred cross.

"They must go and never come back.

"For the peace of this creature of God, who believes in God and glorifies His name each hour of the day and night.

"Full is the earth of His glory. Amen."

My impulse was to rip the book in two. Bringing it to Valter's congregation struck me as little different from carrying a disease into their midst. But it was the book he wanted. Long ago, I had found this entry in Gide's journal, copying it out even as I was judging it a dubious proposition and decidedly overwrought. This day I very nearly agreed with it:

"Certainly the *secret aim* of mythology was to prevent the development of science."

Deoclides motioned me into the men's roncó to change my clothes. Last time I had overheard Valter asking him whether I knew that I must dress entirely in white, and I could tell that the younger man was uneasy about putting me to the expense and nuisance of finding white trousers.

But I could assure him that I had a pair, purchased in California for my visit to the Long Beach terreiro and not worn since. Now I stepped into the roncó and drew them on. I wore a pair of white cotton socks as well, and a white long-sleeved shirt.

Valter and Deoclides were waiting at the altar of the abasé with my white rooster at their feet. As I entered, one of Valter's daughters unfurled a curtain of white cloth. With the help of an old woman, she held it across my back as a shield against influences beyond the door.

Tonight, Ogum came readily, greeting us and invoking God in a long prayer. That done, he took up a small sharp knife and made four minute incisions in the shape of a cross on the skin over my collarbone.

As he was cutting, Ogum said, "Your body will be closed by day and night in the name of the Virgin Mary.

"Your body will be closed with your light.

"Your body will be closed, Jack,

"In the name of Jesus."

With this last phrase, he rubbed in a pinch of green powder. There was no bleeding and no scar afterward.

The cock was a tough one. It cawed like a crow and struggled in my grasp as Deoclides cut its throat and drained its blood into a glass and then a basin.

"Kneel," Deoclides whispered.

I got down on one leg in the fashion of knights, but he gestured for me to place both knees on the floor. At the altar, he was pouring into the glass of warm blood a measure of the tonic called vinho recoris-lituinte Silva Araujo. When it was almost full, he added drops from the jar of honey I had brought the past week.

Ogum took command of the glass and held it to my lips. "Drink," he said.

I obeyed. The tonic had the taste of a light red wine. The cock's blood only thickened the texture and gave the wine body. By putting out of my mind the white feathered corpse on the floor, I could, with a little hesitation but no real nausea, drink the substance down.

At the very end, a stringy white clot like albumen floated to the surface. That I swallowed, too. Had there been another glass of blood waiting, I would have drunk it.

Ogum took my hand to help me rise and stationed me in front of the basin of blood. Deoclides had added a pitcherful of water strewn with herbs. Now Ogum took my vial of perfume and splashed it across the surface in the four corners of a cross. He motioned for me to lower my head.

I had known that at some stage of the ritual I would have to drink fresh blood. Over the weeks I had been bracing for that moment, possibly even curious about the taste or at least my reaction to it.

What I had not expected was to have my head smeared with cock's blood. Rationally it should have been less noxious than the drinking. But I wasn't behaving rationally tonight. It took a force of will to dip my hair into the red fluid.

The mixture reeked of the cheap floral essence I had brought. Ogum thoroughly rinsed my hair with blood, down to the back of my neck. Then the women came forward with the white sheet, draping it over my crown and patting at my hair until the worst of the dripping had ended.

At that moment I was not thinking of ancient gods or of my spiritual development. I was thinking only about getting back to Camamu—how I would go to the shower in the empty house, how I would scrub my head and rinse my hair, how I would scrub again.

Ogum unwrapped the white ribbon from a candle I had brought and handed it to me. With a sweeping gesture, he indicated the statues on the altar. "Which god do you wish to have it?"

I raised my eyes and saw the placid queen of waters. Her white robes matched my ribbon and the gentle slope to her bosom was right for receiving it. "Iemanjá."

He took the band of cloth away again. Stretching, because she rested on the second tier of saints, Ogum draped the ribbon around her neck.

Once more he bid me kneel. As he prayed, he paused that I might repeat the words after him. It took prompting from Deoclides but we got through the short stanza:

"O God, King, Love!

"May this light be

"My life.

"And in my death,

"Like the divine spirit,

"May you come to take your son

"In the name of God the Father,

"God the Son,

"God the Holy Spirit."

"You may ask a final question," said Ogum of the Seven Swords.

"What do the spirits want of me?"

"No," Ogum said, "the question is what you want of us. Together you and I can accomplish anything. But remember: whatever you ask henceforth will remain your responsibility. It will stay on your conscience."

Ogum studied me from behind his fluttering lashes. He spoke of my return. O Templo would determine then, he said, how long I must remain in seclusion. The duration would depend upon the spirits that protected me. When I came back— He paused inquiringly.

I shook my head and said nothing.

More to Deoclides than to me, the spirit said, "Leave me alone."

Deoclides handed me my candle and took me to O Templo. The night was loud with stars but otherwise there was no sound but the doves under the eaves, murmuring in their sleep.

At the base of the thick tree, I lighted my candle and pressed it into a residue of white wax on the flagstones. A thousand others had burned down here and gutted out, as mine would do when I was already on the road home.

Inside, we found Valter's body racing around the terreiro. It was jumping and skipping and hugging itself and rolling its eyes naughtily. Deoclides beamed at the sight. "Do you recognize the spirit?"

"Rei da Matinha menino?"

"Yes, it is he—the king as a small boy."

"I remember you!" piped the child. "The americanese!"

"That is right," said Deoclides. I wondered whether he had ever looked so indulgently at his own five girls.

Geraldo was waiting by the outer door. "You cannot take him away," the menino said, dancing in front of the driver and shaking his finger. "You cannot go now. I just got here."

"He is getting a bus tomorrow morning," Deoclides said. "He is going to Rio de Janeiro."

"No! No! He cannot go! Why should he go? Why can he not stay and play with me?"

"I leave at five hours," I said. "That is very early."

"Oh!" the child cried pettishly. "Oh, then I will go, too. I will not stay here all alone."

The child moved toward the abasé. But he paused at the threshold and hung on the door, swinging back and forth.

"What are they going to think of the americanese in Estados Unidos?" he asked mischievously. "What are they going to say when they find out he is a filho do santo?"

He popped behind the door. In a moment we heard catches to Valter's breathing that meant his spirit was dismounting. Deoclides hurried for a glass of water.

Geraldo had gone to the jeep and started the engine. It chugged impatiently at the door.

I went a last time into the abasé. Deoclides was bent over Valter, pressing water on him as he trembled and groaned.

"I do not understand," I said, "what the child was saying about me at the end. I have not gone into isolation in the roncó. I have not had a confirmation on New Year's Day. So I cannot—"

"When your head was washed tonight with blood, that was your consecration," Deoclides said.

Valter took a sip of water and shook his head to clear it. They were both smiling, pleased with their surprise for me. Deoclides looked to Valter to tell me.

He said, "You are a filho do santo now."

A son of the saint, and thus protected by the spirits for a lifetime.

We were twenty minutes away from Valter's terreiro when the jeep gave a tubercular cough and died in the road. By then it was midnight. Geraldo laughed nervously and slouched behind the wheel to sleep.

There will be no cars on the road till dawn, he said.

I cursed and got out. At least I would be ready if Geraldo was wrong. But there was nothing and I would miss the five o'clock bus to Salvador. The chicken blood had dried; my hair felt varnished.

I considered walking the thirteen miles to Camamu but the road ahead was a black tunnel. Those brilliant stars had faded when I left Valter. Now they were barely mocking my foolish white pants.

It had become crucial that I get out of Bahia that morning. One more plate of beans, one more sight of the prosecutor or the toothless postman and I knew I'd start to rant and flail. I had to get away from the town, from the scrutiny. Away from the mud—red, not black; Freud was mistaken—of occultism.

From the jeep I could hear Geraldo's regular breathing. I stood helplessly in the road and spoke to Ogum of the Seven Swords.

Graças a Deus, Ogum. I don't expect to find a purer spiritism than I have met in Valter's terreiro and it was tempting, for a while, the idea of going backward to a lost mystery.

But we cannot. Not we norte-americanos, nor you brasileiros. Your famous novelist said it long ago: "We are condemned to civilization." The prospect of going ahead often seems dismal but it is the only direction for us.

Maybe we will meet again, Ogum. But it will have to be after Valter's shudders have been calibrated while he receives his spirit, after his gasping has been recorded on graph paper. I will come looking for you again when a neurosurgeon with a rubber-tipped pointer can locate on enlarged photographs of Luzia's brain those forests where the King of Snows roams and the oceans that harbor Sereia on a pink conch shell.

I'm not sorry I spent these months searching after spirits. Where I went wrong was in not recognizing that the mystery lay closer to hand than a forest in Bahia. Writing fiction is my communion with spirits; it is all one mystery. And since I have known better than to analyze my own impulse too closely, I should simply accept and enjoy the Brazilian effort to recast and gladden an unsatisfactory world, at least until science overtakes us all.

On the horizon, I saw headlights and went to shake Geraldo. He

264

staggered into the road and flagged down a pickup truck that gave us a ride into Camamu. Once there I had no time to wash, only to grab my suitcase and run down the hill to the bus.

As I took a seat, I added a postscript to my prayer: I am very grateful for this much, Ogum. The timing will be close, but you have seen to it that I will catch my flight to Rio after all.

At first sunlight we pulled away from the riverbank. Through the dirty windows, Camamu got dimmer and disappeared. I settled back to dream of invisibility the next noon on Copacabana Beach.

Ten miles from Valença, the bus blew its left front tire.

MAJOR GODS OF
AFRO-BRAZILIAN SPIRITISM

Aganjú. Both brother and husband to Iemanjá, Aganjú lost rank in the transfer from Africa and little has been heard about him in Brazil. His name meant "desert" or "waste land."

Ajê Shaluga. The Yoruban god of gold and wealth, he was one of thirteen children that resulted from the rape of Iemanjá by her son.

Babalawo. Considered by the Yorubas a priest, not a god, he was a trustee of the odú, a body of learning comprised of 256 individual chapters. Each had its own stories and verses, and since the priest was required to know them by heart, the name Babalawo translated as "father who knows the cult."

When the faithful came for divination, the Babalawo threw sixteen palm nuts and sticks onto a board sprinkled with sand. For each number he read in the sand, he recited the appropriate prophecy.

The Yorubas thought of him as the servant and oracle of the spirit called Ifá, and a Babalawo accepted no money for his services. That tradition has continued in modern Umbanda and the chief of an Umbanda center may be called Babaluaé.

Dada. Another of Iemanjá's children, Dada was the Yorubas' god of vegetables.

Exú. (Pronounced esch-oo) The Yorubas saw Eshú less as a devil than as a tempter, and in Africa he exercised limited influence, chiefly as intermediary and messenger for the other òrìsàs. Taken for a phallic god in the thirteenth century, he was courted by his worshipers with human sacrifices. In later ages he has contented himself with fowl and goat and, when he can get it, bull.

Dwelling among the Yorubas, Eshú was hot-tempered but easily fooled. His aversion to the oil made from palm kernels was well known. A troublemaker might approach his shrine and tell him, "I have come from my neighbor with this gift for you." Then he would lay down a bowl of the hated oil and gloat as Eshú rushed off to punish the transgressor.

In Brazil, Exú grew wilier, and with the stature conferred on him by a confusion with the Christian devil, he became infinitely more powerful. In Quimbanda, the sect devoted to his worship, practitioners seldom call upon King Exú for favors. He is altogether too formidable for men to conjure with. But his surrogates are available. Exú Manqueira will often appear at a terreiro, speaking French, demanding fine wine—or at the least a pale beer—as his price for curing an ailment. For those who know the charm, Manqueira is also prepared to kill.

Exú Marabo prefers absinthe and cigars, and he affects a slow drawl. Exú Pemba and Exú Brasa are the spirits who will further an adulterous affair. Exú Pagão thrives on hatred, instigating quarrels until he can rejoice at the sight of blows being traded. Pomba-Cira, a female Exú who visits Umbanda centers, usually takes over the bodies of men. In the spiritist stalls around Copacabana, she is represented as having horns on her head and splendid breasts beneath her red jersey.

The most telling story about Exú comes from neither Yoruban nor Brazilian lore but from a Rio newspaper published in March 1972. A man from the town of Nova Iguaçu hired a taxi to take him and a black goat to a crossroads at midnight. He intended to make a sacrifice to Exú, and he had brought along a wooden hammer to crush the goat's skull. They reached the chosen spot. The man asked the taxi driver to get out and help by holding the goat in place. Then, according to *The Brazil Herald:* "The demon Exú played one of those tricks in which he notoriously likes to indulge. The hammer, instead of landing on the goat's head, landed on the head of the driver, who dropped dead. . . ."

Ibeji. The twins of the Yorubas, the Ibeji are known in Brazil as São Cosme and São Damião. African tribes never resolved whether twins were evidence of the spirits' bounty or an unnatural freakishness. Brazilians take only delight in double births.

Iemanjá. (Pronounced ee-mahn-JAH) Daughter of Oxalá and Odudua, she ranks highest among the female gods, for lurid circumstances destined Iemanjá (or Yemanja; yeye for mother, eja for fish) to become a celebrated dam.

That she bore her brother, Aganjú, a son was not in itself an ignominy, given the limited number of sires available to the second woman on earth. But this son, Orungan—the name meant noon—fell desperately in love with his mother. The boy waited until his father was away hunting to make his approach. Iemanjá was horrified and fled. Orungan pursued and raped her. Recovering, Iemanjá ran off again, calling for her husband. But in the tangle of the forest she stumbled and fell. Her breasts ripped open to make twin rivers that ran together and formed a lake. Her womb voided and out sprang the eleven òrìsàs, along with Orun, who was the sun, and Oshú, the moon.

During the festa in Camamu, a black man I hadn't met pulled up a chair in the café and told the crowd at the table the story of Iemanjá's rape, speaking as though it had happened last week and to a member of his family. He also contributed the new and credible detail that at the time of the attack Orungan was seventeen.

In Candomblé, Iemanjá is goddess of water. Umbandists have merged her with Saint Anne and put her at the head of a line of gods and saints that includes Diana the huntress, Mary Magdalene, and such mermaids of the sea as Sereia.

Iemanjá's fetishes are seashells and stars. Saturday is her day for worship. And she has her own greeting: when a son or daughter of the saint receives her spirit, the terreiro must welcome Iemanjá with cries of Odóia! As colors, she favors white robes worn with clouded blue beads. In Salvador, her fête is the fifteenth of August. But in Rio on the last night of the year, women bearing candles line the beaches for miles to wade into the water and pour wine for the goddess and scatter flowers across her waves.

Ifá. A master of divination, Ifá has never been assigned a Christian identity. That may explain why he has been less exalted in Brazil than in Africa. Among the Yorubas, he was the highest of priests, possibly even a brother to Oxalá, and he received all prayers and directed them to their proper destinations. If Obatalá is the Father, Oxalá the Son, may Ifá be the Holy Ghost? Some spiritists say so.

Inhasã or Yansã. The goddess of storms, she is called Santa Barbara by the Umbandists.

Legbara, Leba, Elegara. They are other names for the demon Exú. In Haitian voodoo, Legba is a name for the male principle, the lion, the sun, and Christ.

Obá. Another of Iemanjá's children, sometimes she is called Saint Catherine. She is the goddess of a river called Obá.

Obatalá. In one African legend of the creation, God, called by the name Olorun, created only two òrìsàs. The male, Obatalá, represented the unsoiled sky. His mate, Odudua, signified both the female principle and its less pure domain, the earth.

This black Adam evolved slowly through the centuries in Africa from Obatalá to a spirit called Orisalá, who was later transported to Brazil as Oxalá, or Jesus.

Obaluaé. In Candomblé, this god keeps his face and body hidden behind veils of straw because he is god of diseases and his disfigurements have made him loathsome to see. His antecedents resemble those of Shapanan, the god of smallpox.

268

Odudua. The mate of Obatalá, she has been linked with Venus.

Ogum. (oh-GOOM) He is an equivocal god. As the master of iron, it was Ogum who gave man the cutlass that let him cut through the forest and clear a place for his home. The scalpel also belongs to this spirit since he is the god of surgery.

But in Candomblé, where he may be called Saint Anthony, Ogum is also the god of war. And in this century the Yorubas have come to consider him as the patron of the automobile. Once, no Yoruba tribesman would set off for battle without making human sacrifices to win Ogum's support. Now he accepts a slaughtered dog.

Umbanda terreiros recognize him as the Saint George of Christianity, not Santo Antonio. They cast his statue mounted on horseback with his lance at the ready. Ogum's fetish is a pair of crossed swords; his color is red; his day is Thursday. His foods are fresh goat or fighting cock. His line of subordinate spirits includes the god Mars.

Scholars usually spell his name Ogun. But in Ituberá and Camamu, his worshipers insist on Ogum, a difference in spoken Portuguese that is all but imperceptible.

Okê. Another son of Iemanjá, he is god of hills and mountains.

Olódùmarè. This god figures in an alternative version of creation: the powerful Òrìsà-nlá was given the task of creating men, shaping their forms from clay. But only another potent spirit, Olódùmarè, knew how to put life into these figures. Jealous of that gift, Òrìsà-nlá hid himself to spy out how it was done. But while he waited, he fell asleep and never learned the secret.

Olokun. The Yoruban Neptune, he was another of the children that resulted from Iemanjá's rape. Once, angered by mankind, Olokun sent torrents of water that wiped man from the earth. But the kindly god Obatalá intervened and banished Olokun to the depths of the sea.

Omulu. The king of cemeteries, Omulu presides over a phalanx that includes Saint Lazarus and Saturn. The Brazilian spiritist Pedro McGregor puts Omulu at the head of one of the seven major lines of Umbanda spirits but acknowledges that other authorities claim that since Omulu has the final decision over who will die, he is a spirit working with all lines and should not be assigned as chief of any one of them.

Omulu's fetish is a sickle. His colors are yellow and black. Saturday is his day, although it is on Mondays that he is receptive to specific requests. In Umbanda, Omulu has charge of the Exús of the graveyard, and through his link with Lazarus also has ties with the god of smallpox.

269

Òrìsà-nlá. This most unapproachable of African deities was a king of heaven who visited earth on occasion because he found the hunting good. His fellow gods assigned him only a small patch of land, but he brought with him a five-toed hen that scratched and spread his soil until the spirit's domain covered the globe.

Later, after men had been created, Òrìsà-nlá entrusted his garden to a slave to tend. The man proved diligent, the garden flourished. But he contrived to roll a boulder to the top of a hill and when Òrìsà-nlá came to inspect his work, he smashed the god to bits. Another god, Orunmila, gathered up the remains and spread them throughout Yorubaland, which explained how each tribe could possess a small fragment of the god.

Orishakô. Another child of Iemanjá and god of agriculture, he was considered a fertility god in Africa. At the time of a harvest or new moon, his celebrations were the occasion for sexual license among his worshipers.

Orungan. The son of Iemanjá and, as her attacker, the father of the òrìsàs.

Orunmila. The Yoruban god of knowledge, Orunmila was the spirit identified with the body of learning called the odù. For his offerings, Orunmila preferred rats. In his *Religions of Africa*, Noel Q. King wrote, "In Cuba, the gentle and helpful Orunmila becomes St. Francis."

Oshun. Goddess of the river Oshun, daughter of Iemanjá, she was very probably the beloved second wife of Xangô.

Oxalá. (oh-shah-LA) After God himself, Oxalá stood at the head of the Yoruban divinities. His beauty suggested Apollo, his reputation for purity was unsullied, his devotees always dressed in white. And so the African slaves could readily accept that Portuguese settlers might call their same great spirit by the name Jesus. In Brazil, Oxalá continues to prefer the color white. His fetish is a gold ring. Although his day of worship falls on Sunday, special pleaders have found him receptive on Fridays. Tradition identifies his favorite food as canjica, which is made of corn. But the novelist Jorge Amado is more explicit:

"What he eats is ojojó of yams, mustard greens with white corn, snails and porridge. Oxalá does not like spiced things; he uses no oil or salt."

Oxóssi. (oh-SHAH-see) The god of hunting and the jungle, Oxóssi is one spirit who fared better in Brazil than in Africa, where he held no special rank.

In Candomblé, it is Oxóssi, not Ogum, who has been identified with Saint George. From a lapse of logic, Umbanda takes Oxóssi to be Sebastian and represents this supreme hunter as a tortured youth with arrows piercing his flesh.

Predictably, a bow and arrow form Oxóssi's fetish. He eats peanuts and coconut. Jorge Amado suggests that he is "very picky" about food and won't touch fish that does not have scales. Amado, a member of a Candomblé in

Salvador, also warns that Oxóssi does not want windows in his house because "his window is the forest."

Ôxun. The goddess of fresh water, she has become Our Lady of the Conception in some Brazilian terreiros and thus near the apex of Christian hierarchy. Other centers call her simply Saint Catherine and place her under the command of Iemanjá.

Was she once Oshun, Xangô's scheming wife? If so, she has reformed over the ages and her statues are now among the most beautiful in Candomblé. Her fetish is delicately colored stones.

Skeptical of Ôxun's new graces, Jorge Amado says, "With mirror and fan, all touchy and affected, Ôxun likes fried bean cakes and yams cooked with onion and shrimp. And with the goat, which is her favorite meat, serve her cornmeal cooked in dendê oil and honey."

Sometimes her name is written Oxum, which might imply—incorrectly—a connection with Oxumaré, the bisexual spirit of the rainbow and the snake.

Oya. Daughter of Iemanjá, luckless wife to Xangô, in one legend she became goddess of the river Niger.

Preto Velho, Preta Velha. The old black man and the old black woman are not gods but wise African spirits who return to counsel human beings and intervene modestly in their affairs.

Umbandist statues generally show the old man seated meditatively, a figure that seldom varies whether the individual spirit is called Pai José or Pai Miguel or any of a hundred African or Portuguese names. Pure Candomblé admits no pretos velhos.

Shapanan. The god of smallpox, Shapanan was given a Dahomey name that meant "the one who kills slowly." Horrible as Shapanan's weapon was, the god justified using it because of his own affliction. It seems that he was lame. Yet when the other gods held a fête, he insisted not only upon attending but upon dancing. He fell. The gods laughed. Pulling himself up, he infected them all with the disease he controlled, a scourge so dreadful that it took Obatalá with a magic sword to dispel it. Shapanan was expelled from the company of gods and since that time has walked alone, tended by one loyal servant.

Tupã. In Ituberá, Senhor Valter's terreiro used this Indian name to designate the supreme spirit.

Tupinamba. An Indian chieftain of the Tupininkuin tribe of northern Brazil, his spirit returns to guide Umbandists in Bahia. Brothers of Tupinamba include Itubarajá, Iará, and Ibará.

Ubiraja. Another Indian chief, lamed in a hunting accident, he mounted mediums in both Long Beach, California, and Valença, Brazil. Ubiraja once told the Long Beach terreiro that he had been dead for about four hundred years and that he regularly visited spiritist centers as far away as Morocco.

Xangô. (shan-go) Called Sàngo by the Yorubas, he was their god of thunder, a title he won through a tragic circumstance. Once he held the enviable post of King of Oyo. But his wives and his subjects gave him great trouble and in despair Sàngo went to the forest and hanged himself from a tall tree.

One of these wives was Oyá, a fierce-tempered woman with vestiges of a beard. She found his body and for the first time her legendary courage failed her. Rushing to get away from the corpse, she ran faster, faster, until she became the river Niger.

Despite the turmoil in his nation, the king was survived by supporters who hoped to conceal the disgrace of his suicide. In the streets, they announced, "Sàngo has not died. He has become an òrìsà."

But word of the king's death had already reached his enemies, and they chanted, "Oba So!" The king has killed himself!

"Oba Ko So!" the king's friends shouted. The king has not killed himself!

The triumphant "Oba So!" was louder. Until across the sky came a terrible burst of thunder and lightning. You see, said the friends, that is Sàngo from heaven, answering you disbelievers.

In the years that followed, Sàngo would sometimes hurl down stones from the sky to strike his enemies dead, and other versions of his story gave clues to why his people were hostile to their king. He was haughty, according to the legends, and in a mocking, offhand way he was cruel.

His grandfather, who was Obatalá, had heard reports of Sàngo's hard heart. Taking the disguise of an impoverished old man, he went to investigate. Upon entering the land of Oyo, the first thing Obatalá saw was a starving horse, and he gathered up grasses and fed the poor beast.

He had barely finished when Sàngo's guards appeared. Using the pretext that the horse had been stolen, they beat Obatalá for his kind deed and dragged him before the king for sentencing.

Sàngo laughed at the old man's plight. Indolently he ordered that Obatalá be thrown into prison. It was a sentence the king had seven years to regret. For during that time, the harvests failed throughout Oyo. Lakes went dry, dead fish stank in the riverbeds. Sàngo himself became impotent and his wives infertile. At last, his soothsayers told him about the man who had been unjustly imprisoned. Although he still did not recognize him, Sàngo ordered his grandfather released. Whereupon the kingdom bloomed once more.

In his book *Drum and Candle*, David St. Clair contributes a gruesome story from Sàngo's court that other researchers missed:

The king's second wife, Oshun, was not only prettier than Oyá, which said little, but she was a good deal cleverer. Oyá could not help but see that her husband preferred this rival, and one day, trusting to female loyalty, she begged Oshun for her secret.

"Soup," Oshun replied, "soup is my secret. Come back tonight and I will show you how to prepare a broth that will win you Sàngo's love."

Oyá returned to find Oshun, head bandaged, stirring a pot with bits of white pulp floating along its surface. "Now you know my secret," Oshun said. "Our king likes his soup garnished with pieces of human ear. Make him a kettleful like this and he will be yours forever."

Oyá hurried home, cut off her ear, and diced it. At dinner, she carried in the soup tureen to Sàngo and stood back, ready for his praise.

"What is this?" he demanded, nauseated by the flesh on his spoon.

"It is my ear," said Oyá.

The king saw that indeed her head was streaming blood where an ear should have been. "Out of my sight!" he commanded.

The poor woman was rushed out of the dining room. Still unsuspecting, she ran to her rival to ask what had gone wrong.

She found Oshun in her kitchen. The scarf was off her head, both ears were in their proper place, and she was chopping up more of the white mushrooms that might, to a gullible goddess, look like a human ear.

Many Umbandists throughout Brazil identify Xangô with Saint Jerome. Pedro McGregor puts both Jupiter and Saint James in a cadre of spirits headed by Xangô, and he also notes Xangô's resemblance to Thor.

Xangô's fetish is a meteorite, his color imperial purple. He is worshiped on Wednesdays and tempted with dishes of tortoise, cock, goat. At Nesio's consultation in Rio where I had gone only as an onlooker, the macumbeira interrupted the ceremony to recommend a sacrifice she thought I might profitably make to Xangô. Perform it only if you choose to do so, the priestess had added; Umbandists are diffident about offering advice.

I thanked her and she wrote out this procedure: Take a candle, a bottle of dark beer, and an attractively shaped rock to a crossroads. There, light the candle, splash the beer over the ground, and make your appeal to Xangô.

I never did it. But I folded her slip of instructions and for several years afterward carried it around with me, like a prescription one might need in an emergency.